Choosing Church

What Makes a Difference for Teens

Carol E. Lytch

Westminster John Knox Press
LOUISVILLE • LONDON

Scripture quotations, unless otherwise indicated, are from the New Revised Standard Version of the Bible, copyright © 1989 by the Division of Christian Education of the National Council of the Churches of Christ in the U.S.A., and used by permission.

Book design by Sharon Adams
Cover design by Pam Poll Graphic Design
Cover photo: © Jon Feingersh/CORBIS

First edition
Published by Westminster John Knox Press
Louisville, Kentucky

This book is printed on acid-free paper that meets the American National Standards Institute Z39.48 standard. ∞

PRINTED IN THE UNITED STATES OF AMERICA

04 05 06 07 08 09 10 11 12 13 — 10 9 8 7 6 5 4 3 2 1

Library of Congress Cataloging-in-Publication Data

Lytch, Carol E.
    Choosing church : what makes a difference for teens / Carol E. Lytch.— 1st ed.
        p. cm.
    Includes bibliographical references.
    ISBN 0-664-22717-1 (alk. paper)
    1. Christian teenagers—Religious life. I. Title.

BV4531.3.L98 2004
277.3'083'0835—dc22

2003057683

Contents

108206

Figures

Tables

Preface

This study focuses on the religious lives of high school seniors. When I say that, I typically hear, "Oh, is there such a thing?" This skepticism has some empirical support. Studies have documented that church-reared youth start disappearing in high numbers in their junior and senior years of high school.[1] The dropout rate accelerates further after teens graduate.[2] Developmental theorists demonstrate that in the late teen years differentiation from one's family, hometown, church, and other shaping influences is normal.[3] Yet our social context has shifted too. People are conceiving of their self-identity and their affiliations more loosely in relation to their religious traditions and institutions. These developmental and social factors together create a tough challenge for today's churches seeking to take seriously their ministry with older teens.

Many churches today are struggling to keep their older teens. Some appear to have given up on them altogether. Other churches are highly engaged with their teens of all ages. These churches are awakening and deepening the Christian faith of large numbers of teens, even in this tough social climate. They feel that it is when young people are coming of age that they must notch up their ministry with them: "It's the last gas station they'll hit before they go out into the big world." I wanted to learn from the churches that are putting out the extra effort and engaging their teens through the end of their high school years. I wanted to learn from high school seniors—and their parents—what seems to make the crucial difference. In these pages you will read about three churches (Catholic, evangelical, and mainline Protestant) that appeal to high school seniors. You will read, as well, about teens who opt out of these "best-case scenario" churches. You will hear from parents about how their hopes for their children and for themselves as parents are fulfilled and disappointed as their children cross the threshold into adult roles and institutions.

This book began as Ph.D. research. The research methodology is primarily qualitative, which means I left the library and spent most of my time with the teens themselves. My data is my field notes, a sample of which follows.

> We started the afternoon of the retreat by standing in a large circle in the parking lot (over one hundred teens and adult youth leaders). A bubbly young woman coached us to shout, "Bananas of the universe, unite!" We had to follow that shout with body motions replicating the peeling of ourselves as bananas. We raised our hands over our heads, clapped once in unison, and "peeled" ourselves by lowering our arms and swinging our hips. I thought, "I can't believe I have to do this to get my Ph.D."[4]

Qualitative field research differs from other research methods in that it features researchers themselves as "witnesses and instruments" of the research.[5] Instead of relying solely on documents, questionnaires, experimental simulations, and other sources that are at least one level removed, the participant observer gathers data through direct experience. The researcher "understands" in sociologist Max Weber's sense of *verstehen*, that is, with empathy for one's research subjects.[6] The inner perceptions and feelings of subjects are understood in part by extrapolating them from the researcher's own intimate feelings and thoughts in the same setting. My field notes continue, "I felt very ridiculous, but wanted to be a good participant observer. I noticed that not all the youth leaders joined in, and a few of the teens were holding back."[7]

This study of teens and their parents employed qualitative research methods of participant observation and interviews to enable observation and interpretation of the beliefs, attitudes, opinions, and values from the subjects' standpoint. Qualitative research interprets subjective meanings, rather than discovering objective facts.[8] While the researcher does not presume that her experience is the same as the subjects', her experience is a prompt for asking others how they understand things. My field notes continue, "Could they be feeling as silly as I was? I'll have to ask them."[9]

Qualitative research also allows the researcher to understand institutional patterns—in this case, how church leaders with special competencies and resources ritualize, codify, and transmit cultural products such as a religious tradition. In the same example mentioned above, I experienced how the "silliness" of the exercise described helps to separate individuals from their fixed social positions in the social hierarchy and sets the stage for experiencing sacredness.[10] As a researcher, my relationship with my subjects was enhanced as I experienced the discomfort with them. Their interpretations of how their religious faith was awakened, renewed, and deepened on retreat were understandable to me because of my own sense of the religious dimension of the event. (For a discussion of the validity, reliability, and generalization of findings in qualitative research, see Appendix A.)

For ten months, from August 1996 through June 1997, I attempted to attend all the activities in three churches in Louisville, Kentucky, that attracted high numbers of high school seniors. I attended fifty worship services, thirty-seven youth meetings, four retreats, twenty Sunday school classes, Bible studies, and small-group meetings, and eleven choir rehearsals. In addition, I sporadically attended "drop-ins," when the youth gathered informally at the church. I attended two funerals and one marriage engagement party. Beyond the three congregations, I visited worship services, attended youth meetings, and/or interviewed youth ministers in nine other churches.

My field research took me to eleven of the sixteen schools that the teen subjects attended. I visited classes and interviewed principals, guidance counselors, teachers, choir directors, and athletic coaches. Sometimes teens from my churches gave me tours of their schools. Following the recommendations of teens and adults in my sample, I selected additional settings for observation. I attended a Fellowship of Christian Athletes meeting, two high school basketball games, and three performances of the Louisville Youth Choir. I visited youth in places where they performed community service, such as the Presbyterian Community Center and the Louisville Science Museum. I visited youth at their places of work, such as McDonald's, Target, and stores at the mall. Our family, returning from vacation, mingled with spring break traffic—cars overcrowded with sunburned teens clogging the highways from Florida. I watched movies and television shows the teens mentioned, read some teen magazines, and listened to their radio stations. I attended a Christian rock concert held in Louisville's largest public arena, Freedom Hall. I attended the Youth Worker Alliance Resource luncheon, a monthly meeting of youth ministers in the city. In all, I gathered five hundred single-spaced pages of field notes, filling four loose-leaf notebooks. I collected four large boxes of artifacts that include church bulletins, youth newsletters, issues of the megachurch's weekly newspaper, videos, photographs, and assorted objects. Beyond the interviews mentioned above,

I conducted eighty-three formal interviews with teens, their parents, and one set of grandparents who acted as a teen's legal guardians.

I limited the sample to teens who were currently listed on the membership rolls of one of these churches, indicating that there was some influence of a religious community in their lives. By checking with youth leaders in each church, I achieved representation in each congregation of teens who were active in the church and youth program, teens who were nominally active, and teens who were not active at all. I had an almost equal number of males and females (twenty-one males and twenty females) in my interview sample.[11] I controlled for class and race so I could conduct a fine-grained analysis of other variables.[12] (All teens and parents in my interview sample were white. See Appendix A for further discussion.) The range of socioeconomic levels of teens was kept constant across congregations. (See Appendix B for family incomes.)

In the initial stages of data collection I suspended theoretical assumptions about faith transmission and just recorded my observations, subjective feelings, and how I sensed the teens reacting to me in their midst. After only a few weeks, patterns emerged, prompting me to note comparisons and contrasts among the congregations and teens. I made lists, drew diagrams, and sketched out some patterns and themes I observed. All the time, I was reading literature related to theories of intergenerational faith transmission, other empirical studies of teenagers, and the historical development of cultural understandings of adolescence. (See Appendix C, "Theoretical Models of Faith Transmission"; Appendix D, "Previous Studies, New Empirical Research, and My Analysis of Religious Loyalty"; and Appendix E, "Adolescence.") I began to test some theories with some of my subjects. Their responses helped me to refine my questions and revise my own theories.[13]

After completing my data collection, I coded my field notes and interview transcriptions in ninety-eight categories to facilitate its analysis. I also compared my data with that of nationally normed surveys of teens and other qualitative studies of teen religious beliefs and practices. I began to identify how the data generated by my sample both supported and differed from national patterns, and I sought explanations for the differences. I linked the themes and patterns that emerged from the coded data to theoretical frameworks in a series of "integrated memos."[14] From there, the writing of this report began.

As I wrote this analysis over a three-year period, I become a parent of a teenager myself as my oldest child turned thirteen, then fourteen, and entered high school. I found that my parenting was influenced by the findings of my research. For example, when I took her to an event for teens sponsored by our church youth group, I got out of my car to engage in conversation with other parents instead of just dropping her off. I tried to foster closure to her social network at our church and at her school as I intentionally set out to befriend the parents of her friends. Some of my interpretations of my data changed in the course of the writing period as I experienced the parenting of a teenager. I grew in my awareness of how difficult it is to keep a teen involved in a church youth group when the youth minister leaves and the web of social relationships among teens in the church loosens.

Over the writing period, a friend who teaches at a small Methodist college in Virginia assigned an early version of Part III, "Seven Styles of Being Religious . . . or Not," as reading for a class of freshmen. These young adults, the same generational group as my sample now in their first year of college, verified that what they read described people they knew—even themselves. In addition, I tested the chapter about parents with parents in my church. I presented portions of my research at the Society for the Scientific Study of Religion, at the Religious Research Association, and at conferences at Louisville Presbyterian Theological Seminary and Princeton Theological Seminary. During the writing period I collaborated on several projects on teen religious life funded by the Lilly Endowment. The work and critique of colleagues refined my analysis and conclusions.

In particular, I would like to thank the following people. Steven M. Tipton, director of the original study as a Ph.D. dissertation, shaped the best of this work in the most formative ways and has been a model of kindness. I am honored to be a student of Nancy Tatom Ammerman. She has invited me into the community of scholars in the most gracious way. Nancy L. Eiesland is my guarantor and generous guide to this field as well as to doctoral student life. Charles R. Foster has taught me Christian pedagogy, and I hope to put into practice what he exemplifies.

John M. Mulder has facilitated this study through his encouragement and hospitality. I am grateful for the office he provided at Louisville Presbyterian Theological Seminary and for the community of conversation partners this gave me.

I thank the Lilly Endowment for the three-year fellowship that underwrote the costs of the research.

I wish to thank my early interlocutors on this work: Diana Garland, Jim Lewis, Joe Coalter, Charles Brockwell, Nancy Ramsay, and David Hester. I appreciate other colleagues who read and/or discussed parts of the work while it was in process: Lynn Schofield Clark, Steve Warner, Scott Thumma, Joe Reiff, Don Richter, and Brad Wigger. The influence of another group of experts on the religious life of teens is evident in this text—ones I met through consultations of the Valparaiso Project: Dorothy Bass, Don Richter (again), Tom Beaudoin, Kenda Creasy Dean, Ron Foster, Pat Hersch, Bob McCarty, Evelyn Parker, Julia Speller, David White, Mark Yaconelli, Sue Briehl, Carol Lakey Hess, Joyce Hollyday, Roger Nishioka, Nancy Pineda, Frank Rogers, Don Saliers, Emily Saliers, Melissa Wiginton, and Mark Monk Winstanley.

I also acknowledge the influence on this work of Craig Dykstra, Chris Coble, Kathleen Cahalan, and a host of theological educators across the United States and Canada who have launched fifty seminary-sponsored theological programs for high school youth funded by Lilly Endowment. We have been impressed by the capacities of teenagers to engage in serious theological study and to reflect theologically their sense of vocation.

My church community, Second Presbyterian Church, provided a sustaining source of enthusiasm and support, as well as grist for the mill in my thinking about teenagers. For their reading of my chapters and/or comments on my ideas, I thank Karen Hadley, Ginny Jones, Larry Jones, Elizabeth Clay, Dick Clay, Leslie Taylor, Jud Hendrix, the Committee on Youth Ministry led by Liz Seaman, the Youth Minister Search Committee led by Clay Edwards, and the Parents of Teens Sunday school class. Later, when our church hired a youth minister, I benefited from comments on my first chapter offered by Michael Harper.

Nancy Fuller's assistance in the production of the original document made an arduous task fun. Debbie Townsend laughed and cried with me as she transcribed the interviews of teens and parents, and I thank her, April Armor, and Sue Freidenstine for their efforts. I thank Martha Youngquist for copyediting the study in its original format.

Kim Maphis Early recognized the potential of this work for publication and passed it on to the most capable hands of Janice Catron at Westminster John Knox and Geneva Press. I thank Janice, my editor, for all her work and for envisioning a broader audience for this research.

My loved ones provided the support that made this possible: my parents, Cornelia Wilson Eichling and William H. Eichling; my in-laws, Lois Stephens Lytch and R. Gilbert Lytch; my sister and brother and in-law siblings, Ruth Pulliam, Russ Pulliam, Peter Eichling, Cindy Eichling, and David Lytch; my terrific tribe of nieces and nephews, Christy Pulliam, Daniel Pulliam, John Pulliam, Sarah Pulliam, David Pulliam, Anna

Pulliam, Elizabeth Eichling, Linda Eichling, Susie Eichling, and Amy Eichling; and my godchildren, David Lee and Allison Moder.

This work is dedicated to the glory of God and to those who jollied me to the finish line: my husband, Stephens Gilbert Lytch, and my children, Katherine Louise Lytch and William Gilbert Lytch. As I reworked my study into a book, my daughter became a high school senior and I joined the population in my study. I often think back to the church leaders, school professionals, teens, and parents who are the subjects of this research. They remain my teachers as I strive to fulfill my vocation as a parent. They deserve to be named but the parameters of this research prevent it. I chose them because they are outstanding, and I hope they feel rewarded as their ministry is extended to the wider community through this work.

Introduction

Whitney Richards,[1] an active teen at First United Methodist, was quoted in the local paper one week as part of a teen panel on religion. She said, "I don't really consider myself a Christian, but my parents force me to go to church and youth group and choir. And I'm not sure if they didn't make me that I would stop going, because the community, the friends that you get while you're there, that's what keeps me going, even though I don't necessarily believe all that they believe."

When Whitney appeared at church later that week, the choir director decided not to ask her about her comment in the newspaper. In the course of their rehearsal he invited teens to request their favorite anthems for inclusion in the program of their concert tour. He was jolted when Whitney's hand shot up with a request for one of the more devotional anthems. The choir director told me later, "I wanted to say, 'Hello, Whitney, are you the same person who dissed God in the newspaper this week?'"

It is not unusual for teens to switch off religious belief in certain settings. Whitney just got caught doing it very publicly. Many teens today view their religious affiliation as secondary, something that can be switched off and on in different contexts. Hammond[2] explains that two generations ago, in contrast, religious identity was more often considered primary, something into which one was born, like a family. Religious identity tended to be a given, like race and ethnic identity. The church was one's "primary group," that is, where one's core identity was derived from primary stable, ongoing relationships and reinforced by social ties that overlapped in other local institutional settings. Today, a heightened sense of personal autonomy fosters looser, less-overlapping configurations of social ties, and that, in turn, has undercut the church's role as the primary

1

group. How the church negotiates in this new social context is the theme of this book.

This Study: Passing on the Faith to the Next Generation

This study addresses an audience of church leaders who want to pass on to Whitney and to all of her generation the most truthful and precious thing they know—that is, the Christian faith. It addresses parents who take seriously the commitments they made, formally or otherwise, to rear their children in the Christian faith. What I offer here, however, is not a theology of Christian formation. This work is intended to complement the contributions of theologians and Christian educators by offering the results of a fine-grained sociological analysis of teens who have been reared in the church. This study reports the findings from a one-year study of Catholic, evangelical Protestant, and mainline Protestant high school seniors who are on the active membership rolls of three churches in Louisville, Kentucky. This study names what holds teens in their churches through their later years in high school—just when the dropout period begins. It portrays the different ways three churches nurture maturity in commitment. It examines the distinct challenges that parents and church leaders face as they impart Christian faith in a changed society.

This study also addresses an audience of scholars. This work falls into the established category of research on intergenerational faith transmission and religious loyalty. Sociologist Wade Clark Roof distinguishes "growing up in faith" from "growing in faith."[3] In this research I focus on the former category, the phenomenon of growing up in a historic, institutionalized religious faith. I describe patterns that emerge in teen religious identity and loyalty. I seek to understand why and in what ways teens decide to embrace the tradition handed down by their religious community. I show the variety of countervailing influences on religious loyalty as they appear today.

So What's New?

Andrea, a member of the Church of the Transfiguration, describes how she perceives religious faith to be held differently in three generations of her Catholic family. She remembers her grandmother as "a saint," the person called on to pray for the sick and for students taking important exams. The grandmother wore out a St. Jude's novena booklet of intercessory prayers through her regular usage of it.

Andrea describes her parents as less religious than her grandmother. She says they are "religious on the outside." While her mother still says the rosary every morning, her parents differ with the church on some social issues, like the unmarried priesthood and birth control. Andrea's father elected to have a vasectomy after Andrea's mother endured a life-threatening pregnancy that resulted in the loss of the baby.

Andrea describes herself as even less religious than her parents. "You can have your own sense of faith without the rituals, without going to church," she asserts. "Faith is having a relationship with God. It is thanking him for what he's given you." Andrea opts to attend youth group at Transfiguration instead of weekly mass. She says she may attend church more often when she goes off to college next year, but she's curious to explore other religions, and she will not attend the Catholic church automatically.

Andrea's family illustrates how a heightened sense of personal autonomy has affected the way church membership has evolved over three generations and how it is perceived differently by many of the younger generation today. Andrea's grandmother is what Dolan[4] would call a "devotional Catholic," committed to the "four pillars" of the church: the authority of the church, a sense of sin, ritual, and openness to the miraculous. Andrea's parents are what D'Antonio et al. call "Vatican II Catholics,"[5] those who have one foot in the "old church" and one in the "new church" (after Vatican II). They still affirm their confidence in the pope and bishops of the church, but consider the church less important in their lives. They attend mass, but pray less often. They disagree with some of the social teachings of the church. Andrea, a "post-Vatican II Catholic," exhibits an even lower level of commitment to the religious institution and a heightened sense of personal autonomy. Now, as she adheres to her religious tradition, she does so voluntarily and selectively.

> **Autonomy:** In Greek, a word meaning "self-regulation." An autonomous person has principles that he or she uses in organizing responses to events in everyday life. The heightened awareness of personal autonomy in teens means that they increasingly understand themselves as individuals who can make their own decisions about what to believe, what groups to join, and how and where they will place their loyalty.

While Andrea's family illustrates a distinctly Catholic type of religious declension, they also exemplify a general shift in the way that people are religious. Instead of adhering to a religious tradition, they choose how to be spiritual. This may or may not include holding a religious tradition that has been passed on within a religious community. Even teens like Andrea who have been reared within a religious community now expect to choose how they put together their "own sense of faith." They rarely take the package of beliefs and practices of their religious tradition without revising it, selecting from it, and in some cases detaching it from the religious institution that passed it on to them.

Even for teens who are loyal to the religious tradition in which they were reared and comfortable within religious institutions, a heightened sense of personal autonomy fosters an expectation that they must assemble for themselves a set of structures and relationships that support their chosen religious commitment. They do not necessarily attend a church in their local area. They are not limited to a unitary social world that is anchored in the face-to-face relationships of their neighborhood.

C.J., another teen in my study, chooses to live in three distinct "social worlds."[6] He and his family attend an evangelical megachurch, Riverland Heights, the third church in my sample. C.J. travels forty minutes to church each Sunday, bypassing many other churches closer to where he lives, because Riverland Heights offers "good teaching."

C.J. also attends a school that is located far from home. He drives thirty minutes each way to a Catholic high school that he and his family chose because they like its structure and discipline. C.J. finds these two religious environments dissonant with each other, as he considers few of his fellow students at the Catholic high school to be true Christians.

C.J.'s third social world is based closer to his home, with the friends who participate with him in a 4-H Club. In his 4-H activities the topic of religion is not raised. Of these three social worlds, C.J. considers the church to be the most important. Even if he no longer has many close friends at church, since many of them have gone off to college, he considers his "true friends" to be the people at his church. They share what is most important, their Christian faith.

The segmentation of teens' lives into several distinct and sometimes dissonant social worlds occurs because of several factors. The new option of attending a megachurch[7] is one factor, because it draws its large memberships from a wide geographic area. Teens at Riverland Heights come from over thirty different high schools, some located across the Ohio River in Indiana. Another factor in the segmentation of life into distinct social worlds is school choice. In the late 1970s the structure of the public school system in Louisville was altered drastically when children were bused out of their neighborhoods to racially integrate the city's schools.

Later, this effort evolved into a policy of public school choice, affording youth a choice to attend magnet schools located outside their neighborhoods as long as racial quotas were met voluntarily. Before megachurches, and before busing and school choice, teens attended the schools and churches located near their residence. The church could expect that most of its high school members would attend the same school. Church, school, and neighborhood friendships overlapped. When "multiplex relations"[8] exist through overlapping social ties, individuals tend to be more consistent in their religious identity across different settings.

Whitney, Andrea, and C.J. illustrate how a heightened sense of personal autonomy has altered for teenagers the nature of religious identity and what it means to belong to a religious tradition. Whitney switches her religious identity on and off, depending on the context. Andrea defines for herself what is essential to being a Catholic, excluding from that definition mass attendance, a practice that her church defines as an essential obligation. C.J. chooses to live in three dissonant social worlds, giving priority to his church world, even if he spends the least amount of time there.

Is there a thread running through these portraits? Yes, the common theme in the patterns of religiosity displayed by church-related teens is the presence of a heightened sense of personal autonomy. Teens, as individuals, choose their faith.[9]

The Shift to Individual Choice

Scholars of American culture have noted a shift in the balance between individual and community identity. A sense of self is no longer derived primarily from communal memberships. Americans conceive of themselves as individuals who endow their own lives with meaning on the basis of perceived needs and wants. For religious traditions, this means that religious membership is construed differently. Instead of having "a formative claim on one's very sense of self," religious membership may be "merely instrumental to individual self-fulfillment."[10] The mechanism driving the shift to individualism is *personal autonomy*, with its guiding motto, "I choose to go to church" rather than "I must go to church."[11] Religious choice is now the obligation of individuals; it is the "heretical imperative."[12]

Religion has always been a choice for Protestants. Now it is for Catholics and Jews as well. Some call this a "protestantizing" effect. A fundamental premise of Protestant theology is that each individual is responsible for his or her relationship to God. This assumption can be finessed to foster a suspicion of any authority beyond the self. A high regard for the sovereignty of the individual's conscience goes along with this premise. The last half century's interpretations of the United States Constitution underscore and institutionalize this view. An expanded interpretation of the principle of religious liberty enshrined in the Constitution recognizes that "conscience" is entitled to the same rights as "religion."[13]

Even when individuals do look beyond the self for religious authority, they tend to turn to multiple sources for it. They conceive of religion in a highly personal way, which is less tethered to a single historic religious tradition. They pick and choose the beliefs and practices that make sense to them. They construct a sense of the whole that enables them to interpret their own religious experience, even if that worldview lacks conceptual coherence. Terms for selective adherents have entered our vocabulary. For example, the "communal Catholic" is one who remains Catholic but considers herself or himself the final arbiter of what is to be believed and practiced.[14]

Other changes in how Americans are religious demonstrate affinity with a heightened sense of personal autonomy. Since the late 1960s, sociologists have noted a shift away from historic, formal, institutionalized religious traditions and toward a diffused sense of religion in society.[15] Will Herberg's widely quoted assertion that to be American is to be Protestant, Catholic, or Jewish[16] seems quaint in contemporary America. Not only is there a greater plurality of major religious traditions to consider, today's experts on American religion cast doubt on the ability of historic institutionalized religious traditions to give power and endurance to Americans' religious lives.[17] While Gallup polls consistently report that belief in God is high, public opinion also says people should define their own "spirituality" instead of following the dictates of any religious institution.[18]

The word "spirituality" frequently replaces "religion" as the preferred term for describing how people relate to the sacred.[19] The metaphor of *seeking* expresses the spiritual quest of these times. Seeking evokes images of journeying on a road, of shopping around a mall, of finding authenticity through choice, of glimpsing spirituality through miraculous encounters with angels. *Dwelling*, the metaphor for earlier decades, evokes images of a habitat, of habits, of familiar and secure places, and of the sacred spaces of a tradition.[20]

National survey data measuring the religious attitudes and levels of affiliation with religious congregations of high school youth illustrate this shift to an individualistic appropriation of religion. On the one hand, the large majority of American twelfth-graders surveyed in 1996 did not appear to be particularly alienated from or hostile toward organized religion in America. Only about 10 percent of them revealed some strong dissatisfaction for the religion of their parents or religious congregations. In fact, evidence gathered over twenty years indicates that there is little change in this view.[21] On the other hand, religious affiliation among this group has declined over the last twenty years. It has declined among Protestants by 10 percent and among Catholics by 1 percent. The proportion of American youth who affiliate with other traditions or with no religious tradition has grown noticeably, by 5 percent each.[22]

On an institutional level, religious traditions have suffered from eroding norms of church affiliation and relaxed expectations of denominational loyalty.[23] The challenges to eroding norms of church affiliation are nuanced for the three Christian traditions I studied. For Catholics, the challenge is to cope with pressure from the laity to democratize decision making in the church and to balance church authority with respect for the sovereignty of the individual conscience—especially on social issues like birth control and divorce.[24]

For the mainline Protestant tradition, the urgent concern is the decrease in church affiliation among those reared in its congregations.[25] This crisis is partly explained by what Wheeler observes:

> Mainline Protestantism does not have enough of a culture. By comparison with the prolix popular culture of the evangelicals, mainline Protestantism's inventory of symbols, manners, iconic leaders, images of leadership, distinctive language, decorations, and sounds is very low indeed. Without these elements of culture, mainline Protestantism cannot create something a religious tradition must have to survive: a piety, . . . shared practices, a catalog of virtues, models of Christian adequacy in the church and the world.[26]

Mainline Protestants seem to maintain a taboo against religious talk and value tolerance of other religions in a way that makes their absolute claims to religious truth ambiguous.[27]

While the evangelical Protestant tradition, more than the other two traditions, appears both to keep its tradition intact and to retain its offspring in a distinctive subculture,[28] there are indications it does so only through strenuous efforts to simultaneously shelter teens from outside influences and engage with modern society. The challenge to the evangelical Protestant tradition is best summed up by Berger's "cultural broadening thesis" modified by Christian Smith as maintaining the "sacred umbrella." While it is no longer possible to imagine religion providing an overarching "sacred canopy" that shelters the members of an entire society from chaos and terror, religion does thrive in the form of a "sacred umbrella," a small, handheld, and portable religious reference group under which beliefs make complete sense to a smaller group.[29]

Relaxed expectations of denominational loyalty are a part of the changed religious context on the institutional level. A poll taken in 1955 showed that only 4 percent of adults reared in a faith tradition left it; thirty years later, a similar poll showed that one-third left.[30] With increased religious pluralism, people choose a church more freely among increased options in an "open religious market."[31] Overall, Catholics still retain more of their adult offspring than do mainline Protestants, 50 percent as compared to 39 percent. Conservative Protestants, however, are the most successful at retention, keeping 55 percent within the fold.[32]

Churches Negotiating with Choosers

The comparative design of my study shows how each of these three traditions (Catholic, evangelical Protestant, and mainline Protestant) negotiates the climate of heightened religious autonomy and succeeds through different strategies and to different degrees in the task of nurturing faith in the next generation. This is not a simple story of secularization, modernization, and the decline of religious institutions. While the tenor of the scholarly conversations cited above tends to range from sober to pessimistic,[33] my findings point to a more hopeful projection of the prospects for historic religious traditions to provide the web of meanings that inform people's lives. I investigated cases where religious traditions were not just making accommodations to the changed religious climate; they were vitalized as a new generation of teens experiencing greater personal autonomy remade timeless religious truths and practices as they appropriated them.

The theoretical framework of the sociologist Anthony Giddens is particularly useful to an understanding of the heightened personal autonomy in teens. He views the heightened sense of personal autonomy as part of a larger change in how the whole of the self-identity is reconceived today as "the posttraditional self." He argues that today individuals are less likely to choose to be shaped by religious traditions; instead, a "lifestyle" is selected from possible ways of life standardized by abstract systems, such as money and government regulation. A "lifeplan" develops from lifestyle to channel action along standardized career paths and to prepare a course of action that minimizes risks. The self carves out a "practical consciousness" as a protective cocoon in which daily life can proceed through its routines amidst the risks of overload and complex uncertainty. "Risks" are managed by professional fields such as medicine, law, finance, and psychotherapy. In fact, the heightened sense of personal autonomy is a false consciousness. For the posttraditional self, choice is limited to standardized options.

Along with evidence confirming the existence of the posttraditional self, I found other evidence to support the continuing existence of the tradition-formed self. To greater and lesser degrees I found teens for whom the Christian tradition creates a sense of firmness to the world, orders time and space, and offers narratives on which to base their autobiographies. The Christian tradition organizes social life and articulates right action. While Giddens expects that a residue of religion should persist and continue to shape self-identity, even in high modernity, he underestimates the strength and variety of ways it does so in the teens in my sample. For example, the teens in my sample did not just accept or reject the Christian practice of baptism. As it will be seen, they appreciated the many meanings of baptism and appropriated it in new spheres in innovative ways that took it outside official institutional religious structures. The tradition was not just imprinted on them. They negotiated with it and explored its boundaries and elasticity. In doing so, teens experienced the religious tradition as vital and life-shaping.

How Churches Attract Teens

First, I wondered how the congregations that were attracting large numbers of teens were doing it. Given the widely held assumption that institutional religion is less attractive to people today, especially to young people, I sought out three churches that defied expectations and kept high numbers of teens actively participating. I analyzed what attracted teens to these congregations and report these findings in Part I of this book.

Briefly, I found that youth gravitate toward structuring influences that engage them, ones that "grab their attention."[34] Contrary to popular wisdom, the things that grab them are not young, virile youth ministers, activities that are fun and easy, and a contemporary style of music. It is the deeper, more universal things that congregations offer through a variety of means that attract teens: a sense of belonging, a sense of meaning, and opportunities to develop competence.

How Churches Keep Teens

Second, I wondered whether it was still possible for congregations to secure the religious commitment of teens. What happened to foster a long-lasting, durable sense in them that they would continue to be in the church after they left home? In Part II, I report that there are two movements in the development of religious commitment: socialization and religious experience. Congregations that both teach youth the Christian way of life and create conditions where teens feel they meet God tend to have large numbers of teens who predict that they will continue to be active in the church after they leave home. Part II also reports that the process of faith transmission goes two ways: congregations transmit faith to teens and teens transmit back a revised faith that prompts renegotiation about the faith tradition itself. In this renegotiation, the tradition is vitalized.

An unexpected but powerful finding I report in Part II is the distinctiveness of the senior year of high school. On the brink of leaving home, many seventeen- and eighteen-year-olds are overwhelmed with ambivalence about becoming an adult. They are faced with the practical tasks of leaving home, such as writing college applications and deciding what to do, and with the emotional preparatory tasks, such as negotiating familial interdependence and differentiation. Helpful to them were the symbols, rites, and traditions that structured their passage into adulthood and assisted them to express a mature religious commitment. Secular and religious rituals ease the passage by interpreting their departure as part of "what is supposed to happen" in life. The teens' perception of the salience of the faith tradition is enhanced when their religious community offers rites of passage imbued with religious significance.

Seven Styles of Negotiating the Religious Tradition

What about the teens' relationship to the religious tradition? What does their faith look like? What are the different ways that teens "hold" their beliefs? I cast a wide net as I asked teens about religious faith and observed them in different social and institutional contexts. I looked for evidence of a particular religious allegiance, the Christian faith.[35]

Some church-reared teens in my research sample rejected their religious tradition, and others were not well enough socialized into it to have a basis on which to accept or reject it. In Part III, I have called these two types *Rejecters* and *the Lost*, respectively. On the other end of the spectrum, some in my research sample wholly adopted their religious tradition. Others embraced it only after wrestling deeply with it. Still others came back to it after a period of rejecting it. I called these three types, in turn, *Conventionals*, *Classics*, and *Reclaimers*. There were two other types in the middle that were especially interesting because they reflect the sense of self that is ever more possible with a heightened sense of personal autonomy. One I called *Marginalizers* because they held the beliefs consistent with their religious tradition and participated in their church, but their faith was not an important part of their lives, nor was it consistent across social spheres. Marginalizers appeared to have modal selves, transposable to suit their various social worlds. Another type I called *Customizers*. They held the beliefs and participated in the practices of the tradition in an eclectic manner—accepting some aspects and dropping others. Sometimes they augmented their religious tradition with beliefs and practices of other traditions, sometimes with elements they invented or appropriated from popular culture. To organize these seven ways that teens understood their religious identities—specifically, how they viewed the authority of the religious tradition of the church in which they had been baptized—I developed a typology of religious identity. (See fig. 1.)

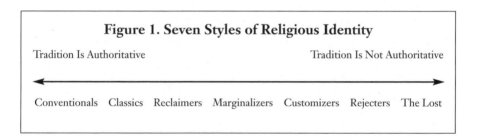

Figure 1. Seven Styles of Religious Identity

Tradition Is Authoritative   Tradition Is Not Authoritative

$\longleftrightarrow$

Conventionals   Classics   Reclaimers   Marginalizers   Customizers   Rejecters   The Lost

Children of Less Religious Parents

Finally, I wondered about the role of the teens' parents in religious socialization. The parents in my sample were baby boomers, a generational group (or cohort) that has been documented to be less religiously loyal than their parents, the World War II generation. (For a discussion of cohort effects, see Appendix G.) I wondered how this generation of less religiously loyal parents was passing on the faith to the next generation. I report the following findings in Part IV.

When teens are reared in families who claim, "In my family, we attend church," they tend to predict that they will remain active in the church after they leave home. Even as high school seniors are less tightly connected to their families—both because of their thinner, more wide-ranging social networks and because they are poised to take up adult roles outside the home—it is possible for some parents to extend their influence a little longer. Some parents make an extra effort to create a teen/parent social network, to maintain a positive relationship with their teen, and to set a religious and moral example. Teens, even high school seniors, usually are not mature enough to sustain a religious commitment without the support of important figures like parents. Additionally, it matters that parents choose a church that is attractive to teens.

The question about parents raises the question about the relative influence of various institutions in teens' lives, including the family. Various institutions compete for the attention of teens, such as the school, the place of part-time employment, the shopping mall, and mass-marketed media. Recent studies show that teens are less influenced by the home than they used to be.[36] The decline has been attributed to the changing nature of family life.[37] In addition, the traditional link between family and church is loosening.[38]

While this may be true, my study finds that the majority of teens still name their parents as the persons who most influence their religious beliefs and practices—for better or worse.

In the Conclusion to this book, I deduce, like Hyde,[39] that parents are the greatest influence on teens who develop loyalty to the religious tradition in which they are reared. While it was beyond the scope of this study to measure religious influence in early childhood, it was evident that the parents' early role of linking the child to the church and teaching the child stories, symbols, and practices had a formative and lasting influence. Teens referred to their "religious foundation" as having shaped their values, faith, and goals.

I found that it matters that parents continue to link the child to the church in their teen years. By the time teens are high school seniors it is rarely possible for parents to enforce a church attendance "rule." If parents have built a warm family climate over time and attend church themselves, however, they can persuade teens to continue to stay with the church.

Together family and church nurture teens in the religious tradition. When teens are held in the church, they learn to see God in their lives. In sociological terms, when there is socialization and religious experience, there tends to be religious loyalty. The key elements related to teen religious loyalty are parents, congregations, socialization, and religious experience. (See below, fig. 2.)

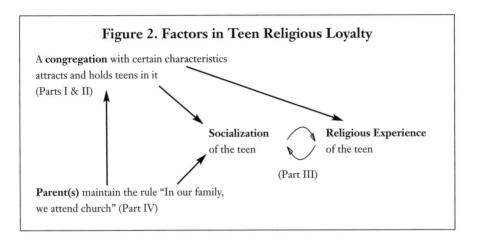

Figure 2. Factors in Teen Religious Loyalty

A **congregation** with certain characteristics
attracts and holds teens in it
(Parts I & II)

Socialization
of the teen

Religious Experience
of the teen

(Part III)

Parent(s) maintain the rule "In our family,
we attend church" (Part IV)

Summing It Up

The transmission of religious faith and society's cultural values to the next generation has been regarded as problematic since ancient times. The Old Testament priest Eli despaired over the apostasy of his sons, Hophni and Phinehas. The seventeenth-century Puritans made compromises to accommodate their less devout offspring through the "Halfway Covenant." H. Richard Niebuhr described how the less isolated, more educated, affluent second-generation children of the founders of sects tended to relax strict religious boundaries to make sects more like churches. Niebuhr observed, "Rarely does a second generation hold the convictions it has inherited with a fervor equal to that of its fathers, who fashioned these convictions in the heat of conflict and at the risk of martyrdom."[40] As sociologist Robert Wuthnow has observed, "The most serious task that the churches have always faced has been the transmission of identity to new generations, and the maintenance of that identity across the life cycle."[41]

Passing on the faith to the next generation is challenging today in a new way. In fact, "passing on the faith" is no longer the task it used to be. Teens *choose* faith instead. American society has changed to favor individual choice of a highly personal religion that is less tethered to religious traditions and institutions. My study demonstrates that churches and Christian families can thrive in this changed context. In plain terms, churches can attract teens if they get beyond the superficial solutions to youth ministry and address teens' deep human needs to belong, to believe, and to be competent. They can hold teens if they get serious about teaching the

faith and introducing teens to an experience of the holy. Churches themselves are revitalized as they pay attention to teens' challenging questions
and radical ideas about Christian commitment. Parents and other adults
can learn from teens how to rekindle their own youthful passion for living the Christian life. Teens have something to teach us about how to live
the Christian faith in this new social context.

Part I

How Churches Attract Teens

Chapter One

Three Congregations

Pastors and church leaders full of the best intentions often base their youth programming on some misguided assumptions about what attracts teens to the church. When searching for someone to lead the youth, they look for a young, virile type who will captivate their interest. They strive to make youth programs fun, eschewing serious and/or controversial theological content because "religious themes" scare away teens. They downplay commitment to the church to make involvement less demanding and therefore more appealing. In this chapter I will show that these assumptions are superficial. The strategies based on them did not prove to be essential characteristics of the three congregations I studied—that is, congregations that were attracting a high number of teens, including high school seniors.

At the time of my study there were approximately 909 religious congregations in Louisville, serving a population of 269,063 within the city limits, rippling out to approximately 984,300 in the larger metropolitan area.[1] Over half of the self-identified "religious" population is either Catholic or Baptist; the other half is mostly other Protestant.[2]

The presence in the city of one of the country's largest Southern Baptist seminaries[3] secures the region's membership in the "Bible Belt," despite the city's marginal location in the upper South.[4] Another significant religious presence is that of four evangelical megachurches.[5] The traffic jams caused by churchgoers on Sunday mornings rival those of business and school traffic on weekdays. On the other hand, with tobacco as the largest crop farmed in the state, the renowned presence of whiskey distilleries, and the horse-racing industry's most famous location (Churchill Downs) in the center of Louisville, Bible Belt religious piety is somewhat moderated.[6] On balance, Louisville's level of religious participation was representative of national patterns. A survey conducted by the main statewide newspaper showed that weekly attendance at churches and synagogues in Kentucky was approximately the same as the national average.[7]

Unlike most southern cities, Louisville has a significant Catholic population.[8] In the nineteenth century, major migrations of Catholic religious orders and missionaries to the Kentucky frontier swelled the Catholic population. One of America's most celebrated Catholic figures, the Trappist monk Thomas Merton, experienced a "turning point," a sudden, heightened religious awareness of social issues and the modern world, in Louisville as he was standing at Fourth and Walnut Streets on March 18, 1958. In the decade and a half before this study, the Roman Catholic Cathedral in Louisville experienced phenomenal growth, from one hundred fifty members to twenty-five hundred, and undertook a complete renovation of its Gothic building.

How did I select from this rich religious landscape a sample of three congregations? Because my goal was to identify what holds church-affiliated youth in their congregations, I did not look for congregations that represented average levels of teen participation. Rather, I sought out the ones that promised to yield a plentiful number of cases of teen religious loyalty. To locate these rich veins, I looked for congregations that were attracting large numbers of teens. In telephone surveys, visits, and preliminary interviews I compiled a list of congregations that appeared to appeal to teens.[9] Second, I looked for congregations that broke out of conventional molds for youth ministry. I was looking for what exceeded the formulas described in manuals of youth ministry. I sought what defied popular wisdom and seemed to garner high teen participation anyway.[10] By investigating some things that struck me as anomalies, I sought to uncover the underlying dynamics of faith transmission to teens.

The Catholic Congregation: "Rituals Keep Them Here"

In a brief telephone survey of thirty-four of the 104 Catholic congregations in Louisville, I was able to estimate the relative activity level of teens in those parishes.[11] In addition, I narrowed the choices through conversations with personal contacts in Catholic churches in Louisville. The names of four congregations regularly surfaced in the telephone survey and in other conversations as the places where the largest numbers of teens participated. One of the four, the Church of the Transfiguration of

Our Lord, attracted forty to one hundred teens to its Sunday night youth group meetings. I also learned that the youth minister at Transfiguration was a fifty-seven-year-old woman whose husband was dying of cancer. That caught my attention. Youth ministers were "supposed" to be young, virile males. How could a female, "the lesser sex" in a male-led institution, and someone at a very different stage in the life cycle, have any appeal to "the youth of raging hormones"?[12]

I made an appointment to meet Angie, the youth minister, at the youth center. I asked her what she did to nurture Christian faith in today's teens. Her immediate answer was "rituals." "It is the way we ritualize the things that are important to kids that keeps them here." Rituals? That was puzzling to me. I had never seen that mentioned in a handbook on youth ministry. Furthermore, according to postmodern sensibilities, life was in a constant state of flux and fragmentation. It is a bricolage of disparate elements. Ritual sounded too stable and traditional to me. I wanted to understand more about how that worked at Transfiguration.[13]

During that initial meeting with Angie, a recent graduate of the youth program happened to drop in to visit her. "What can I do to help you with the retreat?" he asked. He was attending college locally, and was volunteering as an advisor with the high school group. "I'll make some telephone calls for you," he offered. I was impressed. Obviously this young man's experience in Angie's high school youth group was important to him. It was so important, he was volunteering his time at a point in life when most young adults are anxious to shed connections to the church in which they were reared. The puzzle of Transfiguration intrigued me.

The Evangelical Protestant Congregation: "Where They Set the Bar High"

My selection of an evangelical church in which to study faith transmission to teens was perhaps the most obvious of the three choices I had to make. Riverland Heights Evangelical had a widespread reputation in Louisville and beyond as one of the fastest growing megachurches in the country.[14] Church leaders and researchers were curious to know more about it. In 1998 it ranked as one of the ten largest churches in the United States, measured by weekly attendance averaging eleven thousand each weekend. Riverland Heights' proposed new church complex also attracted national attention.[15] What was this megachurch doing to attract so many people, especially younger ones?[16]

One of the ways I probed the possibility of studying at Riverland

Heights was by attending their training session for volunteer adult sponsors of the youth group. What I heard piqued my interest because it was not what I expected. At the first training session, Bret, one of the three full-time paid high school youth leaders, described how he recruited youth for their Sunday night Bible study program. He said, "I tell them, 'Don't come.' I tell the kids, 'If you can't make a serious commitment to the program, don't sign up for it.'" I wondered how this was supposed to attract teens to the youth program. Tell them not to come unless they are serious![17] That defies the popular wisdom about attracting teens to the church. The gist of most of the applied literature on youth ministry advises making activities fun and easy for youth to join in.[18]

Bret reviewed for the sponsors the overall strategy of the youth program at Riverland Heights, highlighting its progressive levels of commitment.[19] At the entry level, the program offers a midweek meeting called Vision, where all are welcome. On average, four hundred high school teens attend. The next level is the Sunday morning/Saturday night class for teaching and discussion called Insight. Youth leaders estimated that if teens like the midweek Vision meetings enough to attend three times, they start to come to Insight and to church services held at five different times on Saturday evening and Sunday morning. When teens are ready to make a serious commitment, they join the third level, the Focus program, with its twin goals of "extreme worship" and "extreme evangelism." To achieve its goals, teens agree to several commitments. Teens must attend one of the church worship services every weekend and the Sunday night Focus meeting that begins with the singing of praise songs accompanied by body movement. Focus teens must have a daily time of prayer, Bible reading, and journaling. In addition, Focus teens must target nonbelievers for evangelism. They must befriend nonbelievers and invite them to the midweek Vision meetings.

Teens choosing the highest level of involvement are held accountable to their commitments in several ways. In small "Focus family groups," teens and sponsors review assigned lessons that they have studied during the week. Leaders look for indicators of enthusiasm, such as whether teens carry their Bibles around with them and whether they quickly locate Bible verses when they are referenced. They notice whether teens dance in worship. Teens report to their Focus family group the names of persons they are "targeting," and together they pray for those specific individuals.

One girl explained how those who accept it view this challenge to extreme worship and extreme evangelism positively. "I love Focus because they set the bar high. You get serious about your commitment to God because God is seriously in love with you. . . ." She went on to refer to her evangelism efforts: "I don't come to Vision meetings to get anything out of it for myself. I come because I'm supposed to bring others to Christ, and I need to support the meeting." She summarized, "The church is not here to entertain me."

These comments indicate that Riverland Heights fostered high levels of religious commitment in teens through its program. As Bret put it, Focus teens are "the owners" not "the consumers" of the youth program. In a marketplace-dominated culture where religion is often construed as a commodity, Riverland Heights finessed the metaphor to shape high levels of ownership in its teens of the ministry of their church.

The Mainline Protestant Congregation: "More Mozart Please"

My third church, the mainline Protestant congregation, was one I kept trying to eliminate as a choice. I did not want to study First United Methodist because it was without a youth minister at the time I began my study. The previous youth minister had been fired over the summer and the youth minister search committee was having difficulty finding someone to take the job.[20] One of the teens' mothers volunteered to keep the youth program going during the interim, juggling that with her full-time job as a preschool teacher. Furthermore, the church building was scheduled to be torn up and renovated during the year. Members were supposed to park at a nearby mall and take chartered shuttle buses to the church facility to save for visitors the few parking spaces not roped off in the construction site.[21] Despite these irregularities and inconveniences, I found myself hooked on this church after my first visit.

One hot Sunday at the beginning of August, I slipped into the balcony at First United Methodist for its eleven o'clock service. For most churches, attendance plummets in the month of August, with many parishioners out of town and those remaining less willing to exert themselves in the hot weather. Often the musical offerings in worship are at a low ebb as well. Soloists and small choir sections regularly provide the "special music" in place of the choir. With that low expectation, I was surprised to see a relatively full sanctuary of worshipers, numbering approximately four hundred. I was even more surprised to see a large choir numbering eighty-five in the chancel. I noted the excellent quality of the music they performed and their versatility at alternating between traditional and contemporary pieces. Most of all, I was struck by the visibility of teens leading worship. There were twelve people in the choir who appeared to be of high school age. The last hymn was accompanied by teens playing electric guitars.

Even though I continued to investigate other mainline Protestant churches for this study, I kept returning to First United Methodist because of its appeal through music to its teens. In time, I decided that even if the high school youth group at this church was not functioning at a high level, the music ministry held teens in the church in significant ways. That in itself offered something worthy of investigation.

I had heard the music program at First United Methodist described by others in the community as the proverbial "tail that wags the dog." A very popular pair of music directors generated excitement in this congregation, especially with youth. The high school choir averaged thirty-five members during the school year. The high school bell choir averaged twelve. At First United Methodist the teens were so serious about their music that they went on a retreat every February so they could rehearse, build relationships, and give attention to the Christian message of their music. Every June, the high school choir traveled "on tour" for the period of a week.

Most intriguing to me at First United Methodist was how the teens found the full range of musical literature appealing. It is commonly accepted wisdom in youth ministry that a contemporary style of music is crucial to attracting teens. Riverland Heights Evangelical is often held up as an example of a church that successfully attracts younger people, including teens, through its contemporary music and worship. At First United Methodist, however, the music that the high school choir performed was more often traditional than contemporary. When the choir director invited the teens to choose their favorite piece from their repertoire to finish out their year, they chose a piece in Latin written by Mozart. In a group interview I conducted with the high school bell choir, I asked them what they thought about different styles of music. One girl admitted that she tried attending Riverland Heights with a friend, but found the contemporary style of music "too boring" in the repetition of its lyrics and simple melodies. "It's just 'praise God, praise God, praise God,'" she claimed. "We have our niche that is different than Riverland Heights's," the choir director at First United Methodist explained. "We need to be ourselves."[22]

Each of these three congregations made me curious to understand how they could hold so many teens in the church when they flaunted the shibboleths of youth ministry. Young, virile, male, youth ministers are not required to attract teens. It is not true that "fun and easy" brings out the teens. Contemporary music is not the crucial ingredient for youth worship. While many churches choose young adult males to be role models and leaders of their youth groups, while many teens cite boredom as the reason for staying away from church, and while most American teens find contemporary music more appealing than other styles, these factors are superficial. Focusing on these surface aspects of church life trivializes the deeper processes of religious meaning making, identity formation, and communal attachment that occur in the church lives of teens. The elements of church life that engage teens are more fundamental.

I could have subtitled this chapter "Three Good Ways to Do Youth Ministry," because each of these three congregations holds teenaged youth in its religious institution in impressive ways. I discovered on closer examination, however, that youth ministers themselves do not view their programs as perfect. As I describe what works, I also will describe some of the struggles, as well as the contradictions I observed.

Chapter Two

What Attracts Teens to Churches

My bottom-line interview question to teens, parents, school person-nel, and church leaders who worked with teens was: "What most influences what teens believe about God and how they practice their faith?" Some of the replies were "peers," "their parents," "music," and "mass media." (See fig. 3.) One response summarized these replies and expressed what I observed in my research. The high school principal at St. Peter said, "It's what engages them most. That's what they'll gravitate to."

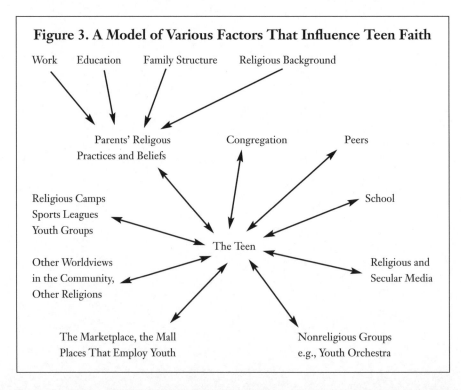

Figure 3. A Model of Various Factors That Influence Teen Faith

Work   Education   Family Structure   Religious Background

Parents' Religous Practices and Beliefs   Congregation   Peers

Religious Camps
Sports Leagues
Youth Groups

School

The Teen

Other Worldviews
in the Community,
Other Religions

Religious and
Secular Media

The Marketplace, the Mall
Places That Employ Youth

Nonreligious Groups
e.g., Youth Orchestra

Csikszentmihalyi and Larson (1984) find that "catching teens' attention" is the first step in engaging them. They coined the term "flow" (or negentropy) to describe the state of being caught, or totally engaged. It is a state of "self-transcendence" in which teens experience "harmony between dimensions of consciousness: between goals, thoughts, emotions, and activations." They found that flow was more commonly associated with leisure activities than with time spent in school. They discovered that regardless of a student's ability, performance was best in classes that were enjoyable.

While Csikszentmihalyi and Larson did not focus on teen reports of their experiences in religious institutions, their basic theory of motivation is useful for understanding teens in this context. What engages teens in their religious institutions is what catches their attention and produces "flow." What "motivates" teens to pursue the religious life is experiencing an intense state of divine transcendence in which goals, thoughts, emotions, and activations are united.

Csikszentmihalyi and Larson note that catching teens' attention is a "reciprocal exchange between growing persons and their environments." "If there is a process of 'catching,' it is as much the teenager as the adult who must do it."[1] It involves a transformation from one type of consciousness to another, a restructuring of the teens' instincts, habits, and values. The "energies" of youth can be reallocated from selfish goals to societal goals. This occurs when youth learn to experience flow in situations that lead toward maturity, like learning a musical instrument as compared to getting high. Plato observed two thousand years ago that the highest goal of education is to train youths to find pleasure and pain in the right objects.[2] Similarly, a curiosity and interest in religious questions is cultivated when attention is turned to God as the object. Engagement in one's religious tradition requires the teen to order his or her complex array of opportunities to give priority to seeking flow in the Christian life.

I concluded from my year of research that when teens are attracted to churches, they are attracted because the churches engage them in intense states of self-transcendence uniting emotional and cognitive processes. Churches "catch" them on three hooks: a sense of belonging, a sense of meaning, and opportunities to develop competence. When churches' ministries with youth include these components, teens will restructure their time and attention to participate in them. (See fig. 4.) I discovered that teens stayed engaged in their congregations if they perceived that they offered, at a minimum, either a sense of belonging or a coherence of meaning. The third component, the opportunity to develop competence, was optional but very desirable. Teens participated at highest levels in their churches when they perceived them to offer all three of these components.

Before I describe how I observed this, I note that the first two components, belonging and believing, are regularly identified as two essential components of religious life. Greeley (1972) calls "belonging" and "meaning" the twin aspects of religious commitment. Roof (1978) appro-

**Figure 4. Three Components of Congregations
That Attract Teen Participation**

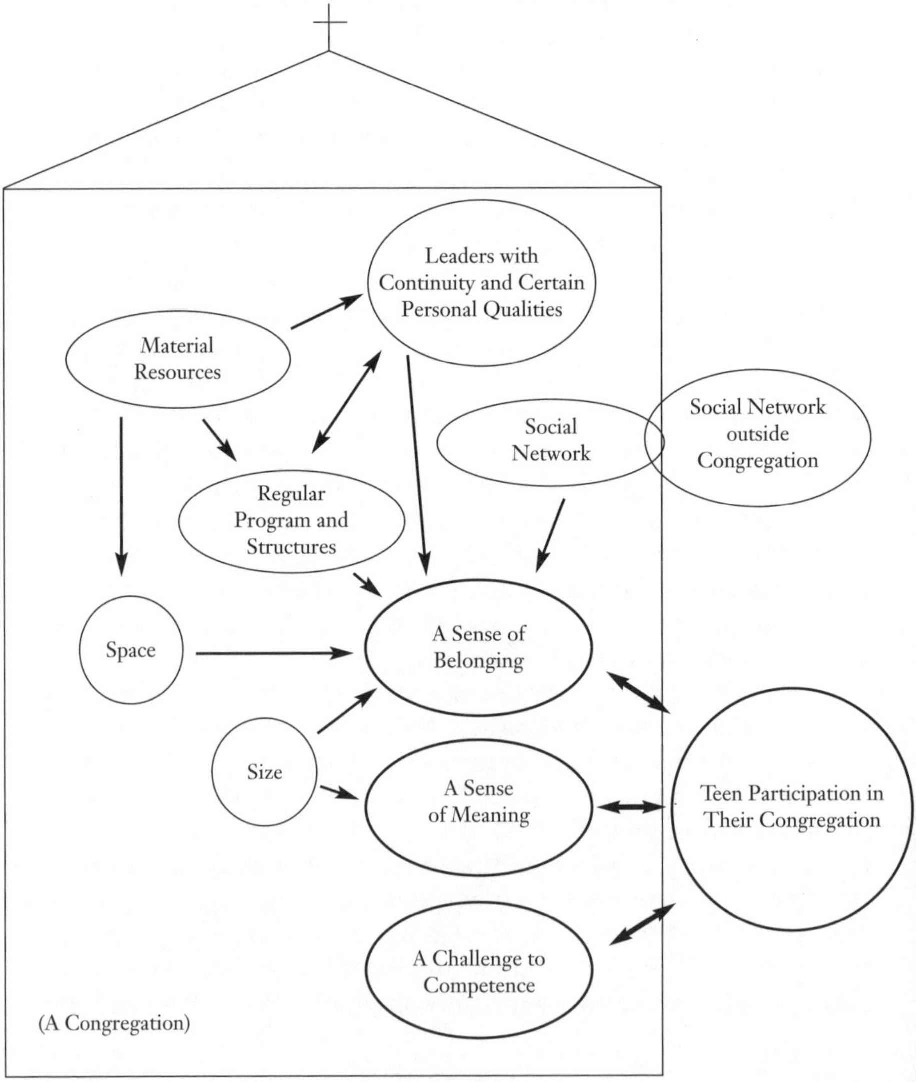

priates this twofold framework in his study of religious commitment.[3] What I identify as a third component, the challenge to develop competence, emerges as significant with this population of high school seniors because of their stage in the life cycle. They anticipate their imminent departure from their families of origin. They want to develop competencies that will enable them to live away from home and participate in the larger, more public institutions of the adult world. (A fuller description of how adolescence has come to be understood is found in Appendix E.)

A Sense of Belonging

"Youth group is where I get my once-a-week hug," said Paul, a senior at Transfiguration. Churches are social institutions, and one of the key reasons people are attracted to them is for the social relationships they offer.[4] That may be true for people of all ages, but it is true for teens in a particular way.[5] Social relationships, especially peer group relations, are important to teens.[6]

Congregations do not always attract and hold their youth in their social network. The lament "We are losing our youth" rings forth from many congregations in the country.[7] In the case of these three congregations, however, this was not the situation. Here I offer an analysis of what enabled the three congregations in my sample to foster significant levels of belonging in an impressive number of their teens.

Structures and Resources

First and most obvious, each of these three congregations has in common an age-graded structure to facilitate the formation of community for youth. As Dean and Yost note, by far the most common structure of almost all denominational youth programs among both Christians and Jews is the "youth group," a clublike gathering of young people who meet for socializing, study, community service, and worship.[8] At First United Methodist, teens also could belong to age-graded choirs and Sunday school classes. Riverland Heights offers all these opportunities, and teen sports leagues as well. While there are religious congregations across the country in which teens have a strong sense of belonging without these age-graded groups, in the congregations I studied many teens who reported that they felt strong attachment to their church related a sense of belonging to a teen subgroup within the congregation.[9]

Certain demographic characteristics favor the formation of subgroups of teens in churches. It is no coincidence that the three congregations I chose to study are well funded and large, with each of them having a membership well over the two-hundred-member national average for congregations.[10] A 1988 Search Institute survey of junior high youth groups in Christian congregations found that 55 percent of these programs were located in suburban churches with memberships averaging over two thousand. Sixty percent of these churches considered themselves "wealthy."[11]

"The bigger, the better" needs qualification, however. When a church increases its membership, the relational dynamics change. Some at Riverland Heights found that this desirable outcome of their evangelistic efforts had reached the point of diminishing returns for their own sense of belonging. At Riverland Heights the families who had been with the church since their teens were infants often expressed disappointment that they were not as well known in their congregation as they used to be when the church membership was smaller. When there was slippage, it occurred most at the megachurch because teens were not missed when they stopped attending. One girl who had been active in youth group in her early years of high school expressed hurt that earlier that year the youth leaders walked by her at a funeral without any recognition or acknowledgment. With over one thousand names on the mailing list of the high school youth program and a 25 percent turnover each year with high school graduation, it is not surprising that she was forgotten.[12] As I worked with the mailing list of seniors, I noted some errors in it that youth leaders might have caught had they been able to know each of these youth as individuals, as youth were known at Transfiguration and First United Methodist.

Few churches face Riverland Heights's problem of having so many teens on the rolls that they cannot be known. More common is the problem of having too few teens on the rolls of the congregation or mailing list from which to build a viable social group. Generally congregations of all sizes do not get 100 percent of their teens to participate in church youth activities. After accounting for the inevitable percentage of inactives, there still must be a sufficient number of active youth to form a critical mass of teens who can be counted on to support youth activities in the church. Transfiguration, with approximately five hundred teens in grades nine through twelve on the mailing list, could count on having enough youth show up at their events for them to come off. Needless to say, this was true of Riverland Heights as well. The megachurch had a base of high school youth on the rolls that was larger than most churches' total congregational membership. Just the number of high school seniors, 260, exceeds the average size of an entire congregation.[13] First United Methodist also had a large enough roll of teens, approximately one hundred, to provide a dependable core group for their activities, even though this was considered a "slump year" for the youth group.

Besides having numerical potential for teen participation, churches must offer a sufficient number of activities for the youth to meet frequently and regularly enough to develop friendships. Each of the churches I studied offered regular opportunities for youth to meet at least three times per week. Youth established habits of attending these activities at particular times, and they became dependable attendees. Frequency of social contact is essential to building the strong relationships that youth will consider primary friendships, the ones they rely on to sustain them in the rocky years of high school. (See Appendix I.)

Having physical space at the church dedicated to the youth program was a key resource for teens' sense of belonging. The previous spring, a generous donor gave Transfiguration money to build a separate two-story youth center on its property. Teens contributed the "sweat equity" of their physical labor in its construction. The result was an attractive fifteen-hundred-square-foot structure with a large, carpeted meeting area upstairs focused on a stone fireplace and a recreational area downstairs with a pool table, a place to play board games, bookshelves for reading material, office space, and comfortable couches. There were kitchenettes upstairs and downstairs.

The youth center at Transfiguration was highly charged with a symbolic significance that became evident when it became a battleground. Adult members of the parish scheduled activities at the youth center when it was not used by the youth. One night, teens arrived at youth group to find that tables, folding chairs, and a piano had been moved in for the adult activities. The adults had encroached too far, and the youth deposited the items back at the main building. Their immediate and dramatic reaction indicated the strength of their feelings about having ownership of their space at the church.[14]

At Riverland Heights, senior high and junior high teens met in the structure that had been the church building ten years ago, when the congregation outgrew their facilities and built a bigger complex a quarter mile down the street. The youth minister and teens referred to the main complex of church buildings as "down the street," and they called the corporate worship held there "big church." The physical separation of the two locations of ministry accentuated the segmentation of the youth ministry from the rest of the congregation. It was often the case that families came to church in separate cars, with some going "down the street" and others going to the youth complex. Sometimes family members did not see each other at all during the time they were in church, unless they made plans to meet at "big church." Paradoxically, while teens were more separated physically from their parents and other adults at Riverland Heights than at the two other churches, Riverland Heights had the highest percentage of "family attenders," a variable that predicts teen religious loyalty. (This will be defined and discussed in Part IV.)

First United Methodist was in the process of constructing a new wing of the building, which included six rooms dedicated to the junior and senior high ministry. Just as the teen area was physically connected to the whole church building, Methodist teens (as compared to Catholic and evangelical teens in this study) were more connected and integrated into the general worship and program life of their church. Teens served as officers on the church boards. On Stewardship Sunday they joined the line of members depositing their pledge envelopes in the collection box at the altar. One of the teens chaired the Advent devotional booklet committee for the whole congregation. Another teen was responsible for decorating the chrismon tree that adorned the sanctuary at Christmas. During Lent, high school teens carried a heavy wooden cross down the center aisle at the beginning of the service. To teens at First United Methodist, the physical space of the whole church was their space, as well as the new rooms that were under construction.

Material resources assisted the teens to have a sense of belonging to their church in one other significant way. Each of the churches in my sample had the means to hire staff to work with teens. Each congregation dedicated significant human resources to the youth ministry, both paid professionals and volunteer leaders who were guided by professionals.[15] Two things were notable about the leadership of these programs that attracted many youth: the continuity of leadership in these programs and the personal qualities of the leaders.

The average tenure of a youth minister has been estimated to be only two and one-half years.[16] Two out of three of these churches were able to maintain their leaders for much longer periods. Angie was involved in youth ministry at Transfiguration for twenty-two years. The head youth minister had been at Riverland Heights for seven years. First United Methodist's turnover of youth ministers was closer to the norm. First United Methodist compensated, however. The choir director had been there seven years and the bell choir director had been there almost as long. The Sunday school teacher of the high school juniors and seniors had been teaching the class almost continuously for twenty years. Continuity of leadership is a positive factor that holds teens in their churches. I noted that when teens at First United Methodist described the point at which they became inactive, they tended to link it with the departure of a youth minister. When a youth minister leaves, it is like a train making a stop at a station. It creates an opportunity for teens to get off, even if they did not particularly like the youth minister.

The clergy and key leaders working with youth in each of these congregations also displayed common personal qualities that superseded denominational traditions. They were more humble than arrogant. They appeared to be vulnerable instead of perfect. They cultivated "warm"[17] relations among their colleagues and volunteer adults who worked with them in youth ministry. They impressed teens by doing something that was outside their "job description."

The humility of the senior pastor at Riverland Heights was striking to me, for example, especially in comparison to what I had read about Earl Paulk, the pastor of a smaller megachurch, who openly reveled in the accolades of his congregation.[18] Bill West shunned public displays of Riverland Heights's boundless admiration for him. Once West was absent for two weeks on a mission trip to India. While he was away, he developed phlebitis, a life-threatening physical condition. The congregation tensely awaited his safe return for ten days. When he stepped up to the podium in the worship auditorium for the first time after recovering, I expected sustained applause and a standing ovation to greet him. Instead, West launched directly into his sermon without a pause, preempting that possibility. His message hardly made reference to the hardship he had endured.[19]

Vulnerability was exemplified by Craig, the youth minister at Riverland Heights. I had observed him for two months before I knew that his wife was clinically depressed and that he had been a de facto single parent for the last three years while she lay in bed. I learned about it by reading an article on the front page of Riverland Heights's weekly newspaper, a publication with a circulation of 15,000 reaching an estimated readership of 35,000. The story did not boast a happy ending, either, as it reported that Craig's wife still struggled to overcome her condition by relying on God. The very public vulnerability of Craig and his wife eclipsed any illusions of their perfection. I observed teens on the retreat gathering around Craig's wife. Her openness about her disabling condition touched them.

Warmth in staff relationships was also exemplified by Roderick, the choir director at First United Methodist, who refers to his colleagues on the church staff as his "best friends." Roderick writes hilarious lyrics to songs to honor staff members on their birthdays. Quips of humor, much of it corny, constantly passed among them. Mimi, the bell choir director, appeared at Roderick's door with a picture frame and nail in hand: "Roderick, do you have a hammer?" "If I had a hammer . . . ," the choir director sang in reply. The merriment of the staff was contagious. The members of the choir created a "soapbox" for Roderick to stand on while he directed them, a box covered with soapbox labels. Roderick, like all the paid staff working with youth in these three congregations, built a congenial community of volunteers who enjoyed working together and with the teens.[20]

Teens were always impressed when youth leaders were willing to go outside their job descriptions to show their interest or trust in them in large and small ways.[21] One boy appreciated the way Craig allowed him to borrow some of Riverland Heights's sound equipment. Another teen mentioned that Roderick gave her a ride to choir rehearsals. An indication of Angie's "second mile" ministry is revealed in a story her adult daughter happened to tell me. According to my notes:

> Halloween had always been a big deal at their house, "ten times bigger than Christmas." They had the front hall decorated. Trick-or-treaters came inside to receive their candy from a bucket lowered from the ceiling by a pulley and bedsheet they had rigged up to look like a ghost. Last Halloween, after Angie's husband was diagnosed with cancer, they had fewer decorations than usual. Angie just handed out candy at the door. She was surprised when she opened the door once to find a man in a business suit standing there. She wondered, Did he come for candy? Should I give him candy? He told her he was in her youth group twenty years ago when she first started doing youth ministry. He was back in town on business and he had a powerful urge to come by and see her. She had had a lasting influence on his life, and he wanted to thank her.[22]

In all, the personal characteristics of the leaders in these three congregations, as illustrated above, offer indications of the elements of church-based youth ministry programs that hold their teens. The gender or age of the youth minister did not correlate with effectiveness in attracting youth. I noted that Angie hired a young adult male to be her assistant. Likewise, the head youth minister at Riverland Heights, a male, was complemented by a female who had a key responsibility with youth. While

Roderick, a male, was perhaps the key charismatic leader with youth at First United Methodist, his magnetism had much more to do with his high level of energy, intelligence, interpersonal skills, and talent than did his gender.

Social Networks within Congregations: Openness and Tightness

A second feature of these three congregations that associates positively with teens' social attachment to them—beyond the structural features of the congregation and characteristics of its leadership—is the quality of the peer social network itself. The significant factor is having an optimal degree of openness in the web of social relationships in the congregation. On the one hand, church groups can be so tight that a newcomer cannot join in. On the other hand, groups can be so loose that there is nothing to hold people in.[23] Finding the right degree of openness is hard to define and difficult to achieve. Each of the three congregations was perceived by different teens as both succeeding and failing in this.

Transfiguration was generally the tightest of the three groups I studied. The bonds of friendship among its members appeared to be strongest as indicated by several factors. Their depth of sharing and their degree of vulnerability about personal, sensitive topics was striking.[24] The outward affection teens demonstrated to one another was notable in comparison with the two other groups. It was not unusual for someone to be greeted with hugs on entering the youth center at Transfiguration. I found myself unconsciously imitating this gesture toward the end of my field research at Transfiguration.

Some teens, however, reported that they did not feel included at Transfiguration's youth group. One of the markers of inclusion was how close one's friendship had been with Maureen, the girl who died the previous spring. One thing that united this group was its grief over her death. The closer one was to her, the more one had a "right to grieve,"[25] and to be in the inner circle. At times, members would raise for group discussion the issue of cliquishness within the youth group. Angie expended a lot of effort to counter clique exclusion of outsiders by assigning teens to work in discussion and planning subgroups that mixed people outside their cliques.

Various individual roles and statuses emerged in the youth groups that were similar to those outside the church. Marketing research names and stratifies teens in the following order of status (from top down) as "influencers or channelers," "edge," "conformers," and "passives." The majority of teens, the "conformers," are always watching the "influencers" to know how to act and what to wear and to try to get to a higher level themselves.[26] Similarly, in my interviews with teens in all three of the congregations, they identified particular teens in the church as influencers, and sometimes agonized that they were not closer to one of them. The influencers themselves tended to report satisfaction with their relationships. As one said, "In youth group, I have forty best friends."

Angie worked hard, not just to counter the cliques and exclusion of less popular teens, but also to create openings for newcomers at Transfiguration. She always took time to make introductions at the beginning of meetings and to lead a hearty applause of welcome. Like the shepherd going after the hundredth sheep, she combed the list of teens in the parish and labored to get each one involved. A common story told by teens about Angie was about how she kept calling them on the telephone until they finally relented and tried youth group. She found out who their friends were and what interests they had. One boy told me she snagged him by telling him he was needed as a guitarist to revive the youth group band for the upcoming retreat.

"Flirting for God" was another one of Angie's strategies. She arranged for an inactive girl to be called by an attractive boy who offered her a ride to youth group. Catholic high schools in Louisville are single sex, and this adds incentive for teens to find places to meet in extracurricular settings.

Some of Angie's recruitment efforts involved whole families. To get the Tubbs's three teens to try youth group, she invited the father to assist in distributing the sacrament at the mass celebrated on the retreat. When the family of five showed up at the retreat, Angie introduced each family member individually in such an effusively complimentary manner it was humorous to me. Youth group regulars, familiar with Angie's warm style, did not find it unusual.

As a researcher, I was sensitive to how different groups included and excluded me as well. Transfiguration was the hardest group for me to break into, because the teens guarded their cherished friendships from interlopers.[27] At the other extreme, I was included so readily in First United Methodist's group that at times I felt I was fulfilling an unmet need for friendship on the part of some of the youth. I also discovered that the web of relationships in each congregation was not uniformly tight or loose. Within each of the youth groups, there were tight subgroups (or cliques) that did not welcome newcomers. Within each of the youth groups, there were loners only too happy to glom onto a friendly researcher.

Youth group, like home, is "the place where . . . they have to take you in." There were teens in each of the three groups who did not have highly developed social skills and came to their church because it was the one group that had to take them in. Most times, these kids were relegated to an outer ring surrounding the inner circle of popular teens. Sometimes these less socially skilled teens were able to move closer inside as they stuck with the group over time.[28]

Others, even some who were popular in their high schools and other settings, gave up on feeling accepted at youth group. Chad and Tiffany, for example, a varsity football player and his Jennifer Aniston[29] look-alike girlfriend, were popular enough in their high school to be elected king and queen of their prom. They found the inner circle of the youth group at Riverland Heights too hard to break into, however. Instead, they just attended church services and played on the intramural sports teams at the church. As observed above, the large size of the megachurch church can be a liability in the formation of social networks that are tight enough to hold people in. The sheer number of potentially active teens at Riverland Heights was so great that there were too many teens for the leaders to pursue and woo, as Angie did at Transfiguration. The fabric of relationships at the megachurch church was looser, and likelihood was greater for teens to slip through the holes in the loose weave.

Multiplex Relations

Finally, the sense of belonging among teens in a church was tested by how the relationships endured outside the official activities of the church. As one mother at First United Methodist put it, "The kids in this youth group enjoy each other. They even get together outside of church." In each of these congregations, there was evidence that the friendships exceeded the bounds of scheduled church functions. Informal groups of teens went out to eat after youth meetings. Teens from the same church were friends in school as well as at church. Teens from the same church went to the prom together. When the relationships were "multiplex,"[30] church friends tended to become the teens' "primary group."[31] School-based parachurch organizations like Campus Life and Fellowship of Christian Athletes, as well as events like Rock the Pole,[32] provided opportunities for a sense of belonging to a religious community to extend to a setting beyond the congregation.

The sense of belonging, more than interesting activities, attracted and held teens in the church. Numerous manuals on youth ministry emphasize planning novel, exciting, and attention-getting activities to keep youth interested. In the course of my study, I saw many teens coming to church to perform some routine, programming, administrative, and/or maintenance activities, like breaking into small groups to brainstorm how they could attract more people to youth group, planning segments of a retreat, assembling a picnic table for the patio of the youth building, and rehearsing their music. They were willing to engage in what some would call "boring activities" because they were tied into the group through the sense of belonging.[33] "The friendship factor," along with the structures that support it, are the key variables in teen attachment to their churches.

A Sense of Meaning

Sociologist Wade Clark Roof argues for the primacy of belonging over believing as the crucial element in maintaining religious commitment. He notes that belief systems always rest on a social base. Beliefs are shaped and reinforced in normal, everyday processes of social interaction. People derive support for their religious convictions in direct and subtle ways as they belong to social networks within religious institutions.[34] My findings about teen religious attachment are consistent with that understanding.

There were some teens I encountered in my study, however, who clearly came to church seeking religious meaning more than the church's social benefits. They did not participate in youth group or in any of the teen-designated social activities of the church. Some teens who attended church were not known by name by anyone in the church. They did not mind being strangers because they came primarily for reinforcement in their sense that the meaning of life was grounded on a belief in God. They came because they wanted to study the Bible, receive Communion, and worship God.

Typical of this type was a boy I saw one evening at Riverland Heights sitting alone in the back row of a Sunday school class. I slipped into an empty seat on one side of him and initiated a conversation. I learned that John and his father were planning to transfer their membership from a small Methodist church to Riverland Heights. John's father, a school basketball coach, had been invited by a member of Riverland Heights to accompany the church basketball team as they traveled to Poland on a sports/mission tour. The father had a life-changing experience on the trip. Now father and son were interested in exploring more about what it means to be a Christian. John came to the youth meeting to learn more about God.

As Max Weber asserts, people are meaning makers, not driven solely by needs, as Freud describes them. Nor are they defined only by social conditions, as Marx describes them. Human beings develop understandings of the world—what it demands and allows. They also develop understandings of themselves in the world—what they are to do and be in relation to those demands and permissions. They ask moral questions about how to measure relations among persons and structures of the world, about what is good and what is right. Through the symbols, narratives, ordered relationships, and the structures of their contexts, human beings fashion meaning. Religion offers a ground of being that orients and orders those understandings in the most comprehensive way. More than offering a system of truths, religion encompasses the meanings of the whole of life. Religious institutions offer persons, including teens, a way to make sense out of their comprehensive experience. Unlike the other institutions of teens' lives—their schools, sports, and jobs that focus on a discrete understanding of a segment of life—religious institutions strive to make sense of the whole of life, pointing to a "ground of being" (God) on which all other understandings are built. My research finds that when religious institutions seriously address the questions of meaning, teens are attracted to them.

Like John, Jeff was a loner at Riverland Heights. In fact, he kept so much to himself that the youth leaders identified him as a dropout in their program. Hoping to find someone who could represent the disaffected, I telephoned Jeff for an interview. I discovered that he was, in fact, strong in his religious convictions. He was a loyal member of another church, but he kept his name on the mailing list at Riverland Heights because he enjoyed coming occasionally to midweek Vision meetings. When I saw Jeff at Vision, he was always sitting alone. He said, "I just like being with so many Christian kids, and I like Craig's preaching." In Jeff's own small fundamentalist Bible church, there were only two teens in the entire congregation. He attended an Episcopal Church-related school during the week that he described as "totally secular." He was shored up in the plausibility of his faith by sitting in the presence of his religious peers and hearing the youth leader preach. As Berger and Luckmann (1966) describe, the plausibility of the religious belief is shored up in the religious community. The sheer size of Riverland Heights made it the most effective of the three churches in offering plausibility structures that reinforced religious meaning.

Jeff did not need friends at Riverland Heights; he just needed a Christian reference group, "religious peers," who validated his sense of God and legitimated his Christian values. Usually teens like these have their social needs addressed in other settings. They tend to live more segmented lives, with different sets of friends for different contexts.[35]

Especially at Riverland Heights, teens said they came to church primarily to learn about God. The rigorous commitment to worship and evangelism required of insiders was too great for those who just wanted a place to belong. Even if teens stayed on the periphery of the social networks at Riverland Heights, they could not miss the church's emphasis on the plausibility of a belief in God that permeates every activity. Guidance was given at every gathering for how to view modern culture through a Christian lens. Sermons reduced the dissonance with modern scientific culture by offering arguments for creationism. Clear biblical guidelines for sexual purity were emphasized at midweek youth meetings. Speakers presented programs promoting the pro-life stance on abortion. Teens were told how to respond to the Goth-style bisexual musician Marilyn Manson when he/she visited Louisville that spring. They were advised not to picket the concert, but instead to witness by quietly praying for his/her salvation.

Norms of language and dress at Riverland Heights also shored up belief. Teens readily used first-order religious language. They adopted the WWJD logos on bracelets and T-shirts.[36] In all three churches, the youth leaders were very clear about the theological grounding of their work with youth.[37] They were not running "a social club." They expressed the desired religious outcomes of their youth programs in different ways, however. Craig said that at Riverland Heights the goal is for each teen to have a relationship with Jesus Christ. He cited the parables of the prodigal son and the lost sheep. "We are here to save the lost, and teens today are the most at risk." At Transfiguration, Angie described the goal of the youth ministry as "to reach the hearts of teens to complement the 'head learning' [doctrine] they get at [Catholic] school." Jesus ministered through relationships, she noted, and hers is a "relational theology." In addition, she described herself as "very in tune with the Vatican II documents." She believes all people have a ministry, not just the clergy, and a goal for the teens at Transfiguration is to find their ministry. In a paper she wrote, "Our young people are already ministers."[38] At First United Methodist, the new youth minister told parents that they were in the business of "making disciples." Their ministry with youth would succeed when each teen developed a mature commitment to Christ and developed gifts in the service of God's kingdom.[39]

Evangelicals stressed conversion and personal religion. Catholics and

Methodists placed higher priority on moral maturity.[40] At Transfiguration and First United Methodist, in comparison to Riverland Heights, teens were led through a consciousness-raising process designed to help them articulate for themselves a moral critique of their society and a sense of their role in it.[41] Because these teens claim their own stance, their social views are more diverse than those of teens at Riverland Heights, notably on social issues such as homosexuality, abortion, and interracial dating. Tolerance for differences of opinion was highly valued.

Theological heterodoxy also was tolerated more readily at Transfiguration and First United Methodist than it was at Riverland Heights. Some teens openly voiced their doubts about the authority of the Bible and the absolute claims of the Christian faith in a pluralistic world. This was disturbing to other teens in those churches, however. As one teen at First United Methodist expressed it, "I wish that the Sunday school teacher would not leave the discussions so open-ended." Adult leaders generally did not assert a clear orthodox position as definitive guidance to resolve questions or differences of opinion expressed by the teens. There was comment by some teens at both Transfiguration and at First United Methodist that the youth group was more social than "religious." One teen at Transfiguration clarified the sense in which she viewed youth group as religious: "It gets at religion through unconditional acceptance."

Beyond teaching and small-group discussion, teens at Transfiguration and First United Methodist derived a sense of theological meaning from the worship and opportunities for service. Their quest for understanding ultimate meanings led them to engage in the sacraments, rituals, music, and rhythm of worship that these churches offered. In chapter 3, I will show how teens in these churches were attracted to the meanings they derived from worship in the three congregations, albeit in different degrees and in different ways.

A Challenge to Competence

Generally when teens described their reasons for participating in church, they mentioned either the sense of belonging they enjoyed there or the church's worship and teaching, which offered meaning to their lives. Very often teens cited both belonging and believing as their reasons for their participation. There was a third reason (often given in conjunction with the other two) that surfaced frequently enough to merit a separate discussion. Teens were drawn to these three churches because they offered a challenge to develop competence. Teens were attracted to high goals, standards of excellence, demands worthy of their attention and energy, and rites of passage marking steps toward their adulthood.

At Transfiguration, teens learned how to be competent leaders. Seniors reported that they liked being the leaders of the high school youth group and role models to younger teens. Angie explained to me in my first meeting with her that the youth themselves run the high school program. She divides them into small groups to plan retreats and to do the programming. "I just reserve space for the spring and fall retreats, and then let the retreat themes evolve from the teens." She says that sometimes they plan things she knows will not work, but they have to learn from their mistakes. She allowed them to plan a mass for the retreat that was too long, followed by a talk. Everyone struggled to stay awake through it all. They got to bed at 2:00 A.M. They joked about it the next day as they realized their error.

I observed a big difference in the leadership skills and abilities of the seniors as compared to the freshmen. In one freshman group I observed on the retreat, several of the boys were trying to disrupt the assigned activity. Blindfolded, they were supposed to reach into a paper bag and describe what they touched. One boy wanted to be tied up with the scarves used as blindfolds, and he sat in the center of the circle as another boy tied him up. Youth group leaders patiently worked with the younger teens to develop their leadership skills. As my notes indicate:

> Karen, one of the youth leaders, told me about working with a group of sophomore boys planning an event. They had to goof off for a while before they got down to business. One boy in the group suggested that they get Alex O'Day, one of the seniors, to help them. She said no. She wanted to teach these sophomores to do their own work instead of automatically turning to the seniors.[42]

I observed the advanced skills of the seniors as they stood up to speak in front of the group with great poise and humor. They presented original skits with satiric wit, performed original music, organized retreat schedules, and worked as mentors with younger teens.

The practice of giving affirmation and encouragement heightened the motivation of the teens. One instance was evident in their preparation for the retreat for eighth-grade confirmands:

> The group began to discuss the upcoming confirmation retreat. A freshman spoke up and said how much it meant to her to have senior highs lead the retreat last year when she was a confirmand. A couple

of other freshmen said the same thing. Angie explained how middle school kids look up to high school kids. "You may think you have faults, but eighth-graders think you are perfect. And they want to be just like you." Angie asked for volunteers who could commit to leading the confirmation retreat. Thirty teens raised their hands. Nobody's arm had been twisted.[43]

At the confirmation retreat, each of the senior highs was assigned two eighth-graders to mentor by spending time with them throughout the day. The eighth-graders had written letters to their mentors describing themselves. The retreat concluded with a closing worship in which the high school mentors gave each eighth-grader a ribbon of a certain color, signifying a gift of the Spirit that the mentor had observed in them during the day.

> The teen mentor led one or two confirmands assigned to him or her to the podium. The mentor spoke to all the parents sitting in the pews, telling what color ribbon was selected for the confirmand, and why. Most of the comments were sincere and touching. Some were also very funny. The eighth-graders seemed genuinely pleased as they were presented with their colored ribbon. The parents smiled, laughed, and seemed to enjoy it tremendously too. One of the eighth-graders concluded the worship with a reading from 1 Corinthians 12:1–11 about spiritual gifts.[44]

The same day of the confirmation retreat, news spread that a senior at St. Peter High School had died in a car accident late the night before. The boy was a member of another parish, but he occasionally attended youth group at Transfiguration. Some of the seniors were late arriving at the retreat because they drove over to visit the crash site. A few seniors skipped the retreat to gather at another boy's house to grieve. We heard that some were planning a prayer service at the church youth center for later that night, after the confirmation retreat would end. Angie said, "I don't have to plan this for them. Isn't it wonderful that they can do it themselves?"

At Transfiguration the older teens were the leaders, and the adults were the facilitators. At Riverland Heights, in contrast, the paid adult youth ministers were the leaders responsible for the programming, the speaking, and the organization of the program, but the opportunity to develop competence was offered in another way. At Riverland Heights they had high standards of excellence in living the Christian life. They also had structures in place to hold teens accountable to those standards. The challenge to meet those standards attracted teens who wanted to grow in their faith and commitment to God.

The youth minister at Riverland Heights described how he viewed the teens who came through the door of the youth complex at Riverland Heights as follows: Teens who were not Christians were told about abundant life in Christ, about forgiveness, and "that God meets them where they are." A main goal of the youth ministry at Riverland Heights is to introduce unbelievers to Christ. More is expected of teens after that. "Once you are saved, you're no longer the client, you're on the team." Craig expects that "changed behavior will follow from changed hearts." He says,

> With Christian kids, kids who are believers and know better, I'm merciless. Kind of like Jesus was with the Pharisees, the Christian kid who says, "I've been raised in the church and I know what God wants and I'm going to do this anyway," I don't have any mercy . . . I lay them on the carpet . . . . I'll say, "You have twenty-four hours to tell your parents [about smoking cigarettes, drinking, smoking pot, or something else] or three of us are going to go over to your house and we're going to sit in your living room and we're going to talk about this with your mom and dad."[45]

At Riverland Heights, teens said they liked rising to the challenge of "setting the bar high."[46] Establishing adult-teen relationships of accountability was one of the key ways adult leaders tracked teens in their growth. A cadre of approximately forty adults had been trained to work as volunteer sponsors with the youth program. Beyond that, there were countless others who understood that it was their Christian obligation to mentor teens in the Christian life.[47]

Brian was one teen who benefited from having an informal relationship with an adult mentor. Abandoned by his father before he was born, Brian found a father figure in Coach Bond, a physical education teacher, football coach, faculty advisor to the Fellowship of Christian Athletes, and fellow member at Riverland Heights. Brian and Coach Bond met at a restaurant every Sunday morning for breakfast. This relationship offered Brian more than just affirmation of his leadership of Fellowship of Christian Athletes and his other successes. Brian reported, with tears in his eyes, that once Coach told him he was acting "too proud." Accountability could be painful, but Brian expressed gratitude for the discipline.

At First United Methodist, teens were attracted to opportunities to achieve competence in yet another way. They rose to the challenge of achieving excellence in choral music, bells, and other instruments. "It is cool" to work hard to meet high standards of musical performance, lead the congregation in worship, and travel to other cities to perform in urban churches, homeless shelters, and nursing homes.

By observing choir and bell choir rehearsals, my appreciation grew for the skill and hard work it took to achieve a high level of musical performance. For example, bell choir members were relied on to ring several specific bells and chimes. Sometimes they had to hold two bells in one hand at a time. They also had to master different techniques for ringing their instruments. One motion produced a knocking sound, another a ring, and another a thump. The complexity of this challenge and the respectful way the choir director gave them the direct responsibility for finding solutions to their problems was evident in the following observation:

> Marianna told Mimi, the director, that she had trouble playing all of her notes because she had to play one note and turn a page at the same time. Mimi said, "Well, perhaps the boy next to you can ring that note. Why don't we talk it over and see if we can solve this problem together." The boy said, "Yes, I can ring that note, but I have to turn my page too." They agreed that since the boy was sharing his score with another boy, that it would become the second boy's responsibility to turn the page. To solve the problem of ringing one note, they had shifted the playing of it to another person, and the page turning to a third person. How amazing to involve three people in choreographing the playing of a single note![48]

Once I observed the bell choir director trying to make a piece easier for the teens to play.

> Mimi said to the choir, "We're having difficulty with this passage. I'm going to make it easier by having you ring the bells through this part instead of the chimes." One of the teens piped up, "No, don't make it easier. We want it difficult."[49]

The fact that the music was difficult was a key to its attraction. Teens took pride in the high level of excellence in musical performance that they were able to accomplish together.

Both the bell choir and the choir that performed choral music were so important to teens that the election of choir officers was hotly contested.

Ten of the thirty-five teens in the choral music choir offered themselves as candidates for the six offices in the choir, requiring them to submit written statements of intent and make campaign speeches to the assembled choir. I was impressed that this conventional church activity could stir up such a demonstration of interest on the part of teens.

In summary, teens were attracted to their religious institutions when they were offered a significant sense of belonging, a serious way to make coherent meaning out of the disparate elements of their lives, and a challenge to develop competence—even excellence—in their capacities for participating in the adult world which they would face shortly. These particular congregations attracted teens to their offerings in different ways, however. The patterns of teen participation in the sample congregations varied because of the relative strengths of their resources and circumstances at a particular time. They also varied because of differences in how youth viewed church participation within their own theological tradition. Next I will describe in greater detail the patterns of church participation that I observed, and offer the accounts teens gave for why they did or did not participate in their congregations.

Chapter Three

The Complex Logic of Why Teens Do (and Do Not) Participate

M any pastors and church leaders agonize over how to garner the participation of teens in worship and youth programs. There are so many variables that affect attendance; the phenomenon almost appears random. A careful analysis of patterns in these three churches names some key variables that are present in many church contexts. This analysis also illustrates the interaction of various countervailing factors. Even when some key positive factors are present, there may be others that moderate the high participation level that is expected.

Patterns and levels of teen involvement in these churches varied widely in comparison to each other and to national trends. They can be summarized briefly as follows: At Transfiguration, mass attendance was below average in comparison to national samples of Catholic teens, but youth group participation among high school seniors was high, even higher than at Riverland Heights or First United Methodist. The pattern was exactly reversed at Riverland Heights, with worship attendance high in comparison to national samples of teens, and youth group participation low among high school seniors in comparison to the two other congregations in my sample. At First United Methodist, the most striking pattern was the high correlation between choir membership and general participation in church.

Worship Attendance

More than 58 percent of all teens in my interview sample attend church corporate worship services every week. (See table 1.) This frequency is much higher than what most national surveys of teens report[1] because my sample is comprised of teens who are on the membership rolls of a church, and because they come from churches that were selected because they were attracting teens. On the other hand, the frequencies in this sample reflect the worship attendance of the older segment of the teen population, only the seventeen- and eighteen-year-old teens.[2]

**Table 1.   Frequency of Worship Attendance
of High School Seniors by Church**

Average Frequency of Attendance at Church Worship	All Teens in Interview Sample		Transfiguration[3]		Riverland Heights		First United Methodist	
	N	Percent	N	Percent	N	Percent	N	Percent
Every week	24	59%	5	42%	12	71%	7	58%
Once a month[4]	5	12%	0	0%	2	12%	3	25%
1–2 times/year or never	12	29%	7	58%	3	18%	2	17%
Totals	41	100%	12	100%	17	101%*	12	100%

*Total exceeds 100 percent due to rounding.

*Where Are They? Not at the Parish Mass: Patterns of Worship Attendance
among Teens at Transfiguration*

It is notable that for Catholic teens in my sample there were basically two patterns of church attendance, weekly (42 percent) or rarely (58 percent). There was no middle frequency of attendance, as there was for evangelicals and mainliners, who sometimes attended once or twice a month. Further, attendance at mass at Transfiguration was the lowest in comparison to attendance at worship at Riverland Heights and at First United Methodist. More than half of Transfiguration teens (58 percent) reported that they attended mass only once or twice a year. The percentage of teens at Riverland Heights and First United Methodist reporting these low attendance patterns was much smaller, 18 percent of evangelicals and 17 percent of mainline Protestants. This finding is especially significant because attending mass is considered "an obligation" within the Catholic tradition; it is viewed less as a voluntary activity than it is within Protestantism.

What accounts for this low attendance at mass among Transfiguration teens? First, I explored the possibility that teens counted their worship and instruction at Catholic schools as a substitute for attending mass at their parish. Ten of the twelve Catholics in the interview sample attended Catholic schools, where mass was celebrated periodically, approximately four times a year.[5] Daily religion class was required in their schools as well. While Catholic teens do worship outside their parish and receive extra training in their beliefs and practices through parochial schools, I discovered that Catholic school was not regarded by parents as a substitute for mass attendance. Four Catholic parents whose teens attended Catholic schools reported that they wished they could enforce a weekly church attendance rule. Parents found they were unable to fight their teens' determined resistance to attending mass.[6]

A fuller explanation of low attendance by teens at mass was offered in interviews with teens. Eight out of twelve Catholic teens reported that the parish mass itself was not appealing to them. A typical response was, "Church doesn't do anything. I feel close to God without it." Two teens reported that they preferred to attend worship in churches of other denominations. Four reported that while they did not like mass celebrated at their parish, they loved youth masses celebrated on youth retreats because they were "personal" and "meant something." Some attended weekend masses celebrated in other parishes. I concluded overall that worship is important to many Transfiguration teens, but they are not drawn to the worship that is offered in their parish service.[7]

"Worship That Makes a Chill Go down Your Spine": Patterns of Worship Attendance among Teens at Riverland Heights

Another striking variation by church in teen worship attendance is the relatively high level of weekly attendance exhibited by evangelical teens (71 percent) compared to the attendance of teens in other churches in my sample and to national samples of teens.[8] While more than half of these teens (53 percent) were required to go by their parents, all the evangelicals who attended church either weekly or monthly assessed their worship experience at Riverland Heights positively. For the purpose of comparison in this research, I counted attending worship as attending "big church," the service offered five times each weekend at the main worship auditorium, and excluded the segments of worship that were incorporated into Vision and Focus gatherings at the youth complex.

The reason teens gave most often for liking big church was that they "learned something." They described both of the preaching ministers[9] as good preachers, and sometimes could recall messages that were particularly meaningful to them. The dramas performed during worship were cited often as high points of the service. They loved the music, especially the more contemporary selections. At big church they occasionally sang traditional hymns, used the organ, and had a bell choir. One boy said he disliked the more traditional elements, and once when he was late for church was glad that he only missed a performance of the bells. Another said, "Worship is good when it makes a chill go down your spine," and that happened most often for him through the music. Some teens also mentioned that celebrating Communion was meaningful, especially the opportunity to pray in the quiet moments surrounding it. Others cited witnessing the baptisms. The only negative comment came from one teen who said the ministers asked for money in the sermons too often.[10] Apart from that, the experience of worship was highly rated by all teens. As one boy described worship at Riverland Heights, "It's probably one of the best services in the country."

"I'm Needed to Sing the Bass Line": Patterns of Worship Attendance among Teens at First United Methodist

Two-thirds of the comments from teens at First United Methodist about their corporate worship were positive. More than half said they liked the minister. What mattered more, however, was belonging to the choir and their experience of worship as music leaders. Eight of the ten seniors who attended worship weekly or monthly sang in the high school choir. Many teens named singing in the choir as the part of worship that was most meaningful to them. Some went to worship only when they were singing in the choir. As one boy put it, "I go because I'm needed to sing the bass line." Another boy would turn down the big tips he could earn as a caddy on the golf course Sunday mornings if that was a Sunday he was expected to sing in the choir.

Youth Group Attendance

A cursory glance at the average numbers of teens in all classes (freshman, sophomore, junior, and senior) attending the general weekly gatherings of teens at the three churches exhibits the overwhelming appeal of the Riverland Heights program (attracting four hundred) in comparison to the other two (attracting seventy and forty). (See table 2.) Looking more closely, however, it appears that Transfiguration kept the highest percentage of their seniors on the mailing list active to the end of high school.

Table 2. Average Youth Group Attendance in Three Congregations

	Transfiguration	Riverland Heights	First United Methodist
Average youth group attendance (freshmen, sophomores, juniors and seniors)	70	400 at Vision meetings; 100 at Focus meetings	20 before the new youth minister arrived; 40 after his arrival

Beyond raw attendance figures, a comparison of church "members" in these three congregations is problematic, because the churches used different methods to determine who "their" youth were. The mailing list used by the churches to communicate with teens about upcoming events is the closest common measurement of the teen population served.[11] (See table 3.)

Table 3. Numbers of Seniors on the Mailing Lists and Attending Year-End Recognitions in Three Congregations

	Transfiguration	Riverland Heights	First United Methodist
Seniors on mailing list	132	260	24
Seniors attending year-end recognition	54 (41% of mailing list)	44 (17% of mailing list)	9 (38% of mailing list)

I have taken as a measurement of active membership in the youth program the attendance figure from the event sponsored by each of the three churches to honor its graduating seniors.[12] Forty-one percent of the teens on the mailing list at Transfiguration identified enough with the youth group to attend and be recognized, as compared to 17 percent and 38 percent of the teens at Riverland Heights and First United Methodist respectively. Therefore Transfiguration held the highest percentage of its seniors in youth group to the end of their high school years.

Unusual Bonds of Friendship: Youth Group Attendance at Transfiguration

While teen church attendance at Transfiguration was lowest of the three churches in this study, the percentage of teens who remained active in the youth group at Transfiguration through their senior year was the highest.[13]

Churches generally notice a dramatic drop-off in numbers of seniors who attend youth activities, with the younger three classes of high school freshmen, sophomores, and juniors comprising the bulk of their attendees.[14] Having such a large number of seniors as attendees was exceptional for Transfiguration as well. This fluke can be explained by the unusual bonds of friendship that developed among members of this class as they grieved the death of one of their members the previous spring, by the tender loyalty this class felt to the youth group leader whose husband was dying of cancer over an eighteen-month period culminating in the spring of their senior year, and by the chemistry among the individuals who happened to comprise the class of 1997.

"Because Christ Is Exciting": Youth Group Attendance at Riverland Heights

Senior participation in the youth activities at Riverland Heights followed the more typical pattern. There was a significant group who had been active in middle school, but gradually lost interest by the end of their senior year. Some teens reported that they "grew out of youth group." They got "tired of the same old sermons," particularly about sex and drugs. One Riverland Heights girl admired the Catholic youth group she sometimes attended with her boyfriend because she liked their openness to questioning, "the way they are really looking for answers." Some disliked the music at the youth complex, some because it was too far out and others because it was too tame. Some were scared off in their freshman year when a particularly rough crowd started to attend and police were stationed at the doors. Many said they gave up attending youth activities when they realized they could not meet the high expectations for increased commitment that came with the graduated levels of involvement built into the Vision-Insight-Focus progression.

Even with a reduced number of seniors active in the youth program, for those who participated their involvement was "everything." As one senior girl active in Focus put it, "The youth program here is exciting because Christ is exciting."

"He Forgives Us": Youth Group Attendance at First United Methodist

Of the nine seniors who were active at First United Methodist, eight were in the high school choir. Six came to Sunday school, some regularly, most not. After the new youth director arrived in January, attendance of seniors at youth group rose slightly, from two to five, off and on. Because First

United Methodist draws from a smaller pool of teens than Transfiguration and Riverland Heights, its fortunes tend to rise and fall more dramatically with the individual teens who happen to be there at the time. More than for the other two churches, the pool of teens is limited to the actual members of the church, though members' friends are welcome. The choir director told me that this particular senior class had fewer leaders than in past years.

Because the group was smaller, some of the status group hierarchies of adolescent peer groups appeared in acute form. The "influencers" were mostly from a particular high school, Grinstead, and they dropped out of youth group. Those who stuck with the youth group during its difficulties in the absence of a youth minister tended to be the less popular teens. They stepped into the vacuum created by the inactivity of the more popular kids. There could be no outsiders, because everyone was needed to maintain the critical social mass of the group. There was a significant level of dissatisfaction reported by some who wished the youth group membership would grow and knew it was unlikely to happen because influencers were not present to attract more teens to the group. Ironically, some who articulated this were the less popular kids who were active in the youth group.

The choir, on the other hand, retained its influencers, and was the main social group for teens at First United Methodist. Most seniors who continued to belong to choir cited the attraction of Roderick, the director. They felt allegiance to him. More than one teen commented, "He forgives us," meaning that Roderick persevered with them in choir rehearsals even when they goofed off. There were instances when Roderick lost his temper with the choir, but he never gave up on developing their musical excellence and spirituality. The choir, with its charismatic director, winter retreat, and annual choir tour was clearly the main attraction for seniors in this church.

⚜⚜⚜⚜⚜

In conclusion, while each of the three congregations engaged teens by offering them significant ways to belong, believe, and develop competence, they were stronger in some areas than in others.[15] The variations in patterns of teen participation that were evident in these three congregations show how teens are selectively attracted to the offerings of their congregations.

Religious institutions today can attract teens. The churches that do so work at it with intentionality and dedicate significant resources to youth ministry. Congregations that attract teens do not rely on a teen's sense of duty to their church or on parents to get them there. As Csikszentmihalyi says, "it is what grabs them" that gets teens' attention. Part II of this book explores what comes after teens are attracted to participate in their congregations. In particular, we will examine what gives "staying power" over time—that is, what nurtures in teens a religious commitment that endures as the attraction ebbs and flows.

Part II

How Churches Hold Teens

Chapter Four

Religious Socialization
and Religious Experience

As a younger teen, Beth went to church, Sunday school, youth group, and choir because she was supposed to. Active church participation was an expectation in her churchgoing family. After her confirmation at First United Methodist in the seventh grade, she continued to attend church and Sunday school, but gradually dropped out of choir and youth group. As an older teen, her parents could no longer force her to participate in church activities outside of Sunday morning. She opted for the minimal amount of church participation.

Beth's church involvement changed in the summer before her senior year. She attended a retreat sponsored by a lay-run ecumenical movement called Chrysalis and had an overpowering experience of Christian community. After that, she came to church searching for fresh insights that would draw her closer to God. In addition, she committed herself to supporting the extra activities for the teens of her church. She rearranged her schedule to make time for choir rehearsals. She sacrificed time at her summer job so she could go on the choir mission tour and teach for a week at vacation Bible school. The choir director at First United Methodist confirmed this change in Beth. "She really came back from the summer with a vengeance," he said as a positive affirmation of the change.

Beth's sense of being a Christian had changed at least twice since her confirmation, and each time it grew more fundamental to her sense of self. The summer after her confirmation she attended a Methodist camp and "accepted Christ." This event seems out of sequence, to accept Christ after confirming one's faith. Beth explained, "When I went through confirmation, I really wasn't a Christian, so it didn't mean anything." In fact,

Beth acknowledged that "accepting Christ" was what she had been reared to do, even what the confirmation process taught her to do. Her conversion was a consolidation of all that she had been taught in the course of her life in her religious tradition. Even though there was more continuity than disjuncture in the content of the symbols and structures she appropriated, Beth used the language of conversion to express how radically transformed her life seemed to her. Belief in God became the organizing principle of her view of the world.[1]

With Beth's second dramatic religious experience,[2] at the Chrysalis retreat just before her senior year, once again she personally appropriated her faith in a way that made it seem radically new. The religious community (her church, First United Methodist, in particular) became her "primary group."[3] She moved beyond engaging with what attracted her (as described in Part I). She exhibited a more enduring allegiance to the religious tradition in which she was reared.

Beth's story illustrates how some teens come to conceive of their church as more than something they choose as it attracts them. They come to view church affiliation and participation as a serious lifetime commitment. Their commitment is sustained by renewed intention and discipline over time. The main argument of this study is about religious commitment, or specifically loyalty to one's religious tradition of nurture.[4]

I asked the forty-one teens in my interview sample,[5] "Do you intend to be active in the church after you leave home?"[6] This question was purposely open-ended, allowing teens in their response to clarify whether to them "church" meant their particular congregation, their particular tradition (such as Catholic), or just any religious institution called a "church." I discovered the teens tended to assume that some kind of congregation was implied by the term "church."[7] Moreover, their responses covered a range that I have grouped into five general categories of loyalty. [See table 4.]

So what can pastors, church leaders, and parents do to foster this sense of religious commitment in teens? What are the constituent elements of religious loyalty? This portion of the book reveals the significance of a teen's upbringing in the church. When this is augmented by an experience that the teen considers an encounter with God, a commitment to a church-based faith often follows. For high school seniors, especially, this is primarily done by helping them appropriate the church's rituals and traditions as rites of passage for themselves.

Table 4. A Typology of Loyalty to the Religious Tradition of Nurture

Type of Loyalty	Response to the question, "Do you expect to be active in a church after you leave home?"
Unshakable (Loyalty)	"Yes." In some cases they mention a particular church near the college they expect to attend. Sometimes they say they plan to sing in the choir in their home church when they return on holidays.
Tentative (Loyalty)	"In college I'll go, but not every week. As an adult, yes." "I will go monthly in college, and I want to explore other faiths too."
Conditional (Provisional Loyalty)	"If my friends go." "If time allows."
Postponed (Unlikely Loyalty)	"Yes. I'll go when I'm married." "Not in college." "Maybe later. It depends on my [future] wife."
Alienated (Unlikely Loyalty)	"No."

Loyalty Factors That Apply to Upbringing in the Church

An analysis of the teens' interviews suggested that five key variables relate to their loyalty level in a striking way. These are: church attendance, praying and/or Bible reading, knowledge of the religious tradition, religious experience, and religious rituals. We will look at the first three of these together as factors that form an interpretive grounding for the teens' religious experience.

Church Attendance

The levels of church attendance mentioned in Part I correlate to degrees of loyalty to show that loyalists (both "unshakable" and "tentative" loyalists) have significantly higher levels of church attendance than teens in the other three loyalty groups. All unshakable loyalists and over half of tentative loyalists attended church each week. All but one of the unlikely loyalists and 60 percent of the provisional loyalists attended church only one or two times a year or rarely. (See table 14 in Appendix N.)

Praying and/or Bible Reading

The list of teens who say they pray every day coincides closely with the list of teens in the top three loyalty categories.[8] The list of teens who both pray and read the Bible every day coincides with the list of the most loyal loyalists, the "unshakable" loyalists. I also found that those who attend church more often and exhibit higher frequencies of praying and (for evangelicals and mainline Protestants) Bible reading tend to say more readily and with greater certainty that they intend to remain in the church after they leave home. (See table 15 in Appendix N.)

Knowledge of the Religious Tradition

I measured the third variable, a teen's knowledge of the religious tradition, in different ways to take into account different emphases of the three religious traditions. I asked Catholic teens to recite the Our Father prayer. I asked evangelical teens to recite a Bible verse from memory or, if they could not, tell me their favorite Bible story. I asked mainline Protestant teens to repeat the Apostles' Creed or tell me their favorite Bible story. Thirty-nine of forty-one teens (or 95 percent) passed this rudimentary "test."[9] In addition, I asked teens to compare and contrast their beliefs with those of their church.[10] From the amount of detail in their answers I arrived at a general sense of their knowledge of their religious tradition.

The Effect of Upbringing: Socialization

Socialization is the larger process that builds knowledge of the symbols, rituals, narratives, and texts, and it includes the habits—such as church attendance, praying, and Bible reading—that comprise the Christian life.[11] Socialization occurs through the example and mentoring of others, instruction in the sacred texts, and in worship using the music, art, and drama of the Christian tradition. Socialization is social—it happens as a person lives in the religious community.

Typically for teens, socialization occurs in the regular, ongoing life of the church—that is, in corporate worship, high school Sunday school classes and Bible studies, and youth meetings. It provides the context for interpreting and acting on their own religious experience, as well as for conducting and participating in religious rituals. I came to see that the degree of teen loyalty was intimately connected with the consistency of their religious socialization in church and at home over the span of their current lifetime.[12] Teens with the most consistent exposure to the environment of the church—especially in the areas of church attendance, praying/Bible reading, and knowledge of the tradition—were those most likely to remain in the tradition. (See table 16 in Appendix N.) When this is coupled with meaningful religious experiences, as I discuss below, the degree of religious loyalty increases even more.

But Have They Experienced God?

Another factor that makes a positive difference for religious loyalty is *religious experience*. When teens reported that they had some experience that they considered an encounter with God, I counted it as a religious experience.[13] I was alerted to this variable early on through my first interview with a teen. I concluded my questions to Caroline with: "So who, over all, most influences what you believe about God and how you practice your faith?" She replied, "Well, God does."[14]

In my research, I observed that when teens described religious experiences their churches had mediated, the conditions associated with them had the characteristics of what Victor Turner calls antistructure.[15] Teens reported that they had religious experiences when the regular symbols and rhythms of life were disrupted, intensified, or accented in some way. These experiences happened especially when a routinized symbol was presented differently. For example, one teen at Transfiguration reported how deeply it moved her to have the priest celebrate mass wearing regular clothes instead of clerical vestments. The symbol of the mass was accessible to her as it was offered for the first time by someone who looked more ordinary. In another case, I observed teens sitting forward in their pews at First United Methodist listening more attentively than usual to a sermon delivered not by the minister, but by a football coach. Laity Sunday provided the status reversal that heightened their attention.[16]

As I conducted my research, I found myself noting times when laughter[17] erupted or when tears streamed down the faces of teens. These were two markers of marginality, times when teens had been pushed to the edge in intense emotional states of mirth or sadness. I noted what I began to call the boundary lines or edges. I noted that what teens described as religious experiences were associated with the boundaries.

Typically, these religious experiences happened in places that were geographically on the boundaries, in locations away from home—at camp, on retreats, and even in parking lots located literally on the boundaries of the church. The youth leaders at Riverland Heights stationed themselves in the parking lot of the youth complex to greet the youth, especially those who hesitated to come in. Youth leaders engaged them in winsome conversation with the aim of helping them enter the building. One time I was invited to join some teenaged girls as they sat in a subcompact car in the parking lot of the youth complex at Riverland Heights blasting on the car stereo a song by a Christian musician, Jackie Velasques. It was a religious experience for them. They sang along and cooed to each other, "God is so-o-o-o cool."

Religious experiences seemed to happen most often on retreats. Many teens, like Beth, described how they had a powerful experience of Christian community on a retreat. The following is an extended excerpt from my field notes from a retreat sponsored by Transfiguration, which illustrates the power of a retreat to produce experiences that teens describe as an encounter with God.

> There were about a hundred of us sitting on the wood floor of a retreat center in a remote part of western Kentucky. It was midnight. A single candle illuminated the darkness, shining on the face of one teenager, Tate, who agreed to tell his story to the youth group as it related to the theme of the retreat: the masks we wear.
>
> Tate started by telling about how, when he was in seventh grade, his parents started to fight. Late at night, after drinking, the fights would escalate to episodes of violence between them. One night the police came to their home to follow up on a hang-up of a 911 call his mother managed to make between blows. When an officer came upstairs into Tate's bedroom where he was huddled with his younger brother and sister, Tate smiled at him and said, "Everything's fine." Tate said he is aware now that this was the first time he put on a mask to hide his pain.
>
> I felt exhausted, cold, and achy sitting on the hard wood floor. But I hardly dared even to shift my weight, because the concentration in the room was so intense.
>
> Tate went on to describe his parents' drinking, episodes of abandonment by his parents, their eventual divorce, and his mother's cocaine addiction. A good student at one of the Catholic high schools, Tate's grades took a nosedive when his parents divorced. He told about injuring himself when he tried to commit suicide, about the deaths of his cousin and his aunt, about dropping out of school, about wondering why he could not bring himself to kiss his girlfriend, whom he loved, and about feeling hurt when he and his best friend grew apart. Mark, the best friend, was among those listening.

After a very long prayer session following Tate's talk, focusing on the struggles that kids have—with some kids offering very angry prayers—Angie asked us each to take a candle and light it off of Tate's. It symbolized how Tate showed us how to take off our masks and be real with one another. The first boy who went up to light his candle from Tate's was Mark. It was 1:40 A.M. when I could see my watch again—by the light of a hundred candles.[18]

This episode exhibits most of the elements of *liminality*, a characteristic of antistructure. According to Victor Turner, liminality is a temporary state of ambiguity where statuses and roles are equalized or reversed. "It is likened to death, to being in the womb, to invisibility, to darkness, to bisexuality, to the wilderness, and to an eclipse of the moon."[19] Everything indicating rank, role, or position—property, insignia, types of clothing, and so on—is set aside or becomes invisible. People may even go naked. Behavior is normally passive or humble as people obey and accept arbitrary conditions that reduce them to uniformity, and in the experience an intense social bond is formed.[20]

In this case, the retreat took place in a location set apart from ordinary life, in a wilderness-like setting. It occurred in a "moment in and out of time," as my watch was not visible and I had to forget the normal pace of minutes. The event imposed compliance: I fought physical exhaustion and discomfort to attend to the program. Darkness cloaked any differences of status, class, or gender, to make us equals. There was a sense of nakedness in the exposure of Tate's desperate story—a removal of his mask. The lower-caste person (Tate, the high school dropout) was exalted. The intense social bond that was forged was dramatized in the candle-lighting ceremony and confirmed in spoken affirmations.

The power of such experiences for teens is demonstrated in the high correlation between religious experience and religious loyalty. In my interview sample, all "unshakable loyalist" teens, as well as all the "conditional loyalist" teens, reported that they had some personal experience of God.[21] (See table 17 in Appendix N.)

Putting It Together: The Combined Effect of Consistent Religious Socialization and Religious Experience

The connection between having a religious experience and developing religious loyalty is seen best when it is juxtaposed with my findings on consistent religious socialization. The unshakable loyalists, those with the highest degree of loyalty to the religious tradition, had both religious experience *and* consistent socialization. This was true for no other loyalty type. (See table 18 in Appendix N.)

Why does high religious loyalty seem to grow out of the combination of these two factors? According to Christian educator C. Ellis Nelson, socialization conditions persons to have religious experiences by providing them with the symbols, stories, and practices to use for "sifting" their experiences and interpreting them as religious.[22] Nelson says, "Experience that is religiously interpreted is similar to any other experience; the difference lies in the interpretation and in what we conclude from it."[23] If religious symbols are available to teens, and if they are guided by a religious community that practices the interpretation of their experiences in religious terms, teens tend to interpret their experiences as encounters with God. If they are not thinking in those terms, they may be like the teens the choir director at one of the high schools described by saying, "There are some kids who aren't even asking religious questions."

According to Nelson, religious experience also is necessary to developing religious commitment—what he calls "mature faith." Having an intense, personal encounter with God is a normative expectation of the Christian tradition. It transforms the "acquired faith" that is socialized into the "experienced faith" that is personally appropriated by the individual. According to Nelson, faith is the "residue" of religious experience, the enduring conviction remaining when the intense moment of theophany fades.

Socialization and religious experience work together in a circular fashion, according to Nelson.[24] Socialization in the religious tradition conditions persons to have religious experiences because they have readily available the symbols and models to use for interpreting experiences as religious. Those having a religious experience will seek to be more deeply involved in their religious community as a result. (See fig. 5.)

Religious institutions can and do mediate religious experience.[25] Moreover, the symbols and practices of a religious tradition can help teens recognize an encounter with God and name it as such. In turn, these religious experiences of divine encounter then breathe meaning into old, familiar symbols and practices.

We can see powerful elements of this in the earlier account of the retreat in which Tate told his story. There, the teens perceived the significance of the symbols and practices of the traditions so that they became components of a religious experience.[26] The religious symbol of light, for example, was deepened and given concrete existence through the use of

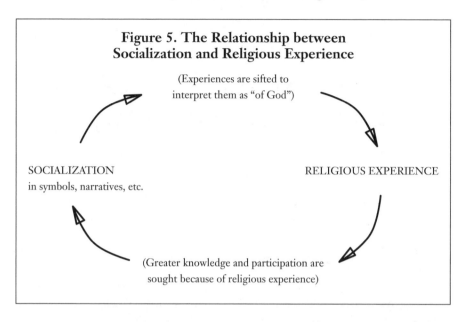

**Figure 5. The Relationship between
Socialization and Religious Experience**

(Experiences are sifted to
interpret them as "of God")

SOCIALIZATION
in symbols, narratives, etc.

RELIGIOUS EXPERIENCE

(Greater knowledge and participation are
sought because of religious experience)

candlelight to affirm Tate in the telling of his story. Teens experienced the power of the Christian practice of testimony as Tate conveyed his painful truth. Through prayer, teens struggled to understand the unknowable wisdom of God. Their sense of brokenness was sanctified in the practice of confession. They participated in the Christian practice of forgiveness as they witnessed the reconciliation of alienated friends. This experience was deemed sacred as it appropriated the symbols and practices the teens knew all their lives through the church. Likewise, the symbols and practices that the church had imparted to them also took on new significance as they became charged with a personal experience of God and Christian community.

Chapter Five

How Three Congregations Hold Teens in Distinctive Ways

Socialization and Religious Experience

Across the three congregations I studied, the combination of socialization and religious experience was crucial to teen religious loyalty, and congregations conveyed it in distinctive ways through their particular traditions. In this chapter, I will describe some of the ways these Catholic, evangelical, and Methodist churches taught teens about the Christian way of life and provided conditions that fostered religious experiences—thus distinguishing themselves as congregations with a higher chance of helping their teens choose to stay connected to their religious tradition.[1]

Reaching the Heart: Socialization and Religious Experience at Transfiguration

In the Catholic tradition, attending mass is the central religious activity for people of all ages, including teens. "Making the sacraments" is a key goal in religious formation. The religious educational component for youth is oriented toward preparing youth to receive the sacraments of First Communion and confirmation. To prepare for these sacraments, children take religious instruction either in parochial school or in weekly classes held at the parish for children who attend public school.[2] After confirmation in eighth grade, teens continue to be socialized in Catholic life as they attend mass and participate in general parish life. A national survey indicates Catholic teens across the country are most involved in their parishes through the following activities (apart from attending mass): religious education, youth retreats, and social events. Catholic teens are less likely to be involved through Bible study, prayer groups, and leadership training programs.[3]

For Catholic teens in my sample, much of their socialization in the Catholic life occurred in parochial schools. A higher than average percentage of teens at Transfiguration, approximately 80 percent, attended Catholic high schools.[4] The influential role of Catholic schools in shaping the lives of teens can hardly be understated. Daily religion classes at the high school level instruct teens in the Bible, sacraments, theology, and ethical decision making. Religion is taken each semester as a requirement, including seminar-style courses at upper levels on moral decision making.

I discovered in my observation of religion classes at two schools that the quality of religious teaching varied widely with the skill level of the instructor. At one school, the religion teacher was adept at incorporating different pedagogical styles into a single class session. I observed her leading a class of seniors through various exercises designed to cultivate in them an ability to critique the messages of the commercial media about gender, and to contrast them with religious understandings. She created a spiritually centered learning environment by starting each class session with a participatory prayer ritual using a candle, music, and relaxation postures. At another school, the religion teacher appeared unable to stay in control of her class. Students came to class late, brought candy and soda to consume during class, and occasionally left their seats to throw wrappers and cans in the wastebasket. The discussion was unfocused and the guidance offered by the teacher veered widely from Catholic theology.[5] Both teachers, the gifted one and the inept one, were former nuns.

Religiously, these schools shaped understandings of Catholic identity through strategies that exceeded traditional classroom instruction. The moral example of the teachers was noted by many teens as having a positive influence on them. Several schools have brothers and nuns living in residence on the school campus, and some teach on the faculty. Religious symbols, such as crucifixes and statues of saints placed prominently throughout the buildings, silently shape teens' religious imaginations. Mass is celebrated on the holy days of the church year by the entire school. In addition, all Catholic schools required community service and offered placement in various settings. They offered teens opportunities to be mentors to youth in Catholic elementary and middle schools as they spoke in classrooms about how to resist peer pressure and to be drug and alcohol free.

Schools also socialize teens into a Catholic identity that exceeds the purely religious elements. There is a culture of Catholic schools that is pervasive and visible to anyone who drives around the city of Louisville. Local residents display their Catholic school logos on their cars and on banners flown outside their front doors, especially to mark key school sports events. The local paper chronicles the long-established rivalries in sports among Catholic schools in the city. Educationally, these schools are considered some of the best in the city, on a par with the public magnet schools[6] and the elite private schools.

What teens mentioned most often about their Catholic education as a positive influence on their religious identity was the retreat program that their school offered. Following a curriculum used widely in Catholic high schools across the United States, most of the parochial high schools in Louisville offered teens the opportunity to attend a class retreat during each of their years of high school. On retreat, teens talked with their teachers about faith and vocation for extended periods of time. They reported that they wrestled with the relevance of God to their lives and with making a serious commitment to a Catholic lifestyle.[7] So moving were these experiences to many teens that they developed phrases that referred to experiences on retreat. For example, the phrase "Remember the fifth" was used by St. Peter boys to allude to a powerful experience they shared on the fifth day of their senior retreat.

On balance, the socialization in a Catholic way of life that these high schools offered was weighted heavily in cognitive learning. While teens did have powerful religious experiences on retreats, and while many teens reported how they admired their teachers' moral example—especially the religious brothers and nuns—the majority of teens expressed resentment about religious instruction at their schools. Typical were the comments, "I don't get anything out of it," and, "We could use the time better if religion classes were replaced with other things."[8]

At Transfiguration, Angie made it her goal to offset the school's emphasis on cognitive learning by reaching the heart. Transfiguration's youth group was widely known by teachers and school administrators because of its importance in their students' lives. As one Catholic high school chaplain observed, "Transfiguration's youth group is larger than life."

One way that the general community became aware of the power of the parish youth group in teens' lives was through reports of how it helped teens cope with the deaths of friends. Tragically, the death of a member of the youth group was an experience shared more than once at Transfiguration. Maureen died in the spring prior to my research. Another member, a boy, was killed in January during the year of the study. In March a boy at St. Peter known to some at Transfiguration was drowned in the floods that ravaged the city that spring. Teens at Transfiguration learned to bear their grief by gathering as a community at the youth center. There they asked the questions of theodicy and anomie that pushed the edges of their faith. (See Appendix K.) They learned to ritualize their grief, sometimes using symbols layered with personal meaning for them through repetition. Stories and traditions from one experience evolved and deepened in subsequent ones.

When Maureen was killed in a car accident in the spring of her junior year, the youth center at Transfiguration became the central place where teens gathered to grieve. According to accounts given to me by the youth director and teens, they spent days and nights there after her death telling stories, weeping together, praying, comforting one another, and ritualizing their loss. Angie bought a flowering tree for the youth center that became the focus of their mourning. Since Transfiguration teens were used to giving colored ribbons as symbols affirming gifts and virtues they recognized in others,[9] Angie provided them with a basket of ribbons for Maureen's tree. In a solemn and tearful ceremony, each in turn selected a ribbon of a color that expressed their memory of Maureen and tied it to the tree. Angie said that the last person to do so was Maureen's father. He wanted a red ribbon, but none was left. Angie silently offered a desperate prayer. As she looked down to pray, there was a red ribbon between her feet. The beribboned tree also went to the funeral home for the calling hours, into the church for the service, and to the grave site. It was planted at the youth center after the burial.

What Transfiguration's youth program did best was offer teens the religious experience component that complemented their socialization. Youth group offered spaces and times of liminality where teens could interpret their lives and experiences using the religious symbols that had been given them over the course of their lives in their parish and schools. Faith transmission was "working" at Transfiguration as teens had powerful experiences that they interpreted as experiences of God. It is no coincidence that these experiences often happened in experiences of death, on retreats (in spaces away from home, at times set apart from the daily rhythm), and during the senior year—a whole twelve months lived on the edge between childhood and adulthood.

"God Is S-o-o-o-o Cool": Socialization and Religious Experience at Riverland Heights

Teens growing up at Riverland Heights have a strong sense that the church is an institution that constantly grows and expands because its truth is so compelling.[10] In the year of my research, Riverland Heights broke ground on yet another church complex, which was completed in December 1998.[11] It is impossible to overstate how the sustained pattern of growth and sheer size of the church reinforced in teens the sense that what Riverland Heights stands for is true. At almost every worship service, individuals, couples, and families were baptized. Evidence was presented that people believe in God and choose the Riverland Heights way of being a Christian.

Riverland Heights shaped in all its members from the time they were infants the enduring sense that being a Christian means that one expects growth—that is, growth in one's personal faith and growth in the church. Like the train rolling down the tracks that brings with it its own rails, being identified with Riverland Heights means that one constantly makes tracks into new mission fields.[12] The most obvious mission field for teens was their own high school. Teens were expected to evangelize in their schools by becoming identified with religious school groups, by inviting friends to Vision meetings at church, by speaking out in class to offer Christian perspectives on topics such as evolution, and by witnessing through a godly lifestyle. When one girl switched from a large public high school to a private Christian school, the youth leader told her he was disappointed. Being an evangelist in one's school is what keeps a teenage Christian growing. Attending a school where there is little challenge to evangelize can make you lose your faith, the youth leader cautioned.[13]

Besides the practice of evangelism, teens at Riverland Heights were socialized into many other spiritual practices that reinforced a distinctive Christian identity, such as worship, prayer, Bible study, and charitable service. More than in the other two churches, Riverland Heights offered unequivocal teaching on controversial social issues such as homosexuality, creationism, and abortion. A regular and important part of each year's curriculum for teens was the topic of appropriate sexual behavior. Teens were taught to date only Christians, to respect limits of sexual intimacy (areas covered by a modest bathing suit were off limits), and to remain sexually pure until marriage. This delicate topic was addressed adroitly by the youth ministers in ways that elicited rapt attention and much laughter.

> Craig talked about the problems we have because we have "parts." "GI Joe and Barbie didn't have parts, and that made it easier. It might be easier for us if we didn't have parts, but then after you got married, it wouldn't be so great. Wouldn't it be great," he said, "if we didn't have parts and could stop at a parts store and get them after we took out a marriage license?"[14]

Many evangelical churches socialize youth into distinctive Christian practices, symbols, and stories with direct and clear strategies. What made Riverland Heights so notable, besides its size, was the way it successfully blended religious experience with its socialization processes. A higher proportion of Riverland Heights teens, as compared to teens at the other two churches, reported that they encountered God through their church. They did not just learn the Christian ways of believing and practicing; they had experiences that they perceived to come from the divine realm. They received not just the structures but also the substance of faith. Together, socialization and religious experience fostered high levels of loyalty to the Christian tradition in teens at Riverland Heights.

Teens at Riverland Heights said they found God on retreats as they did at Transfiguration (as mentioned above), and on mission trips as they did at First United Methodist (as will be described below), but at Riverland Heights teens said they found God especially in the worship that was presented, both the worship at big church[15] and at the youth complex. It was impressive how much teens at Riverland Heights loved to worship. I witnessed one worship time at the youth complex when they sang, danced, prayed, listened to a message, and celebrated Communion for an hour and a half. When the youth minister tried to end the worship, they yelled, "More! More!"

What made the worship at Riverland Heights so effective was its liminality. The worship auditorium at the youth complex looked more like a nightclub than a church. The large, cavernous auditorium had no windows, and generally remained unlit during worship except for the spotlights trained on the stage. In the darkness there was a feeling of anonymity that freed persons from self-consciousness as they participated in the dancing, clapping, hand raising, and body motions that accompanied the music. Because one could follow the lyrics of the songs as they were projected on a screen above the stage without having to hold a hymnbook or song sheet, participation in music could more easily involve the whole body. In addition, the volume of the music was so high it created a physical sensation. My ears hurt if I sat near the front, close to the speakers. I could feel my bones vibrate because of the strong beat of the music. When one sings and moves to music as teens do at the youth complex, the endorphins in the brain produce a high. The powerful effect of the darkness, the sound, and the euphoria minimizes "the world outside." It sharply focuses a person on what is presented on stage. The impact of the message, the music, the drama, the video clips, and the prayer is intensified.[16]

Over the year of my research I grew somewhat accustomed to entering the worship space at the youth complex and adjusting to its liminality. I also built up some stamina to participate in the physical challenge of their worship. I was amused to watch, at the end of the year, the reaction of the parents when they were invited to attend the last event.

> With my eyes already adjusted to the dark, I watched some of the parents as they came into the auditorium. They walked unsteadily into the blackness. One wife gripped the arm of her husband as he blindly groped his way to some seats. It amused me to see the cautious way they proceeded, since it really does take some adjustment to walk into this auditorium. You feel like you've entered a big, vibrating cave. . . . I also noted during the worship that parents were dropping back into their seats with exhaustion before they were supposed to sit down. You have to be in shape to worship at Focus.[17]

Another element contributing to liminality at Riverland Heights was evident in the style of humor. Initially puzzling and repulsive to me, "gross-out humor"[18] is exemplified in the following field observation note.

> Craig started the choir rehearsal by reminding the kids about the retreat in two weeks. He described the retreat leader: "He weighs four thousand pounds." "Once when he was in my office he farted and we had to evacuate the whole building. My secretary, Linda, who is pregnant, threw up." The kids laughed. I was surprised at what Craig could get away with. I guess kids like off-color humor like this. To me, it's obscene.[19]

Later I came to understand how the antisanctimonious quality of gross-out humor was consistent with the vulnerability and anticlericalism that characterizes "new paradigm churches," a new type of evangelical church that attends to consumer demand by tuning their worship and organizational style to contemporary culture.[20] Gross-out humor equalizes people by publicizing what is conventionally private. It surprises because it exceeds the norms of propriety, especially when used in public settings by an adult religious authority.

As observed by other keen observers of American church life, many megachurches discard attributes of established religion and strive to be anticlerical.[21] This is true of Riverland Heights as a whole. The traditional church instrument, the organ, was used very sparingly. There was no pulpit, nor did ministers wear clerical vestments. The youth program, even more, endeavored to be "unchurchy." At the Vision meetings, which targeted nonbelievers, no one was expected to sing. They just performed the music on stage, and chose Christian music with lyrics that "cross over" or secular songs that can be interpreted in a Christian way. One of the youth ministers said she replaced the word "chardonnay" with "lemonade" in a popular song they presented. The teens noticed the substitution. She laughed, "That's good. They learn from that too."

In summary, Riverland Heights exemplified the best of its evangelical tradition in its emphasis on immediate personal experiences of God. It combined that with clear and intense teaching that effectively socialized teens into its religious tradition. The result was that teens reared at Riverland Heights professed high levels of loyalty to their religious tradition. Only at Riverland Heights did any of the teens say they intended to pursue a professional church vocation.

Singing as a Prayer: Socialization and Religious Experience at First United Methodist

In one respect, First United Methodist was better at offering religious socialization to its teens than the other two congregations in my sample. Teens at First United Methodist were more integrated into the worship, leadership, and general life of their congregation than teens at Transfiguration and Riverland Heights. Like adult members, teens at First United Methodist led worship, served as church officers, came forward to offer their pledge envelopes on Stewardship Sunday, and taught vacation Bible school.

On the other hand, even with their significant integration into the life of their church, teens at First United Methodist still did not perceive their church culture to be so different from that of American society in general. The effort of First United Methodist to cultivate a distinctive Christian identity in its teens was undercut by the general social circumstance that hobbles all mainline Protestant churches: the Protestant way of life is historically "established" in American culture. It is so blended with the dominant culture that the distinctive Christian claims and way of life do not stand out as countercultural. As some have suggested, it is not "sectarian" enough to socialize its youth into its distinctive moral and theological practices and beliefs.[22]

As I spent time at First United Methodist, I looked for how that might be true in this congregation. On the one hand, I found evidence of the uncritical tolerance for other religious and secular views, even fostered by religious "authorities," that some scholars say weakens the distinctiveness of mainline Protestant plausibility structures.[23] (Some examples will be offered below in a description of Sunday school.) I also observed that there were few cultural elements of mainline Protestantism that marked it as distinctive.[24] On the other hand, I noted some moments when teens at First United Methodist looked very countercultural. This was evident in a choir presentation as follows.

> Standing there singing, with their earnest, fresh faces, I was struck with how they deviated from the self-absorbed demeanor of celebrities in *People* magazine. In their church clothes—boys in neckties and girls in flowered dresses—they deviated from the dress code of drab colors and prominently displayed name brands dictated by influencers in their high schools. How traditional and inspirational the music sounded in comparison to the raw emotionalism and angry tones that I had been listening to on the radio! One piece they sang was in Latin. The other was classical-sounding and very explicitly Christian in its lyrics. They were so identified with the Christian church, they were countercultural.[25]

During my year of field research, I tried to immerse myself in the cultural media that teens named as what they liked—the television shows and movies, and the radio stations.[26] I found that these media, particularly the movies, did engage teens in discourse about justice, the death penalty, forgiveness, and other moral issues. The three top television shows they named also dealt with moral dilemmas that could prompt moral reflection. The main characters in these television shows, however, mostly exemplified expressive individualism and instrumentalism in personal relationships, orientations that run counter to normative Christian views. Popular music recordings and music videos were the media that offered the greatest dissonance with Christian culture and moral views.[27]

One of the two practices that I observed at First United Methodist, apart from the practice of attending corporate worship, that most socialized teens into a Christian identity and way of life was that of meeting for an hour each week for Sunday school. First United Methodist offered a separate class for high school juniors and seniors that drew five to fifteen teens each Sunday. It was taught by Dwayne Bear, a seventy-year-old grandfather who, despite his snow-white hair, looked vigorous enough to play on the varsity football team, as he did decades ago. Dwayne was legendary because he taught teens in the church on and off for twenty years. College students home on semester break came to the Sunday school class to visit with him. Beth named him as one who most represented to her a model of mature Christian faith.[28] Dwayne made it his business to learn the teens' names and attend the high school youth group fund-raisers and choir performances. Occasionally Dwayne mentioned in class that he had just attended the funeral of one of his lifelong friends, and I would be reminded of the large gap in age between him and the teens. I wondered why, in Dwayne's "golden years," he would bother to be involved with teens, to prepare Sunday school lessons for them and to put up with their tardiness and intermittent attendance at class. He explained that when one of his daughters was a teenager, she became estranged from him. Something about that painful time in his life as a father motivated him to work with teens.[29]

Dwayne's desire to relate with teens came across in his style of teaching. He invited teens to focus on their own experiences and feelings as they intersected with the Bible stories. He asked the teens to describe the previous night's high school field hockey game, where longtime rivals displayed unsporting conduct and one team member was "red-carded" (penalized for a personal foul). They drew analogies between that and the ancient animosities among warring tribes in Palestine that fueled a violence lasting for generations. Discussing David dancing naked in celebration of the ark's arrival in Jerusalem, he asked: "Have your parents ever embarrassed you?" Many teens offered examples. Dwayne tapped into the ambiguous feeling teens have about their parents and other topics. He asked, "Have you ever injured another person on purpose?" He told of a time he had done so. "Did you ever ask yourself if you are causing too much trouble, if your parents would be better off if they didn't have you?" He told of a time when he was in high school and had thought of committing suicide, and was glad that he did not. I noticed that the class grew eerily quiet at the mention of suicide. One girl's eyes widened and locked on Dwayne. He allowed teens to voice their fears and ambivalence to the group and validated their complex feelings. As teens linked these feelings and experiences to the biblical stories, they interpreted who they were through the biblical narratives. Such a Sunday school is what William Myers called a "free place," or what Parks and Keating call a "holding environment."[30] It is where teens can say what they want and shape who they are in Christian symbols.[31]

Once Dwayne overheard a teen whispering to another teen sitting next to him, "Were David and Jonathan lovers?" Instead of glossing over the controversial issue of homosexuality, Dwayne raised it as a topic for general discussion. One girl argued that they were not lovers because God condemns homosexuals, and God would not choose one for a leader in Judah. Another girl agreed. Dwayne offered that David was also an adulterer, something God did not condone. God's leaders were not perfect. The question of homosexuality was left open and unresolved.

Similarly, on Palm Sunday the class discussed the meaning of Jesus' death on the cross. One girl said that it showed that Jesus died like everybody else. Another girl disagreed, and stressed the unique, salvific aspect of Jesus' death. The second girl was frustrated because the teacher had not underscored that point himself. Dwayne's style was to let the teens draw their own conclusions. This openness was especially striking to me in contrast to the teaching style at Riverland Heights, where sometimes the adult leader would give teens an outline of the teaching with fill-in-the-blanks for them to complete as the answers were given in class.

Like all mainline Protestant churches, there was tolerance at First United Methodist for divergent social views and allowance for pluralism, even within the teaching that took place in Sunday school. As sociologist Patrick McNamara noted in the classrooms at the Catholic high school he studied, students were encouraged to question and develop the high level of critical thinking that sometimes undercut the authority of the very tradition in which teens were being reared.[32]

The other regular practice that stands out at First United Methodist as one that socialized teens in the Christian way of life was the experience of participating in the choirs. Teens internalized the lyrics of sacred music, as Roderick expected them to memorize their pieces. He asked them to sing their music as a prayer. He drew attention to the biblical sources for the texts. When they sang a text referring to being carried on eagle's wings, he read aloud its source, chapter 40 of Isaiah, and displayed on an easel next to him a photograph of an eagle to assist the choir in visualizing their music.

Singing in the choir and playing bells also offered occasions for religious experiences, especially on the annual choir tour. One boy told me about a choir tour they had taken two years before. Late at night, after a performance, the choir was relaxing together in the home of a host family in St. Louis. "One person grabbed a pitch pipe and started us off. We started singing our music at the top of our lungs." "It was a religious experience?" I asked. "Yes, definitely." "What was the song?" I asked. "'Many Gifts, One Spirit,' and I always think of that night when we sing it."

On the choir tour, teens experienced strong bonds of community along the lines of what Turner described as the liminal state. Teens were separated from their normal settings and families and bound together to face new experiences in marginal places: homeless shelters, nursing homes, and inner-city churches. Most important, choir tours brought teens into meaningful contact with what Daloz et al. call "the Other": strangers, the homeless, the elderly, neglected children living on the margins of life.[33] One girl reported back to the congregation how affirming one of those experiences of encountering someone very different from herself had been as the choir concert wrapped up the tour.

> Nicole said she talked to a woman at a homeless shelter who told her about her background, and about how unwanted and disregarded she felt by society. "It meant so much to this woman that the choir wanted to come and sing to them. The woman said, 'God bless you, Nicole' to me." Nicole reported to the congregation, "I just bawled."[34]

Another boy told about arriving in Charlotte, North Carolina, to sing and provide vacation Bible school to an inner-city church. The church forgot they were coming, and had sent off all its children to spend a week at a camp. He reported, "So we wondered, what were we supposed to do all week?" The teens went out into the neighborhood projects and knocked on doors to invite other kids to vacation Bible school. "It was like the parable where all the invited guests couldn't come and you went out and got other people to come." At the week's end, as their bus was pulling away, a child ran after them down the street. The bus stopped. The child wanted to give her teddy bear to one of the teens. The teens were deeply touched that they could become so significant to children who were vulnerable and underprivileged in comparison to themselves.

On balance, First United Methodist was better at offering socialization than conditions that fostered religious experience, as far as this could be observed and/or reported during the year of this study.[35] Since most religious experiences that were reported were connected in some way with the choir tour, teens who did not participate in the music program at the church tended not to report notable, specific religious experiences. Sometimes teens, like Beth, said they had life-changing experiences of God on retreats sponsored by parachurch groups. Others mentioned experiences at Christian camps and/or experiences that occurred in connection with religious school clubs like Campus Life and Fellowship of Christian Athletes.

It is notable that the average of all the teens in these three congregations who say they will remain loyal to their religious tradition (over 68
percent) is high in comparison to national samples. (See Appendix P.)
These congregations exemplify methods of socialization and of fostering
religious experience that lead to high religious loyalty in teens.

Chapter Six

Special Challenges of the Senior Year

T he issue of religious loyalty comes into sharp focus during the senior year of high school. It is as if seniors come to a fork in the road where they are presented with the prospect of either dropping out of church or becoming more committed to their community of faith. High school seniors are preparing to leave home. In most cases, they are also leaving their city or town, and therefore also the church of their nurture. If they continue with a church in the years ahead, they will have to exert some effort to find one in their new location.

In the course of my research I became aware, as never before, of how tumultuous this stage in the life cycle can be for many teens. They are marginalized in several key ways. Economically, they face the high costs of college tuition and living independently or semi-independently from parents, but most can earn only minimum wage at part-time jobs. Socially, they are marginalized, particularly in certain social settings. Some teenagers reported that they felt unwelcome at restaurants even when they came dressed up in formal clothes for the prom. They noticed that clerks in stores at the mall eyed them extra vigilantly as they entered.

High school seniors sometimes fail to cope well with their marginalization, and become depressed or unmotivated, especially as their high school graduation approaches.[1] As a researcher, I noticed that it was much easier to get teens to interview with me in the fall (the early part of the senior year) than in the winter or spring. Adults who work with seniors noted that they sometimes begin their final year in high school with great enthusiasm, but grow increasingly disengaged in both school and church. As one school principal described it, "a small window of opportunity" exists in the first month of the senior year to engage seniors' commitment to the school. Teachers had to sign them up for leadership positions and projects at that time because they soon lost interest in the school. There were brief bursts of engagement at particular points during the senior year—at homecoming, Christmas, the prom, and the senior recognition worship services—but for the most part seniors were focused on what lay beyond high school and beyond their home churches, which they would be leaving. "So much of adolescence is an ill-defined dying, an intolerable waiting, a longing for another place and time, another condition," and this is especially true in the senior year of high school.[2]

One obvious way churches influence teens to choose the path of further church involvement after high school is by addressing their ambiguous stage of life between childhood and adulthood with rites of passage, to give their unclear status more definition and imbue it with religious meaning. The educator Ianni has argued that teens are engaged in a "search for structure" to guide their movement from childhood to adulthood.[3] Carnegie Council on Adolescent Development authors argue that communities must offer youth a "charter" providing clear expectations and positive models to guide them as they enter the adult world.[4] In my research I discovered that the secular culture, more than the church, offered high school seniors rites of passage to define their leave-taking from the sheltered institutions of childhood. Yet, when churches offer some symbols and rituals that give this ambiguous state some meaning and structure, teens affirm their religious tradition. Moreover, we will see that teens remake their religious traditions, adding layers of meaning to its symbols and rituals, and they incorporate new elements to fashion rites of passage with religious meaning for themselves.

Secular and Religious Rites of Passage

The spring break trip was the quintessential secular rite of passage for high school seniors. It was the practice of large numbers of Louisville high school seniors to travel with their friends to Panama City, Florida, to sunbathe on the beach during the week they had off from school each March. While not all seniors participated, the more popular "influencers" tended to go, and thus it was widely regarded as an event marking the senior year even for teens who did not participate. Even more than the prom or graduation, this week was a rite of passage, because it extended over a longer period of time (a week) and it clearly stood outside the structure that normally characterized the teens' everyday lives.

This rite occurred in three phases, beginning with separation from home and family, as parents generally did not go with teens on spring break. If parents or other adults went, they were expected to keep their distance. For most teens, it was the first time they had left home for a vacation without their families.

The time on site in Panama City offered the second or "marginal" phase of this rite of passage. Used to comfortable suburban homes, teens stayed in cheap hotel rooms, pooling their resources to make it affordable, often crowding in the maximum number of guests allowed per hotel room.

The time in Panama City was marginal in a moral sense as well. For some, spring break was regarded as a time to test the firmness of one's values in the face of temptation. For others, it was a time to exceed the limits of boundaries they had been taught. Alcohol and drug abuse, promiscuous sex, extended exposure to ultraviolet rays, and other reckless behaviors were the norm. Tragically, teens died or came very near to death during these trips. One high school senior who was a nominal member of Transfiguration's youth group died of a drug overdose on spring break during the year of my study. The school principal at St. Peter vented, "Teens think that what they do on spring break doesn't count. They think that this week is exempt. They act like what they do in Panama City can be bracketed from their real lives."

Finally, at the conclusion of spring break there was evidence that the third phase, the gathering in new roles and identities, had taken place. As one teen described it, "In Panama City you see the same people you see in Louisville. You can walk down the beach in Panama City and see the St. Peter section, the Thomas Merton section, the Grinstead section, and so on." The symbolic demarcations of their hometown high schools were replicated in their new setting. By the time they returned to Louisville, however, some new configurations emerged. Danielle, for example, was excluded from the car in which she thought she was returning home. During the week, one of the girls staying in her hotel room had to be rushed to the emergency room because of alcohol poisoning. Danielle was the one who called the girl's parents and cleaned up the mess in the bathroom while the others left for another party. Danielle, who exhibited responsible behavior, was ostracized, and she had to take a plane home by herself. School counselors were on alert for spring break returnees who were devastated by the upheaval in their lives created by their spring break experiences.

Apart from spring break, there were certain liminal places in the landscape of the senior year where older high school teens tested boundaries as part of their passage out of their school years. One of these was the school parking lot. Just as the church parking lot could be a place to encounter God (as illustrated earlier), the school parking lot was a place to deal drugs, to be robbed, and to display wealth and status in the type of car you drove. A girl explained to me during a tour of her high school that the three parking lots at the school were informally classified to reflect different social groups. They were called the "Jock Lot," the "Pot Lot," and the "Teachers' Lot." The parking lot is associated with both the freedom and the danger that are still fresh and exciting to newly minted drivers.

In all, the senior year is a time that is ripe with opportunity for the church to offer rites of passage to give religious meaning to teens' transition to adulthood. Yet the official institutional rite of passage that the church offers is not synchronized with the timing of the American adolescent in the late twentieth century. The "sacrament" (Catholic) or "rite" (mainline Protestant) of confirmation—when a person is initiated into adult roles in the church—already occurred years ago for most church-related high school seniors. Confirmation takes place in the eighth grade at Transfiguration and in the seventh grade at First United Methodist. Similarly, baptism—a rite that represents for evangelical Protestants the mature discernment of the significance of Jesus' saving death and resurrection—already took place for most evangelical teens. The average age of baptism among teens in my interview sample from Riverland Heights was eight years old.[5] Needless to say, none of the teens in my sample linked either confirmation or baptism to their current transition to adulthood. Many teens in my sample (particularly the Catholic and mainline Protestant teens) had negative assessments of the personal significance of these rites.

All twelve Catholics in my interview sample were confirmed in eighth grade. Only one in twelve cited it as a positive experience, as "neat," and "my decision." The rest were indifferent and said they participated in confirmation because it was an expectation they did not care to challenge. One boy tried to refuse confirmation but relented when his resistance brought him unwanted attention and extra meetings with parochial school personnel. Another boy said he deeply regrets having been confirmed because he does not hold Catholic beliefs. He says he feels he is marked by confirmation, "like a concentration camp inmate with a tattooed number."

Others regretted it for different reasons. One wished she had not been confirmed already because she would like to be confirmed during her senior year of high school, now that she appreciates what it means.[6] Confirmation tended to occur in a real sense for Catholic teens not during the official ceremony in eighth grade but later, when they were leading the confirmation retreat themselves. Both Angie and the director of religious education at Transfiguration observed that teens appropriate the meaning of their confirmation when they lead the confirmation retreat themselves for the eighth-graders.[7]

The confirmation process occurring in seventh grade at First United Methodist was described as a positive experience by only one person. That was the same teen who said she had a real choice in the matter because her older brother had opted not to be confirmed. The others described confirmation as something with which they went along, as the Catholic teens described it. Some said they grew to appreciate their confirmation later. Several mentioned that they liked the confirmation retreat, but the confirmation ritual itself did not mean as much. Beth, mentioned at the beginning of chapter 4, illustrates how the rite of confirmation is not synchronized with her religious experience. She said she "became a Christian" several years after she was confirmed and had publicly claimed her faith. Normally one would expect the sequence to be reversed.

Teens at Riverland Heights are generally more positive in their reports of their memories of their baptisms, even if they say they did not fully understand baptism at the time. They said that what matters more to them than being baptized is that they are saved. The experience of making the choice to be baptized was perceived as a decision for salvation. It is remembered by teens as very positive even if they made that decision when they were too young to grasp its full implications. None reported that they were forced by their parents to be baptized.

Some Riverland Heights teens were baptized more than once if they had been sprinkled as a baby in a mainline Protestant church before they switched to Riverland Heights.[8] One boy was baptized three times, once as a baby in a Presbyterian church, once in the River Jordan when his family was visiting Israel, and lastly (and most important to him) in a swimming pool at a camp by some friends late at night. The last baptism represented his commitment to God. Baptism presented an interesting dilemma for evangelicals. How can it represent the one-time saving decision for Christ when many adherents experience that choice in a series of gradual decisions? While evangelicals practice rebaptism, it is not endorsed in sermons preached at Riverland Heights.

It is very striking, overall, how confirmation was negatively rated by Catholic and mainline Protestant teens, and believer baptism by immersion was rated positively by evangelical teens. It is difficult to delineate the reasons for this difference. Choice seems to be a key positive factor for evangelicals, since they were not baptized as members of a class, as were Catholics and Methodists. It is difficult to say whether immersion is perceived to offer something preferable to sprinkling, the usual practice of the Catholics and Methodists at the time of this study.[9] Clearly what was disliked most about confirmation was the sense that it was routinized. None of the teens had any specific memories to share of the confirmation liturgy, any positive feelings that lingered about the act of standing before the congregation to proclaim their faith, or any deepened sense of belonging that their new status in the church afforded.

Teens Remaking Their Religious Traditions

In different ways, all three congregations compensated for the lack of synchronicity between their official rites of passage and the high school seniors' need for rituals to define their transition to adulthood and/or mature religious commitment. Teens in these three congregations structured local rites of passages from the symbols of their religious traditions. This happened most dramatically at Transfiguration and Riverland Heights and to a lesser degree at First United Methodist.

The senior mass at Transfiguration was one of the nonofficial but regular traditions that teens developed over the years to symbolize the conclusion of their high school years. Over the twenty-two years that Angie worked at Transfiguration, the senior mass evolved and grew in importance to become a defining event of the senior year. While all three churches had senior recognition ceremonies, only Transfiguration's senior mass was designed and executed by the teens themselves. The amount of time and energy that teens invested in its preparation was notable. Teens planned the entire service except for the institution of the sacrament, which was performed by the priest. The youth group band played original music composed for the mass. Seniors designed and painted an elaborate mural that was hung over the altar during the service and kept in the youth center afterward.

To the central ritual of the mass were added particular local rituals and symbols that had been developed over the years by this youth group. For example, it was the custom of these teens to present their parents with a rose taken from the bouquet on the altar to symbolize their love and gratitude. During the presentation, they sang "The Song of the Rose," a ballad from the sound track of a popular movie. The custom of presenting a rose to parents was also practiced regularly at the confirmation retreat in eighth grade and at different ceremonies at the Catholic high schools. When the custom was repeated at the senior mass, it was loaded with memories and meanings of the other significant events. The rose presentation took on a quasi-religious significance for these teens because of all these associations and because it was incorporated into a religious service held in the church.

Another motif that took on quasi-religious significance for this group was the symbol of the butterfly. While the butterfly is not a biblical image or an officially sanctioned symbol of the Catholic Church, at Transfiguration it signified resurrection. On the anniversary of Maureen's death, teens developed a ceremony at the youth center of pinning different-colored butterflies made of feathers on a grapevine wreath. Angie and her adult daughters wore butterfly pins at the funeral of Angie's husband. At the senior mass, teens used the butterfly motif in the mural they made to hang over the altar. The mural portrayed human figures crossing a narrow bridge over a body of water toward a larger human figure in black. The figures were holding hands as they moved toward the end of the bridge. There were butterflies in the sky over the heads of the human figures—butterflies with human faces. The teenaged boy who was the main artist creating the mural explained that the figures represented the seniors taking off and flying because of their transformative experience in youth group.

Evangelical teens in my sample also sacralized certain motifs and developed new rituals, as Catholic teens did. Most striking was their reappropriation of the church's rite of baptism. When baptisms take place at big church at Riverland Heights, only men, usually one of the ministers, perform them. The youth minister explains that baptism by male clergy is "not doctrine, but tradition." Since tradition is less authoritative than doctrine, there is some openness to alternative forms of practice. They have a "really cool elder" in charge of the youth ministry. The elder allows teenagers to baptize other teenagers when it is performed outside big church.

"Sometimes girls baptize other girls," Craig, the youth leader, explained. "It is just natural that the person who has helped lead someone to Christ do the baptizing." Craig described how the experience of baptizing is just as important for the baptizer as it is for the one being baptized. "It is a mark in the life of a Christian to baptize someone else." When a teen baptizes another teen at the youth center, in the ocean on spring break, or in someone's swimming pool, the whole group cheers, claps, hugs, and sings in celebration.

While Riverland Heights does not officially endorse rebaptism, there were instances when teens asked to be baptized again. They sought to acknowledge publicly their commitment to God in a serious, mature way that was not possible when they were baptized at a much younger age. Often this occurred after they had had a powerful religious experience. They sought a way to symbolize publicly that their life would be different thereafter, as they lived "a new life in Christ." The revised, fluid practice of rebaptism exemplifies one of the myriad ways Riverland Heights keeps together the structure of the tradition and the substance of religious experience.

There were fewer instances of teens remaking religious symbols and/or reappropriating church rituals at First United Methodist. Teens at this church were more integrated into the whole congregation, and they tended to find general congregational traditions meaningful as they were practiced. There were a few local customs in this church, however, that marked the teens' passage out of high school, as well as their return on breaks from college. One of these was the midnight candlelight Christmas Eve service. The high school choir always provided the choral music for that service. It was a dramatic and much anticipated moment in the service when all alumnae and alumni of the high school choir rose from their pews and joined the high school choir in the chancel for the same final piece that they sang every year. Similarly, it was a cherished tradition at the choir tour concert held in the sanctuary at First United Methodist for alumnae and alumni in the congregation to join the choir for their final piece, which was always "Goin' Up a Yonder." In the year of my research, teens and alumnae wept as they sang this piece. It was loaded with memories of all their choir tours, the times when they met "the Other," had powerful experiences of community, and grew in their faith and loyalty to their church.

❖❖❖❖❖❖❖❖

In conclusion, churches foster in teens religious loyalty—more than fleeting attraction—when they both socialize their teens in the symbols, stories, rituals, and practices of their tradition and foster the conditions through which teens feel they encounter God. When congregations do both, teens tend to profess strong allegiance to their faith tradition. The senior year is a pivotal time for religious loyalty. High school seniors are fortified in their religious commitment when churches encourage them to use the symbols of their tradition to fashion rites of passage to give definition and religious significance to this ambiguous time. When teens reappropriate traditional practices to represent and deepen their personal experiences of God, the tradition is remade and vitalized. Religious loyalty for contemporary teens is a blending of enduring processes (socialization and religious experience) with new emphases on personal autonomy and choice.

While "religious loyalty" (defined in the Introduction and described extensively here) is an important category to use for assessing how congregations, parents, and others pass on the faith to the next generation, the varied ways teens relate to the religious tradition of their nurture cannot be fully captured by this term. In fact, "loyalty" is rarely mentioned by teens as they describe themselves and their sense of being religious. Instead, self-identity is the main theme of the teens' own stories. In Part III, I describe the distinct patterns that emerged in how teens referenced their religious tradition as a source for self-identity.

Part III

Seven Styles of Being Religious . . . or Not

Chapter Seven

Religious Tradition and Teen Self-Identity

Teens today—like many adults—tend to conceive of religion in a highly personal way that is less tethered to an unquestioned religious authority. They might embrace a historic religious tradition, but they also might pick and choose the beliefs and practices within it that make sense to them. They might go to church, but they might attend various services around the city, depending on what seems to meet their need. As Gallup notes, most youth who attend church claim that they go to religious services not just because their parents insist, but also because they themselves choose to go.[1] Moreover, because of their freedom to choose, their relationship to their tradition may be negotiated in various ways.

Seven patterns emerged in the way church-related teens in my interview sample referred to the religious tradition of their upbringing as a shaping force in their self-identity. For some, the most *conventional* Christians, their faith is the basic framework of their lives, like the frame of a loom on which they weave the different threads of their relationships, goals, and spheres of activity. The basic shape of the tapestry is fixed, and the patterns tend to be uniform. For others, the *"classic* event" of Christ[2] is a theme that dominates their lives in a different way, like the main musical theme of a fugue. It is stated and restated by various ensembles and soloists, in different contexts and moods. Another group of teens *reclaimed* their tradition after a period of rejecting it. Their autobiographies follow the same basic plot. Like the apostle Saul/Paul, they have two selves: one lost, one found. They once were lost from God and now are found by a profound experience of grace. Another group of teens looks at all that life offers and selects their investments of time and psychic energy, as if they were calculating the potential yields and risks of different investments in the stock market. The religious tradition is *marginalized* in their portfolio. It is like an insurance policy that is purchased and set aside for the time being. Other teens *customize* the Christian tradition by taking the parts that have personal meaning and quilting them together with other beliefs and practices of spirituality that appeal to them. Some teens *reject* their tradition altogether, leaving it after childhood as if they were moving away from home to another city better suited to their adult lives. Another group of teens are underexposed to the Christian tradition and *lost* to the church, even though their names appear on the church rolls. For various reasons, the tradition is like a seed planted that never grew. It was trampled underfoot, snatched by birds, choked by weeds, or scorched by the sun.

These seven styles of relating to the religious tradition (named for the terms in italic type above) can be placed on a continuum illustrating the degree to which the Christian tradition is authoritative in shaping that particular self-identity. (See fig. 6.)

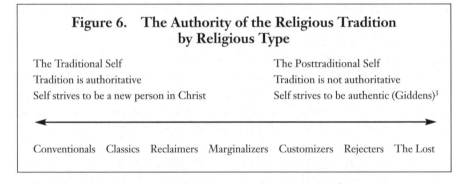

Figure 6.   The Authority of the Religious Tradition by Religious Type

The Traditional Self   The Posttraditional Self
Tradition is authoritative   Tradition is not authoritative
Self strives to be a new person in Christ   Self strives to be authentic (Giddens)[3]

Conventionals   Classics   Reclaimers   Marginalizers   Customizers   Rejecters   The Lost

This continuum can be interposed with another one (Figure 7) constructed from Peter Berger's (1998) understanding of the degree of certainty the individual claims in his or her beliefs about God.

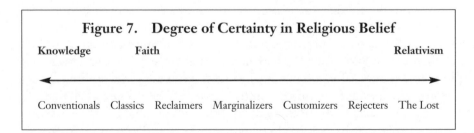

Figure 7.   Degree of Certainty in Religious Belief

Knowledge   Faith   Relativism

Conventionals   Classics   Reclaimers   Marginalizers   Customizers   Rejecters   The Lost

Those at one end "know" God with complete certainty. Typically, Conventionals express this kind of certainty of God. In the categories to the right of the Conventionals and in the left-of-center categories, there is a faith stance, belief based on the "assurance of things not seen." That stance characterizes the Classics and Reclaimers, and to lesser degrees the Marginalizers and Customizers. At the opposite end, there is extreme relativism or nihilism undercutting the possibility of belief in God. Typically what Rejecters say is that it is impossible to affirm the absolute truth of the Christian revelation; Christianity is one religion on a par with all the others. The Lost type, those at the farthest end of this continuum, may express some certainty in Christian beliefs, but they do so without knowledge of what the Christian tradition stands for. The religious expression of the Lost is idiosyncratic.

Self-Identity in Late Modernity

In both Figures 6 and 7, Giddens would argue that the default mode of self-identity in late modernity is represented more by the right end than the left. He believes that persons today are not shaped by authoritative traditions—religious, civic, moral, or otherwise. Belief in communal values is relativistic and not certain. A "thoroughgoing reflexivity" chronically revises knowledge about social life and material relations in the light of ever more new knowledge and information.

Giddens says the shift in how self-identity is constructed in late modern society is most evident as one observes adolescents. As persons make the transition to adulthood, their process of choosing a "lifeplan" (one of the standardized career paths) is most transparent. Giddens argues that adolescents are no longer shaped and guided on the journey to adult self-identity by the religious traditions that used to structure rites of passage in premodern and modern society. Instead, the *posttraditional* self replaces the *traditional* self in late modernity.

The Posttraditional Self

How does one know a posttraditional self when one sees it? Five key characteristics can be extracted from Giddens's extended discussion. These are seen more clearly when contrasted with elements of the traditional self that Giddens says is nearly obsolete. (See table 5.)

**Table 5.   Five Elements of Self-Identity
for Traditional and Posttraditional Selves**

	Intimacy	Bodily Presentation	Grounding of Ontological Security	Rites of Passage to Adulthood	Moral Dilemmas, How Resolved
Traditional Self	Kinship ties	Physical characteristics are accepted as given; demeanor of respect for authority	God, country, religious truth	Rituals and rites of passage dictated by traditions	Normative beliefs, practices, institutions
Posttraditional Self	Pure relationships	Self-mastery of bodily appearance; sensuality	Practical consciousness in day-to-day life that brackets chaos	Self-actualization as an open process	Maximize opportunity and minimize risk to self

First, the posttraditional self conceives of intimacy through "pure relationships" instead of kinship ties and traditional obligations. "Pure relationships" maximize one's interests for intimacy in a rational choice model. In sexuality, marriage, and friendship, "a relationship exists solely for whatever rewards that relationship can deliver."[4] The parent-child relationship generally does not qualify as a pure relationship.[5] Second, the body is "less a given," an entity that one has, and more "a phenomenon of choices and options."[6] A competent self maintains control over the body as a way to maintain one's biography of self-identity and to display one's competence to others. Third, ontological security is not anchored by religious understandings organizing time and space, and defining moral action. Instead routines construct emotional acceptance of the world. "Meaning is not built up through descriptions of external reality . . . rather daily practice forms the necessary condition of what can be said and of the meanings involved in practical consciousness" (1991: 43).[7] Fourth, the trajectory of the self, how it goes through transitions involving loss, is "open experience." Religious rituals and traditional rites of passage fade in importance. Instead, a "lifestyle" growing from a "more or less integrated set of practices . . . gives material form to a particular narrative of self-identity."[8] Fifth, the preeminent value that guides posttraditional selves in moral behavior is authenticity within a framework of self-actualization. Giddens himself finds this disturbing, because genuine moral questions tend to be repressed by the posttraditional self.

He comments that authenticity offers too little for grounding right human relations.

Giddens's description of the components of posttraditional self-identity in late modernity provides a helpful starting point to use for an analysis of self-identity as it is understood by the teens in my interview sample. In the next chapter, I offer my analysis of how teens construct self-identity in reference to their religious tradition and exhibit seven distinct ways of holding (or not holding) their faith. To enable me to draw comparisons with Giddens, I used his five dimensions of the self in my analysis, looking at how church-related teens conceive of intimacy, bodily presentation, the grounding of ontological security, rites of passage to adulthood, and morality.

Using Giddens's categories of the traditional self and the posttraditional self as two poles of identity construction, I expected to find that the teens I interviewed would fall somewhere between these two extremes. I expected to find that the Conventionals were least likely to exhibit elements of the posttraditional self, and conversely that the Lost would exhibit the most. The results were not as clean as expected. Some elements of the posttraditional self are evident even in the most traditional selves, the Conventionals. Some elements of the religious tradition are residual to the Lost's sense of self-identity as well.

In all, the sense of self I discerned in the teens in my sample had greater agency and control over the structures that shaped them than that assumed in Giddens's model.[9] The teens I interviewed did not just accept or reject the Christian tradition. They did not experience their religious tradition or their church as univocal, static, and/or monolithic. As it will be seen, they appreciated the many meanings of the Christian tradition and appropriated it in new spheres and in innovative ways. The tradition was not simply reproduced in them. They negotiated with it, tested its boundaries, and experienced it as life shaping as they remade it.

Chapter Eight

Self-Identity in Seven Religious Types of Church-related Teens

I n this chapter, I sort the teens in my interview sample into categories that developed gradually as I analyzed the teens' sense of identity that emerged in my interviews with them and in my field observations of them. I do not permanently label the teens or assume that they can be summed up by these categories. I view the following as the kind of sorting one might do after taking a series of snapshots. This is more about the range and variety of categories that exist than about labeling particular teens.

At the end of the chapter, there are a chart (table 7) and a conclusion that summarize the findings of this portion of the study.

Type One: The "Conventionals"

Rebecca describes her favorite season of the year as winter, especially when there is a huge snowfall that traps all her family at home. She loves spending the day with her parents and four younger siblings, playing in the snow and roasting marshmallows in the den fireplace. One of Rebecca's most hurtful experiences happened when her father forgot the birthday celebration ritual of standing behind her just before she blew out the candles on the cake to ask God for a special blessing on her in the year ahead. Rebecca is unusual for an eighteen-year-old American in that her family constitutes her inner circle of intimacy.[1]

Rebecca is able to live like this because she is sheltered more than most American teens from the posttraditional influences and institutions of high modernity. She has been home-schooled by her mother all her life. When she first attended Vision, the midweek youth meeting at Riverland Heights, it was "the most secular thing" in which she had ever participated, and "it took a whole lot of getting used to." The style of the event, the raucousness of it, and the diversity of the youth shocked Rebecca. She prefers "soft Christian rock," as, for example, the music of the Christian artist Amy Grant. When the pop-rock music style at Vision shifts occasionally to the alternative Christian style, Rebecca considers it too extreme for her tastes. The only non-Christian adult she has ever known well is her art teacher. All her friends are from Riverland Heights except for one Jewish girl who lives in the neighborhood. Before I was given permission to interview Rebecca, her mother screened me over the telephone to make sure my interview was not designed to undercut what her daughter believed and how she lived.

There are other teens, not quite as sheltered as Rebecca, who still consider their family ties to be primary. These teens tend to live in traditional families with clearly differentiated parent, child, and gender roles. They believe they must obey their parents and respect parental authority, even when their parents disappoint them. That explains why Robin remains loyal to her father even though he committed adultery, and why Emily was able to weather the toughest years of her father's alcoholism before he started his recovery. While many teens would be embarrassed to have a mentally ill mother like Brian's, he brings his friends home to meet her because that is the respectful way sons are supposed to treat parents.

For the conventionally religious, Christian friends form a second ring of intimacy around the core of the biologically related family. The overwhelming majority of the Conventionals in my study were affiliated with the evangelical megachurch, with the remaining few belonging to First United Methodist. (See table 6.) Both churches promoted the understanding that their congregation was like a family; they were "brothers and sisters in Christ."[2]

Intimacy was not just expressed in gestures of mutual affirmation, although there was plenty of that. It was also expressed through the members' "accountability" to one another. Brian described how an adult mentor once criticized him for his pride. Rebecca described how she had to ask forgiveness of a girl in the youth group because Rebecca disliked the rude way she spoke. Achieving intimacy with Christian friends proved difficult for many, and it was all the more disappointing when it was not achieved because the expectation of tight bonds with one's coreligionists is heightened. What I found as often as affirmations of satisfying friendships within the circle of Christian fellowship were expressions of disappointment that intimacy was wanting.

Table 6.   Churches by Seven Religious Types
in Interview Sample of Teens

	Transfiguration (Catholic)		Riverland Heights (Evangelical Protestant)		First United Methodist (Mainline Protestant)	
	N	Percent	N	Percent	N	Percent
Conventionals	0	0%	9	53%	2	17%
Classics	0	0%	2	12%	2	17%
Reclaimers	1	8%	3	18%	0	0%
Marginalizers	6	50%	0	0%	5	42%
Customizers	1	8%	2	12%	1	8%
Rejecters	2	17%	0	0%	1	8%
The Lost	2	17%	1	6%	1	8%
Total of each church	12	100%	17	101%*	12	100%

*Note: Number exceeds 100 percent because of rounding.

"Your body is the temple of God" is a biblical injunction that clearly informs the second element of self-identity, how Conventionals view their bodies. Conventionals are modest and they groom themselves carefully. They generally blend in with their peers by wearing a less extreme version of what is considered stylish in their reference group. For Mitch, a disc jockey at his high school radio station, this means sporting a retro-style haircut with long sideburns, but not the extreme of a ponytail. Long hair on a boy is not just considered rebellious, but effeminate. A few of these teens do stand apart from their peers because they are not stylishly dressed; however, most blend in. Even Rebecca, the most sheltered, would not be viewed as notably different in appearance from other teens in Louisville. She generally wears jeans, leather boot-style shoes, and a drab-colored sweater. She wears her shoulder-length brown hair pulled away from her face, revealing dangling hoop earrings. These teens want to stand out because of their testimony to God, not because they look like nerds.[3]

Susan was impressive in the confidence and forthrightness with which she spoke. She was one of the few teens who extended her hand to me after the interview to signal respect and acknowledgment of our parting. Susan emphasized in the interview how she disliked the way most of her peers lacked respect for adults and people in authority, especially teachers. Susan had internalized the biblical admonition, "Outdo one another in showing honor."

Conventionally religious teens who exhibit clear understandings of the priority of their family ties and of what is appropriate in outward presentation to others also exhibit confidence about their ultimate safety in heaven. Among Conventionals, heaven comes up as a topic in the conversation at least as frequently as God. Going to heaven is presented as a compelling reason to accept Christ, even more often than God's love. Heaven is the place where teens will see their grandparents again. Heaven is one's ultimate destination. Brian agonizes that the girl who died in a car accident the night of homecoming is not in heaven. The boy who was killed in the same crash is safe there. Heaven is also the place where they will meet God and ask him the answers to difficult questions. Lauren says her first question to God in heaven will be "Why isn't everyone here?"

The fifth element of self-identity, rites of passage, is seen ultimately by Conventionals as accepting Christ as Lord and Savior. That is the key transition in one's life that most defines the self. This rite of passage generally does not mark the passage to adulthood, however, since (as mentioned in Part II) the ritual marking this, baptism, occurs for the evangelicals in my sample on average at age eight. Likewise, the rite of confirmation, the closest equivalent for Catholics and Methodists to the evangelical rite of baptism by immersion, is not a rite of passage to adulthood because it also occurs too early (in the seventh or eighth grade) to mark the beginning of adulthood.

Instead, marriage is the rite of passage to adulthood for Conventionals, because it forms the adult family unit. Of all the teens in my sample, Conventionals were the ones who exhibited the most interest in finding not just a girlfriend or a boyfriend, but a future spouse. Brian drew up a list of characteristics he is looking for in his wife. Caroline keeps a journal for her future and yet unidentified husband. She speaks of the importance of "being yoked alike." One of the arguments that weighed in favor of Brynne's family switching to the megachurch was their daughter's remark that she would be more likely to meet a Christian young man there than at a smaller church.

Because adulthood is marked by marriage, there is extra incentive for Conventionals to get married. Unmarried adults, especially the never-marrieds, and most especially the female never-marrieds, occupy an ambiguous status. On the one hand, the church depends on the extra time that these adults can give to be youth leaders in the youth program. On the other hand, they are not held in the same high regard as role models to the teens if they pass their marriageable prime. The thirtyish never-married female youth leader on staff at the megachurch was named only twice as a role model by teens I interviewed, as compared to the seven times her married male colleague was mentioned.

As important as marriage is to Conventionals, none in my sample had plans to be married in the near future. High school graduation and eligibility to attend the "young adult" activities of the church were the intermediate rites of passage that they anticipated.

When I asked teens whom I later grouped as Conventionals various questions relating to ethics,[4] a regular set of examples was used to describe the arenas for testing right and wrong. Predictably, Conventionals mentioned the following: sexual purity; opposition to abortion, evolution, and homosexuality; and living a drug-free and alcohol-free life. Of all these, sexual purity is the crucible.

When I talked to Lauren at Christmas, she was "worried sick" that she would not have a date for the prom in May. She had never dated before, so her fears were well founded. She channeled her anxiety into fervent and frequent prayers. She confided that she thought God was not giving her a boyfriend because she was not sure that she could wait to have sex until she got married. That sounded like an extreme worry, to jump from a mere date to having sex, but Lauren is naive about dating. She admits that she loves reading Christian romance novels. Like some of the other conventionally Christian teens, especially the girls, she wears a "promise ring" in place of an engagement ring to remind her of her pledge to postpone sex until marriage.[5]

Almost as important as remaining sexually pure is showing love for those who have obviously failed. Brian reported that a female member of the Fellowship of Christian Athletes club at his school was pregnant. The entire club offered this girl and her boyfriend "open arms and love because they know they made a mistake." Strong views about preventing abortion go along with this forgiving stance. Typically, Conventionals cited the Ten Commandments, the Bible, WWJD, and what their parents taught them as the guides they use for determining right action.

In all, these teens illustrate how, even in high modernity, the Christian tradition provides conventionally religious teens the structures of their self-identity. In the framework of their religious tradition, these teens establish the boundaries that define their circles of intimacy, the guidelines for outward self-presentation, the anchor that grounds their sense of security, the rites of passage to adulthood, and direction for how to act morally. There is also some evidence to suggest that high modernity disturbs these structures of self-identity, especially for Robin, who struggles with anorexia, and for Brynne, who has an "evangelism problem."

Robin was voted "Miss Highland Park" by her classmates. This title honored her as a model student, as a leader in her service to Highland Park High School, as popular among her peers, and as physically attractive. She also revealed confidentially that she suffered anorexic and bulimic episodes. It is not uncommon for adolescent girls who attempt to conform to unrealistic images of perfection to exhibit self-destructive behavior expressed in their compulsive control of their bodies. Giddens suggests that this condition is evidence of a posttraditional self. While fasting and self-denial have long been a part of religious rituals, extreme bodily regulation can be performed to exert self-mastery "as an emblem of security in an open social environment."[6] Becoming slim and attractive to males gives the female a way to hedge her bets in "masculinist culture," where women's options for success are ambiguous.

High modernity also exposes teens to plural views of truth and diverse examples of how people ground their sense of security. Brynne, the president of a conservative Christian student-led group at her high school, Fellowship of Christian Athletes, has not resolved "the evangelism problem." She has not sorted out how she is supposed to evangelize in her school, much less *to lead others in evangelizing.* A lot of her friends are Mormons, and they evangelize aggressively. She wonders how her way of believing is different from theirs, and how her knowledge of the truth is better than theirs.

While plural religious views do unsettle Conventionals in the ways Giddens suggests it does for all in "high modernity," none of these teens viewed their religion as something given by their background or ascribed by their family as Giddens portrays people who hold on to traditional religion in these times. Even though these, of all the teens in my sample, are the most certain of the absolute truth of their religion, this truth is something they have chosen to accept. They exhibit agency. Typically Conventionals were riled by my question "Do you consider yourself a religious person?" "No," they reply emphatically. As Rebecca explains, "Some people think it is just a set of rules. . . . You go to church on Sundays and you pray before meals and you ta-da-da-da-da-da, you know. . . . It's not a religion, it's a relationship. It's being, not doing." Conventionals consciously chose this way of being. They know they have the option not to believe, and they have made their choice.

Type Two: The "Classics"

Almost all the teens in my interview sample had at least a few tense issues roiling in their relationship with their parents. These were most often curfew, chores, rules about the use of the car, grades, and finishing college applications. Graham was one of the few who could not name a single area of tension with his parents. "They trust me a lot. They know I'm responsible and stuff," he explained. Beth, on the other hand, occasionally causes her parents worry because of her lapses in good judgment. Once she locked her car door with the keys in the ignition and the engine on, and she left the car running in the school parking lot all morning because she had to attend classes. Beth is sorry about that. She explains that she tries to be responsible and to "honor her parents," as it says to in the Ten Commandments.

Graham and Beth are two teens who consciously try to honor their parents and respect their guidance even as they are distancing themselves from them as they prepare to leave home. Graham prefers to attend a different church from his parents'; yet he attends their church periodically because it means so much to them. C.J., another of this type, has learned how to disagree respectfully with his parents. He and his mother watched an episode of the television show *Touched by an Angel* where the homosexual lifestyle was portrayed as forgiven. C.J. notes, "She said, 'That's not what God intends for natural sexual relations,' and I disagreed and explained my view of what God considers sin."

Peer relationships replace the child-parent relationship as the locus of intimacy for these teens. Jeff goes camping some weekends with friends he has had since childhood. They spend hours in conversation with one another as they fish, sharing their most intimate thoughts on all topics, including theology. While these teens respect their parents, they choose to spend time with their friends more often than with their parents.

Classics work hard to be consistent in the Christian example they set as they interact with distinct groups of peer friends. As Beth put it, "I have school friends who are sort of the same as my church friends, but I also have neighborhood friends. I also have work friends that I hang out with for the whole summer." They struggle with the segmentation of their lives into different social worlds and with the integration of who they are as people of religious faith in nonreligious settings like school.[7] C.J., mentioned in the Introduction, lives in three distinct social worlds. Only in his church "world" does he feel comfortable religiously.

Classics feel challenged to keep their Christian identity continuous across all spheres. They tend to belong to Fellowship of Christian Athletes (or its equivalent at their school), though they may dislike some of the more conservative views of some of the guest speakers.[8] They stand out as Christians by attending the annual "Rock the Pole" massive prayer event at their school, and sometimes also by bowing their heads to pray before their lunch in the school cafeteria. They are unlikely, however, to "target" people for evangelizing as the Conventionals do. They witness by example instead. Some reported that they voiced their religious views without hesitation when they related to the topic of a classroom discussion. They said that in public and elite private schools their religious views were not ruled out of order. They were treated respectfully in school when they supported their points with references to their religious beliefs (that is, if they gave more than *ad hominem* responses).

In bodily presentation, Classics do not conform to any particular style. While they are not as uniformly neat as the Conventionals, they tend to avoid extreme display. They are also less concerned to dress in traditionally gendered ways, to conform to an ideal body size, and to exhibit a demeanor of deference toward adults. I was surprised to meet C.J. after first interviewing his distinguished-looking, well-dressed parents. I expected this much-wanted son of older, affluent parents to look conventional, even preppie. Instead C.J. appeared in a sweatshirt and jeans, wearing a necklace with a Christian fish pendant, appearing to be about twenty pounds overweight. If anything, he looked more grunge than preppie. Graham surprised me in a similar way. I met with his well-groomed parents, who were still wearing their tailored suits from Sunday morning. Later that afternoon Graham appeared in a flannel shirt (untucked), navy sweatpants, and sneakers, wearing his thick, curly brown hair tied back in a gingham handkerchief. He had a lot of facial hair and long sideburns. Hair on boys, its longer length and the presence of facial hair, is an indicator separating the Classics from the Conventionals.

Jeff said his mother pulled him out of the private Christian school because teachers were criticizing his shoulder-length hair. "That has nothing to do with being a Christian," Jeff was affirmed by his mother. Classics distinguish what is custom, like hairstyle, from what is "the classic event," the theology at the heart of the Christian tradition—the focus on Jesus as the Christ. Classics are more open to revising "the way we have always done things here" to adapt to contemporary expressions of Jesus and to new theological ethical reflection. Sometimes this leads Classics to hold views that Conventionals would consider too liberal. Classics are open to interracial dating, to reconsidering traditional understandings of homosexuality as sin, and to accepting truth in other religions. Graham, for example, described the anger that welled up in him as he browsed in a Christian bookstore:

[There was] an entire shelf on like how to combat Muslims, you know, why Muslims are wrong, you know, everything that's screwed up about Hindus, and it was like all this hate and I just like stormed out of the place. I was like, man, there was just too much hate within these walls . . . and that's a big thing with churches that kind of bothers me. There's a lot of hate. A lot of division.

Classics are serious about God. They tend to be disciplined in their study of the Bible. They look at the world, their goals, their relationships, and moral issues through the lens of the Christian tradition. They ground their sense of security in their life with God, in the assurance of grace, in the expectation of the coming kingdom of God on earth. Because they do feel secure in their sense of God, Classics tend to shun "career paths" in pursuit of less lucrative, God-given vocations. Graham plans to follow a career path that will afford him a much lower salary than what his father earns in the corporate world. Graham plans to become a high school teacher because "there aren't enough good male role models out there. I mean the only ones I can think of are the immoral athletes. . . . There are so many like single-family homes, single-parent homes and stuff, and I think there is a real need for positive male role models."

What rites of passage signal adulthood for this group? For Classics, the transition to adulthood is marked by their acceptance of adultlike responsibility for themselves, and "coming of age" is symbolized in different ways that signal responsibility. For C.J., adulthood will be marked by his twenty-first birthday. He and his parents have a bargain that if he refrains from drinking until the legal age of twenty-one, they will give him ten thousand dollars. As C.J. describes it, fulfilling a commitment to his parents and the challenge to exhibit responsible behavior motivate him more than the anticipated financial reward. For Beth, leaving home and going off to college means becoming an adult. She is fulfilling a dream and bringing special delight to her parents because she is attending the same college where they met. Jeff won a full scholarship and will no longer be financially dependent on his mother, who until a few years ago was struggling financially as a single parent. Graham thinks it is likely he will choose to attend the local university and live at home. Graham already made the transition to adulthood during his high school years through his responsible behavior. He does not need to leave home to become an adult.

Like Conventionals, Classics are guided by the Ten Commandments, the Bible, and the values of their parents. In addition, they cite the Golden Rule and the question "What would Jesus do?" as they consider what divides right from wrong. The arenas for moral decision making, however, were less predictable for Classics than for Conventionals. Beth, a popular girl in her school who attended a lot of parties, considered it a test to resist the temptation to join in when some at a party were drinking and taking drugs. She was disgusted by some in Fellowship of Christian Athletes who succumbed. Graham was bothered most by racism at his school and by the meaning of his own affluence. He was embarrassed when his mother picked him up from school in her nice car, because some of his friends from the football team lived in the projects and had no family car at all. Graham was also troubled by "hypocrisy" exhibited by people in the church, and described a particularly disturbing example of it that occurred several years ago. Shortly after the church janitor died, his widow accused other church employees on the janitorial staff of sexually abusing her. She sued the church, and Graham's father (one of the church officers) had to help sort out the scandal. The feeling that the church could have done more to make peace with the widow still troubles Graham. In all, this group of teens focuses on the moral dilemmas at hand more than the global or political issues that raise moral questions in a broader context.

In summary, Classics consciously identify with the Christian religious tradition and view it as authoritative for how to live. Unlike the Conventionals, they do not see it as providing a framework for how to live, dictating particular patterns, offering styles, scripts, and uncontested standards. For Classics, the tradition attracts them because they believe it is true and because it is open to reformation. The tradition is revised when it is shown to deviate or detract from the priority of the classic Christian event.

Type Three: The "Reclaimers"

There were certain teens who initially seemed to fit with either the Conventionals or the Classics. They expressed the same strong religious convictions and exhibited concern about the same moral issues as the Conventionals, yet they did not look like them. They dressed sloppily or showed some evidence of rebelliousness. Some of the boys wore earrings. (Conventional boys do not.) Some of the girls wore too much makeup or wrinkled clothes. One girl wore a skirt held together by a safety pin. (Conventional girls are generally understated and neat in their appearance.) And while they looked as if they could be Classics, they used certain phrases that Classics did not use, such as describing someone as "a baby Christian," or as "unsaved." A closer look at these teens revealed that they were more than a hybrid type of the Conventionals and Classics. They also shared a common experience that set them apart: they had broken with the tradition in a significant way before reclaiming it. As I reviewed the basic elements of identity, I noted other differences that distinguish the Reclaimers as well.

Reclaimers do not consider their parents part of their inner circle. Unlike Conventionals, they select from among their family circle certain members with whom they choose to be close instead of their parents or their peers. Paul says he is not close to his parents, but they have "passed the test." When he was arrested for being a passenger in a car that was stopped by the police and found to have drugs hidden in it, his parents stood by him. Despite Paul's gratitude to his parents for the support they gave him, Paul names his older siblings, two brothers and one sister, as his intimates. His parents, immigrants from Poland, are "from a different world."

Caroline may not say so directly, but she feels abandoned by her parents. She calls them "business people," who work long hours to earn a combined income of $350,000 per year. She deliberately calls the place where they live "a house," not "a home." "It is just where we sleep." There is no food in the refrigerator, because no one eats at home. Caroline skips breakfast, eats lunch at school, and catches dinner at a fast-food drive-in since her parents never get home in time to prepare an evening meal. Thinking that there was something wrong with their eating habits, Caroline's parents once hired her grandmother to prepare home-cooked food and leave it in their refrigerator. They eventually "fired" the grandmother because no one was home to eat the food she made. When Caroline speaks of her grandmother and deceased grandfather, she uses affectionate nicknames. Instead of her parents, Caroline has chosen her grandparents and her dog as the family members she considers her intimates. One Sunday morning Caroline's mother was taken suddenly to the hospital because of chest pains. That same morning Caroline asked her Sunday school class to pray for her dog who also was sick, not for her mother.

These youth who are not close to their parents do not appear to be close to their peers either. Paul started coming to youth group only at the end of his junior year. He was liked for his humor and for his role as lead singer in the youth group rock band. When he speaks of his closest friends, however, he names boys outside or on the fringes of the youth group, ones known to use drugs. During the year of my study one of his "best friends" died of a drug overdose. Paul is striving mightily to shift his key friendships to more wholesome ones based in the youth group at Transfiguration.

Like Paul, Caroline feels most comfortable with the teens at school who are "druggies," even though she has not smoked marijuana herself since her freshman year. She speaks respectfully of the anger that druggies exhibit by their self-destructive behavior, even as she witnesses to them about how Christ can save them. She "targets" them for invitations to attend Vision with her. At church Caroline hangs out with the younger girls in the youth group, ones who look up to Caroline as an exemplary evangelist. Making friends with same-age peers seems difficult for her. Every day after school she baby-sits.

As mentioned above, Reclaimers' bodily presentation tends to be sloppy or rebellious in some way. When Matt showed up in church with a small gold hoop pierced through the flesh of his ear, it attracted some gentle teasing. Why would this otherwise conservatively dressed boy get his ear pierced? A private agony torments Matt: a lapse in his witness two years earlier when he and some other boys he had targeted to come to Vision went off together and smoked pot. They continued to do so on and off over that summer. In the fall, when Matt gave up pot, the boys would not return to Vision with him. It is bad enough to take drugs; it is far worse to be a stumbling block to others in their faith. By piercing his flesh, Matt indicates that he is not the goody-goody he might otherwise appear to be.

Reclaimers have an intense experience of being saved by God; this grounds their sense of ontological security. They are often very serious and strident in practicing their faith. Caroline alluded to the painful memory of the time she came to youth group "as high as a kite," and had to be driven home by the youth leaders for a discussion with her parents. The youth minister "slapped me back into place when I needed it." Caroline continued, "And he pretty much told me what tough love was all about and made me understand the whole concept of not being a wet Christian and not being a pew sitter but actually working for Christ, and that when you have a relationship with Christ, how blessed you are." Reclaimers have firsthand experience of the world as a dangerous place. They have walked to the edge of the precipice, faced the abyss, and seen some of their friends destroyed. Their way of being religious has an experiential certainty that comes from being rescued from self-destruction.

Reclaimers already feel like adults because they have lost their naïveté in their experience of nearly destroying themselves. They have tangled with the law and faced the premature deaths of friends. Caroline says, "I don't remember my childhood," as if it happened decades ago. There is little left to mark their crossing over to a distinctly adult life. Like Conventionals, Reclaimers look forward to marriage someday, but not as the rite of passage to adulthood. Unlike the Classics, they do not proceed toward their future with a sense of expectation. I noticed a lack of the normal enthusiasm most teens exude for their plans to attend their universities and Bible colleges. Lacking confidence that he can meet the adult demands that lie ahead, Paul delayed submitting his college applications. He did not apply for the scholarships he needed in order to afford college. Reclaimers take halting steps in their quasi adulthood.

Like Conventionals, Reclaimers view staying alcohol-free, drug-free, and sexually pure as clear moral tests. They speak of these tests as Satan tempting them. Caroline also expresses moral outrage at the practice of abortion. "We were the generation that was not supposed to be born. A third of us were aborted," she says, citing Howe and Strauss's thesis of how the odds are stacked against "thirteeners."[9] Caroline has deep compassion for unwanted children. Reclaimers cite the same religious sources as Conventionals and Classics to guide them in deciding what is moral. They say that sometimes it is difficult to know the difference between right and wrong. God sees your heart, judges your intentions, and forgives.

In all, Reclaimers strive hard to "to put Christ at the center of their lives." They know, however, that the structures of their religious identity could come crashing down, as they have before. Not trusting themselves, they rely on God to shore up these structures. Matt used as his yearbook picture caption the lyrics from a song by the popular Christian musician Steven Curtis Chapman that expresses this struggle:

> I've tried to hold many treasures.
> They keep slipping through my fingers like sand.
> But there's one treasure that means more than breath itself.
> So I'm clinging to it with everything I am.[10]

Reclaimers tend to be evangelicals and Catholics, not mainline Protestants. When a mainline Protestant teen becomes a Reclaimer, he or she might switch to the evangelical megachurch because it offers more support for the notion of a distinct "new life in Christ." For example, the rite of believer baptism by immersion is a powerful public ritual that the evangelical tradition offers to reinforce the division between the old life of sin and the new life in Christ. Some evangelicals are baptized by immersion again when they reclaim Christ after falling away.

Before moving on to the next type of church-related teen, it is important to note something that the three types described above hold in common, exclusive of the four types that will follow. The first three types look deliberately to extrinsic sources, to God and the religious tradition, to shape their self-identity. The teens of the later four types rely more on an intrinsic source, the self, to shape the persons they are and will become. In this way the later four types are more posttraditional as compared to the first three types. Typical of the last four types was Parker, who answered the question about who most influenced what he believes as follows: "I would say myself. I'm really not afraid to be who I am. . . . I would say that in some situations others might influence me. But whether . . . I do it or not, I'm the *only* influence."

While these first three types rely on extrinsic religious sources of self-identity, they consciously exercise a *choice* to believe. For Catholics, choosing to believe was not the norm in their parents' generation, and even less so in their grandparents' generation, as Andrea describes her parents and grandmother (see the Introduction). Today when you ask Conventional, Classic, and Reclaimer teens of all three traditions who most influences what they believe about God and how they practice their faith, they tend to answer the same as Marginalizers, Customizers, Rejecters, and the Lost. They say, "I do." All teens may not exhibit a posttraditional self, but they do believe with a personal autonomy that exceeds that of previous generations.

Type Four: The "Marginalizers"

I interviewed Megan for about an hour, asking her about different areas of her life as well as her views and values, and how she might relate all of that to religious faith. Finally she voiced her exasperation with the topic of the interview: "You know, religion is just not a big part of my life."

Anyone reading a résumé of Megan's family background, education, and involvements would assume otherwise. Megan comes from one of the large Catholic families in Louisville, and she is related by blood or marriage to many other large Catholic families. She has attended Catholic schools all her life. She sees her aunts, uncles, and cousins often as they gather in each others' homes on holidays and sit together at Catholic school sporting events and fund-raisers. Megan marked the passages of Catholic life by all the sacraments up through confirmation. While she only attends mass on Christmas at her parish and four other times a year at school when it is required, she hardly ever misses any of the activities of the parish youth group. The youth minister, who has known Megan since sixth grade, considers her one of the student leaders. She takes time off from her job at a bakery to help lead the confirmation retreat for the eighth-graders. She is a role model in the "Ophelia Project" at her school, a program that takes older girls like Megan into Catholic middle school classrooms where they talk to girls about having a strong positive self-image during the difficult early teen years.[11] Megan plans to attend a Catholic college after high school.

As we talk, Megan seems unaware that she punctuates her conversation with "God" to emphasize a point, a practice that would be considered swearing in some circles. "God, I'm not really religious," she explains. "It doesn't really take up a large part of my life. It's something I've kind of grown up with and gotten used to. It's kind of like going through the motions." She continues, "Every once in a while there will be a moment where, you know, I'll like say a prayer to God, just like, 'God, help me get through this,' or something like that." "Does God get you through it?" I ask. "More times than not, yeah," she says with a laugh. She sees the irony that God hears her prayers even if she marginalizes God in her life.

What distinguishes the Marginalizers from the previous three types is how they view the relative place of religion in their lives. Marginalizers are believers, but belief in God does not dominate their thoughts, nor does it self-consciously shape their lifestyle or life plan. They are looking for a career defined by the market, not a life's work discerned through prayer as "a calling." Many of this group are high achievers in school and see their extracurricular activities as instrumental to building a college résumé. They are what the *Habits of the Heart* authors call utilitarian individualists.[12]

What most distinguishes Marginalizers from the Customizers (the group we discuss next) is the Marginalizers' acceptance of the church's definitions of belief and practice—even if they do not pay much attention to them. Marginalizers still value their connection to the institutional church. That is why they are mistaken by youth leaders as religious virtuosos. They can be counted on to show up and take leadership roles in the church youth program.

For Marginalizers, religious tradition and family are often blended together as one's "background." The majority of Marginalizers in my interview sample (55 percent) were Catholics,[13] but many mainline Protestants fit the profile as well. Nick, who switched from being Lutheran to Methodist when he was a young teenager, has a general sense that he is Protestant. His stepsisters were married in Presbyterian churches. His mother was raised as a Congregationalist. "Denominations don't matter," he was taught. "We could be Lutheran, Methodist, or Presbyterian," his father explains.

For Marginalizers who attend parochial schools, religion and family are blended with a third element: education. The reasons teens and parents give for choosing Catholic schools are mostly nonreligious: the academic superiority of Catholic education, family tradition, and the "structure" that Catholic schools offer. Only one teen attended Catholic schools primarily for the religious training. It is rare to hear Marginalizers praise the religion classes offered in their schools.

How is intimacy conceived by this type? Marginalizers generally show respect for their parents, even in cases where the relationship is strained. Some of the practices that have evolved over the years in the Catholic schools and in the youth group at Transfiguration serve to strengthen and ritualize the parent-teen relationship. At one of the girls' Catholic high schools, the senior class makes scrapbooks to give their mothers at the annual Mother-Daughter Breakfast. Another girls' Catholic high school holds an annual Father-Daughter Valentine's Day Dance. Parents are asked to write letters of affirmation to their teenaged children to be opened on retreats sponsored by the school and/or the church youth group. A Catholic youth who attends both the fall and spring retreats of the church youth group and the annual school retreat might receive as many as three letters of affirmation from his or her parents during the year.

Marginalizers show deference to other adults as well. Among the adults Marginalizers named as influential Christian examples in their lives were the religious brothers at the Catholic school, teachers, the church youth leader and youth group sponsors, the choir director, pastors, and a mother for whom one of the teens baby-sits. Marginalizers acknowledge a hierarchy in social relations. Age and authority figures are treated with respect.

Despite Marginalizers' respectful acknowledgment of adults in their lives, intimacy is clearly reserved for their peers. Marginalizer teens' "core group" is school-based, because the school is the key institution fostering their future success. Larger rings of school friends build around the core. These rings overlap in different degrees with church youth group friends, work friends, and talent-related or sport-related friends. Peer relationships, like adult-teen relationships, are assisted by the structure of the school.

Especially when teens attend Catholic schools, multiplex relations develop.[14] For example, there were eleven teens in my study who had attended Transfiguration's elementary and middle school. Of these eleven, nine went on to four different Catholic high schools, but they maintained their childhood friendships through church youth group and interscholastic events.[15] Childhood friends introduced each other to new friends from different high schools. Because the parochial high schools are single sex, childhood connections are important for building a coed social life. A large web of social connections among teens attending parochial schools is built from the introductions made among childhood school friends. Marginalizers attending parochial school are more likely than the others to attend homecoming and senior prom because their dating patterns rely heavily on annual school-sponsored events. The parochial schools' many formal homecoming dances, Christmas dances, and proms create occasions when teens call on childhood friends of the opposite sex to arrange dates for themselves and their friends so that they can attend. Non-school-sponsored clubs such as scouts, 4-H, and the city-wide youth choir do not create these kinds of occasions. Marginalizers do just "hang out" together, but their informal socializing tends to happen before, after, and between the events on the school calendar.

Marginalizers tend to follow traditional rules in their relationships. For example, sexual intimacy in dating is boundaried. While Csikszentmihalyi and Larson document that by the senior year the preferred type of friendship interaction is the opposite sex dyad,[16] socializing for Marginalizers occurs mostly in groups of males and females. Marginalizers have their sights set on career paths that require deferred gratification. They will skip an activity with peers (same sex or opposite sex) when they have too much homework. Some disappear for weeks at a time while they complete their college applications.

Just as Marginalizers are traditional in their construction of intimacy, they tend to follow moderation in their bodily presentation. Like the Conventionals, they are attentive to their outward appearance, dressing in less extreme styles of their chosen reference group. They are not body piercers or hair dyers. "Dress for success" might be their motto. They are usually athletic in some way and careful in their eating and sleeping habits. They are not consciously guided by any religious understandings of the body or demeanor. Rather, they present themselves outwardly with the same self-mastery they exercise in their résumé building. The youth minister sensed this in Andrea, offering a rare criticism of a teen: "She worries too much about appearance."

What gives Marginalizers a sense of ontological security so they can proceed amid the risks of life to pursue their career plans? They find their protection in the achievements they have already racked up (their grades, SAT and ACT scores, their honors and recognitions) and in their physical assets. On the basis of their talents, along with some good luck and more hard work, they will maximize their assets. If they stay focused on their life plans, these assets in turn will minimize the risk of failing to get on a career path and to find a life partner.

A crack in this security system appeared when a popular girl in the Catholic youth group was killed in a car accident in the spring of their junior year. "It could have been any of us," said Tom soberly. The end of Tom's "year of nonbelieving" coincided with Maureen's death. Tom and his best friend started to talk about whether or not God caused Maureen to die. Tom took the position that God did not. "I don't really blame God. I like math a lot and I just kind of think of it as bad odds. You know, it's going to happen to somebody, and if it happens so many times, it's going to happen to somebody who is good. So, I really don't think of it as punishment or anything like that at all. I just think it's almost . . . not really . . . well, random, I guess."

Tom stays busy and focused on what he needs to achieve. If he depended on God it would be "like a crutch." He does not "pray" as much as "review his day" each night, "with God listening."

> The world is not really affected by God but affected by the people in it. There's really only one way that things can be. The summation of my life, who I am, is because of the summation of my parents' lives. The decisions that they are going to make are going to be one way.

He displays a view of fate and probability similar to the one that Giddens says characterizes the posttraditional self. It is an orientation to the future that favors letting events come as they will.[17]

Rites of passage for Marginalizers relate to their schooling and to the things they are allowed to do that younger teens are not, like driving a car and having a part-time job. Some of the events that signify the uniqueness of the senior year of high school are as follows: submitting college applications, receiving college acceptances, selecting homecoming kings and queens, going on a trip at spring break without close parental supervision, attending the senior prom, being honored at the senior awards assembly at school and at graduation, and being celebrated at graduation parties by relatives. The next stage for this type is not adulthood, because with graduate or professional school they anticipate more than an additional four years of schooling. Their dependence or semidependence on parents is prolonged.

In addition, Marginalizers tend to participate in the rites of passage

offered by their church and parochial school for marking the end of high
school. At their respective churches they attend the Senior Mass at Transfiguration, the Senior Recognition Sunday at First United Methodist, or
Senior Vision, the last Vision meeting of the school year at Riverland
Heights. Marginalizers make a point of attending the senior retreat at the
parochial school as well. More than for most teens, this type's transition
out of high school is marked intentionally by religious symbols and by
religious institutions, even if the religious significance is shrugged off and
considered nominal at the time.

Some of the key ethical concerns of Marginalizers are AIDS awareness,
protection of the environment, and the plight of the disadvantaged.
Andrea belongs to an environmental club at school. As part of the Governor's Scholars Program the previous summer, she raised awareness in
the community about clean air. The need to earn service hours for honorary societies such as Beta Club and National Honor Society prompts
many to work at soup kitchens and at tutorial programs with inner-city
youth. Once Marginalizers get involved, they tend to say that they gain
great satisfaction in serving. Sometimes their volunteering exceeds what
is required. I visited with Brad as he dried aluminum pots in the kitchen
at the Presbyterian Community Center, located in a rough section of the
inner city. He claims to love coming there to work in the kitchen. He did
not say he was serving God by doing something for "the least of these,"
nor did he feel that he was making a difference in the intractable problem
of urban poverty. Absent from his service, as from other Marginalizers'
descriptions of their volunteer work, was a story that framed service in
religious terms. Like many teens, Brad offers no narrative to tell what his
caring means.[18] He was performing "service hours" and could not say why
it was satisfying.

In summary, Marginalizers are shaped by their religious traditions in
formative ways through their families, churches, and parochial schools.
They take these tradition-bearing institutions for granted, however, and
do not consciously embrace the radical religious message or lifestyle that
Conventionals, Classics, and Reclaimers find crucial to their self-identity.

Type Five: The "Customizers"

If Marginalizers are the ones who take the religious institution without
the belief, then Customizers are the ones who take the belief without the
religious institution. Customizers are "seekers," in Wade Clark Roof's
terms,[19] those keenly aware of their personal need for meaning and con-

nection to God. They want spirituality, not institutional religion with its standards, doctrines, rituals, and obligations. "If I'm not going to church I still feel fine because I can still pray with God . . . and I know it doesn't mean less to him in my beliefs than if I would go to church," said Kevin.

While the religious institution does not have authority in itself for Customizers, particular priests, ministers, or congregations may be appealing if they offer something that engages the Customizer personally. Michelle loves a particular priest who has been a family friend since before she was born. They fly him back from Florida where he now lives for their family baptisms, confirmations, and house blessings. She likes him because he is more than a priest filling a role. He is a personal friend who knows her and cares about her. Sometimes Customizers will participate in a congregation because their particular talents are needed there. Tara goes to choir because she is needed to carry the alto section. Church is also the place where they need her to work with children, her passion in life along with music. Customizers can be pressured too much by the church, however. Kevin stopped participating in the megachurch youth program when he felt burdened by the high expectations to attend more regularly and to bring a friend to evangelize. For most Customizers, churchgoing is random. As one boy put it, "Whenever I go to a church it's kind of like I stumble into it more than getting up and going."

If Marginalizers are the utilitarian individualists, Customizers are the expressive individualists. They crave a personal experience of God, especially in prayer, in dreams, and in signs of nature. Like Conventionals, they talk a lot about heaven. Unlike Conventionals they commune with angels as often as with God, and find God's word in texts and images outside the Christian tradition. Some of the literature, movies, and music that they cited as having religious meaning were *The Velveteen Rabbit, Chicken Soup for the Soul, Field of Dreams*, and Joan Osborne's song *One of Us*. They are what Turkle (1995) calls "bricoleurs." They assemble a collage of heterogeneous symbols, stories, texts, and codes from religious and secular sources to express their "personal" sense of God.

"When you talk about God, you don't use a lot of traditional language," I observed to Michelle during our second interview. "I'm not traditional," she replied. I continued, "I don't hear you talking about Jesus and he died for our sins and Mary and some of the things that are traditionally religious. Do those stories mean something to you?" Michelle paused and said thoughtfully, "Every one of them means something to me. But to me, God is the Man in the Moon. That's what I look at him as. He's the man that sits up on the moon and he's there in my dreams and I don't really look at him as like a superior being. I think of him more as like a grand-father, you know, like somebody that's there to protect you and nurture you and take care of you. And he's always there for you." I pursued, "But kind of remote?" "No. He's not remote to me."

Some Customizers are original thinkers, like Michelle. She writes poetry about God, using biblical narratives and diverse popular sources. She has created a "cleansing ritual" that she practices several times a month, involving lit candles, music, and meditation on the glow-in-the-dark stars she has pasted to the ceiling of her bedroom. She experiences freedom to customize her Catholic tradition to meet the needs of her personal life. She brackets out the formal elements, such as the liturgy when it is said without feeling. She excludes the doctrines with which she disagrees. She includes the beauty that can be experienced by the senses in the mass and the warm feelings of fellowship in personal relationships at church.

Unlike Michelle, Parker is prompted by circumstances more than by his own creativity to select what he believes. He has been reared in two different religious traditions. Parker's father is a Catholic, and Parker attends one of the Catholic high schools. He also participates as a student leader in the Catholic church youth group. Living near the church youth center, he is trusted to hold a key to the building and to lock up after meetings. In fact, Parker is so outstanding as a leader in the youth group that the youth minister invited him to represent Transfiguration's youth at a luncheon hosted by the archbishop for prospective candidates for religious vocations. The youth minister was shocked when Parker declined, saying, "I'm not a Catholic." Parker's mother, reared Baptist, is a member of Riverland Heights. Parker attended the megachurch growing up, and still goes there occasionally. He was baptized by immersion at the megachurch when he was eight years old. Even if he prays the Lord's Prayer like a Catholic, without the traditional Protestant ending, he talks like an evangelical describing how he "accepted Jesus as Lord and Savior." When I asked Parker if he was a Catholic or an evangelical Christian, he replied that he would probably marry a Catholic and most likely end up choosing Catholic. Right now he is eclectic. He doesn't embrace a single tradition as much as pick and choose what he thinks is right in each of them.

Picking and choosing is also how Customizers construct their circle of intimates, and in doing so they pick and choose outside traditional categories. Michelle considers her mother "more like a sister or friend because I talk to her so much and a lot of people don't talk to their moms that much and I mean, I just love her. I mean, we have just this special bond that's great." Michelle's relationship with her mother is what Giddens calls "a pure relationship." While Michelle might be loyal to her mother even if they did not have the "special bond," she awards her the additional titles of sister and friend. Michelle is posttraditional as she bases intimacy on "special bonds," not family ties of obligation.

Kevin also relates to his mother as a sibling. For Christmas they went out together and got their ears pierced and ankles tattooed. Kevin's equal relationship with his mother has more to do with circumstance than choice. His mother was divorced when he was a baby, and for many years the mother and son had to live with the mother's parents. Kevin speaks of his grandfather as "like a father." Because his mother was finishing school as he was in school, Kevin says that he and his mother "grew up together." The parent-child relationship between them is leveled to one of equality.

Either way, by choice or by circumstance, Michelle's and Kevin's leveling of the traditional hierarchy in the parent-child relationship goes along with other posttraditional perspectives on self-identity. Race and gender constructions are two other notable examples of categories that are constructed outside traditional definitions. Michelle describes an African American friend as "not black." She says, "Everything he does is white, except for the way he looks." Parker makes his father nervous because he does not seem masculine enough. Most of Parker's friends are girls. Parker enjoys art and spends time with his aunt in her art studio instead of going to the lake with his father and his male friends.

Sexual intimacy also is less bounded by traditional rules. Customizers were some of the most sexually active teens in my study. Some teens were unembarrassed to talk about their sexual activity; others were discreet. Tara was one who wanted to discuss her conflicted feelings about her relationship with Drew. She had contracted a sexually transmitted disease from him, and now was trying to convince herself that she should trust his avowal of fidelity to her. Similarly, Allison spent much of our interview describing her inner turmoil over relationships with boys. She was deeply wounded by a previous relationship in which her boyfriend "raped" her, a designation she worries over because it happened twice. "The thing that really bothered me was wondering if I was to blame because I let it happen again." Allison struggled to sort out her dilemma by using religious symbols for comfort without the religious prohibitions against nonmarital sexual intimacy that are usually attached to them. She said that after the second time "I was crying and I looked up and there was a picture of Jesus on the wall in his house. . . . That really changed my faith around. . . . I don't know if you have ever heard of 'Footprints,' the poem. I felt like Jesus was there. . . . He was carrying me through my hard time." A Conventional teen looking up at a picture of Jesus on the wall at just that moment might have felt shame.

As an interviewer, I experienced Customizers' lack of boundaries in the way they tended to ignore my direction and jump off from my interview questions toward the topic that most interested them. Tara and Allison, in particular, managed to turn almost every question I asked toward the subject of their boyfriends. In general, Customizers are heavily invested in relationships and claim to have serious romantic relationships, as well as many "best friends."

Bodily presentation is a venue of self-expression and individuality that is relished by Customizers. While there was no particular style that characterized the way they dressed, they looked more flamboyant and sensual than Conventionals and Marginalizers. Instead of dressing in denim and drab colors like most teens, Tara liked wearing tea-length dresses in pastel shades adorned with pearl buttons and gold jewelry. Parker expressed his artistic predilection for vivid color and for variation in texture as he sported bright flannel shirts and plush corduroys.

Customizers also altered their appearance as a way of experimenting with self-identity. These teens were the ones in my study who tended to participate in drama and the visual arts. To perform as "Dorcas" the clown, Tara fashioned a costume that included a purple polka-dot dress, orange lightbulb earrings, a complex braided hairstyle, and decorative buttons. I observed to her, "For someone who describes herself as serious, that sounds pretty silly." She replied, "I've discovered I'm a person that finds it very hard to be myself. I'm really not serious. When I'm a clown I have a different face. I love it when a little kid comes up and starts touching your makeup and says, 'Who are you? What is your real name?'" As a child, Tara was thrust early into the role of caretaker for her younger siblings while her parents worked. She says she did not get to enjoy her own childhood as much as she would have liked. "Dorcas" is the lighthearted, nonserious child that Tara wishes to be. Kevin also enjoys acting. I was surprised to discover that side of his personality. As a big, brawny two-hundred-pound varsity baseball player, he did not look like the sensitive artistic type. Allison also tries on alternative identities by modeling. She says she "puts on a different face with every outfit."

Customizers exhibit fewer prohibitions when it comes to introducing controlled substances into their bodies. They made reference to their own alcohol and marijuana use. The part of the message of the anti–substance abuse campaign that seems to have registered most with Customizers is the danger of driving while under the influence of alcohol and drugs. They designate certain teens at parties to be the drivers. "Taking care of a friend" means watching that they do not harm themselves when they are drunk or stoned. It does not mean trying to talk them out of using controlled substances.

Customizers find a sense of security in the dependable love and support of committed relationships. Death destroys these secure buffers against loneliness, and is particularly shattering for Customizers. While Tom, a Marginalizer, was shaken by Maureen's death because "it could have been any of us," Michelle, a Customizer, was devastated by it. She describes the pain of her loss in cosmic terms and draws comfort in the religious significance of signs of nature. Michelle fashioned for me her account of the night of Maureen's fatal car accident. As Michelle and her boyfriend were sitting on her porch watching the night sky, she noticed:

> It was the most perfect night I've ever had . . . and there was this star and it was shining so bright and it was just, like, right there. And at 9:30, which was when she died, a cloud, like, went over the whole sky. But, like, two minutes later the only thing that was open was this, like, little star. . . . [Later] I realized that was Maureen. I decided that star was Maureen and she was still there. And that was her way of saying good-bye to me. . . . So every night I would have to go outside and look up at that star and just say good night. . . . It was there for, like, a month.

Progressively deeper levels of sexual intimacy mark the passage to adulthood for Customizers. The traditional religious understanding of chastity in singleness is dismissed as one of the standards that make religion too legalistic. Allison believes sexual intimacy is appropriate when there is "mutual love," but she also promised herself that she would wait to have sex until she was sixteen. The first time she was raped by her boyfriend, she was one week short of turning sixteen. That shortcoming confirmed for her that she had not consented to the act.

Gifts signify the level of intimacy, and therefore are indicators of rites of passage. Tara's boyfriend gave her a tennis bracelet for Christmas. "My dad said, 'I'm surprised it's not an engagement ring,' and Drew said, 'Oh, that's for her birthday.' And I thought he'd be game enough to do it." Drew has already proposed to Tara, and she has accepted, but she doubts that he means it. An engagement ring signifies that he means it. Before the engagement ring, however, comes "the living together stage." Drew's parents have agreed to help them get an apartment together. Tara says they will "try a living together situation before we do anything."

Michelle was the one Customizer who was engaged in the larger political arena as she expressed her moral values through public action. She was president of the Republican club at her school and the student representative on the state pro-life organization's steering committee. She went to Washington one weekend to lobby her state congressional delegation on the topic of abortion. She framed the issue in typical Catholic language: the ethical concern was to respect an unborn life. For someone who thought of God as "the Man in the Moon," she was able to switch to standard Catholic language when the setting called for it.

Customizers, for all their expressive individualism, could be very focused on others. Moral action is not so much behavior based in separating right from wrong as it is going the "second mile" by helping others when it is not required. Customizers were notable for the amount of time they gave serving meals at soup kitchens, teaching crafts after school in downtown community centers, tutoring, collecting money for charity, taking meals to elderly relatives or families with members in the hospital, and coaching sports teams for younger children. Unlike the Marginalizers, who logged "service hours" to meet the requirements of their school honorary societies, Customizers often did not get "credit" for their hours. Parker said he volunteered as a tutor for over three hundred hours during his high school years, far exceeding the minimum standard of ten hours per year that the chapter of National Honor Society at his school would require of him were he a member. Kevin made it clear that he was doing nothing to "win over God" in his volunteer work with the elderly in a nursing home. Having been a Lutheran before he joined the evangelical megachurch, he knew he was not going to be saved by works. "I'm doing it for someone else and not for myself," he stated. Tara drew the connection, however loose, between her service and God. "I show my belief more than a lot of people do 'cause I think honestly what I do believe is seen in my clowning [a volunteer activity at church events], and I don't think I could do that if I didn't have God or somebody around."

At the end of my interview with Tara I offered her the opportunity to add anything she wished. She surprised me by lobbing an invective at two other girls, the only two Conventionals among the seniors at First United Methodist. Tara said:

> I don't think there's a teenager in the world that has faith, or a lot of it. Even people like Vicky and Emily. I don't know crud about the

Bible, and they were obviously taught the Bible. But the two of them don't have a lot of faith. Yes, they read the Bible. And yes, they know the stories. But I don't think that they really believe. I really don't think you can find a youth that can say, "There's no doubt in my mind I believe in God."

Unlike the girls she scorns, Tara speaks openly of her doubts about God. She finds the certainty exhibited by Conventionals to be "fake." The sermons she likes most are the ones that leave the questions unanswered. The next group to follow, the ones who reject the Christian tradition altogether, accentuate the dignity of their doubt even more than Tara.

Type Six: The "Rejecters"

Alex reports that around fifth or sixth grade he looked for evidence of "this God fellow." "I'd go to church and I'd be, like, concentrating real hard and I'd close my eyes and hold my breath and try to feel this feeling that everybody talked about that you get, and I just didn't feel anything." By eighth grade Alex had made up his mind that religion did not matter to him. "It's not like I have strong beliefs contradicting, it's just that I don't see, like, much of the use in anything." Marginalizers also say that religion is unimportant to them, but Alex and other Rejecters go farther to identify themselves as agnostic. Alex is willing to engage in debates with peers and argue that there is not enough evidence to believe in God. At times he feels "assaulted by Baptists and others who start yelling, saying, 'I used to be like you but now I'm saved.'" At the Governor's Scholars Program in which Alex participated over the summer with other top students from around the state, he was surprised to meet "so many people who were so interested in religion and took it so seriously." He gained a reputation as the one who argued the evolutionist position against the creationists during late-night conversations in the dormitory lounge.

Alex attends a Catholic high school and is one of the leaders in the youth group at Transfiguration. He is able to "filter out the religious stuff" that he does not want from "the spiritual things" that he accepts. For example, when they pray at youth group, he participates at a surface level. During the group intercessory prayer time he listens to what others are troubled about and feels grateful for how "good" he has it. As he sees it, prayer functions to "calm everyone down." When mass is celebrated on retreat it has meaning for him, but "not religious meaning." Rather, "It just seemed like me looking at how it might be for somebody that did believe in all the Catholic religion and all that stuff."

While Alex reports that he cannot identify a particular time in his life when he consciously broke with religion, Ian can point to a particular incident associated with his decision to drop Christianity: the departure of the youth minister at First United Methodist. Ian was angry that the church would not pay a higher salary to keep this man who was "like a father" to him. In addition, Ian did not like the "atmosphere" in the youth group, the lack of serious commitment and the way kids sneaked away to "make out" whenever they were not being watched. Ian admits feeling regret for participating in that behavior. He feels "degraded." He went to the youth minister to talk about it and felt better for having done so. From the youth minister he received "profound kindness."

After the youth minister left, Ian replaced church with a different community, one that revolves around rock music. "In eighth grade, I was overweight, wore glasses, sat in the back of the class, and never said a word. And then one of my brother's older friends who was really into the music scene talked to me." Four years later he summarizes, "My life is music. . . . It takes up all of my time and money." He is a guitarist in a "hard-core" rock band, meaning, "The music is just real intense and the musicians believe so strongly in what they say and how they practice it. It just comes through."

Ian now identifies himself as a Buddhist. He finds peace at the end of the day when he meditates in his room for thirty to forty-five minutes. What he finds attractive in Buddhism is "inner peace and not being material and the loss of anger and temptation. It is more like what I strive to be than what everyone considers to be perfect in the eyes of God." Ian read *Zen and the Art of Motorcycle Maintenance* and articles on meditation recommended by his English teacher. He finds satisfactory Stephen Hawking's scientific explanation that the world just evolved.

Tim's departure from his church is even more painful and conflicted than Ian's. He is enraged with the church for failing to protect him from "brutal things" he experienced in parochial school, humiliations that go back to middle school.

> Like, if I came to school and, like, I had a new pair of shoes and other kids didn't like them so when we went out and it was recess and it was muddy out and I would stay on the pavement, like, to try to keep my shoes from being dirty, everybody would come up and . . . hold me down while they would scuff up my shoes with mud. And you

know it seems, you know, well, clean off the shoes. . . . [But] it's much more . . . the thing that really gets to me is not the actual thing that people are doing but the motivations behind it and the ideas that they express of, "I devalue you so much as a person that I devalue your property, stuff that isn't even associated with you besides the only fact that you're wearing it." To me, that means a whole lot more to me than the actual action of it, because you can clean off the mud, but . . . there is a whole lot of representation within that.

Tim continued to be estranged from his peers as he went on to Catholic high school. In his junior year he brought to the attention of school officials the fact that there was a car in the school parking lot that had a Confederate battle flag emblem on its front license plate. He argued that allowing this symbol of racism to be displayed on school property was an affront to the religious values for which the school stood. When the school officials took no action in response to his complaint, Tim and another boy got the local television station to run a story about how the school refused to respond to racist emblems displayed on school property. The television station aired footage of the car and its license plate. Soon thereafter, Tim found his own car scratched and dented when he returned to it in the school parking lot.

Tim does not separate who God is from Catholicism, or Catholicism from his hurtful Catholic school peers. I asked him if he knew anything of the base movements of poor Catholics in Latin America and of Catholic priests working for justice for the poor. He replied that he knew mostly stories of how the Catholic church has been co-opted by corrupt governments and how it perpetuates the misery of the poor by assuring them of a reward in heaven.

While individual Rejecters state different reasons for opting out of the Christian tradition in which they were reared, they construct elements of their self-identity in similar ways, including the way they conceive of intimacy. Rejecters consider their intimates those who support them in the values they have chosen as critical to their self-identity. "Intimates" can be parents, but not because of ties of blood. In the last years of high school, Ian has grown closer to his father because they enjoy discussing books of mutual interest. Tim, on the other hand, does not count his parents as intimates. His relationship with his devout Catholic parents is combative because of his agnosticism. He says his parents accuse him of disowning the family. "They thought I'd always be Catholic once I was confirmed, kind of like you're always a Jew once you get that number tattooed on your hand in the concentration camps."

Unlike Customizers with their serious romances and many "best friends," Rejecters strictly limit their circle of intimates to a small number and establish a high threshold for friendship. "I have a limited group of what I consider friends," says Ian, "only three or four." As an elected representative to student council, Ian obviously stays friendly with a wider circle of people in his high school, but he limits those he calls his "friends." They are the members of his rock band. "It's like a marriage with four other people."

Tim is also highly selective of his friends. His best friend is one of his older sisters. Other than her, his friends are the people he knows from the clubs he visits on the weekends. Intimacy is based on posttraditional "pure relationships."[20] Tim's friends are those who share his rage and vent it in mosh pits. His friends are also those who volunteer with him in the Fairness Campaign to enact legislation prohibiting discrimination against homosexuals in housing in Louisville. Tim's friends are not from traditional settings like his school, his church, his neighborhood, or his place of work. Nor are they necessarily those of his own age group. Sometimes Tim does not know his friends' last names.

Just as they are deliberate in defining criteria for membership in their circle of intimacy, Rejecters have given thoughtful consideration to the integrity of their physical bodies. While all teens who reject the Christian tradition of their nurture may not be as strict, the Rejecters I got to know best were nonsmokers, nondrinkers, drug free, and vegetarians. Ian identifies with a movement called "straightedge" that was started in the early 1980s "by kids who were rockers who were disgusted with their parents who were alcoholics and doing drugs." While Ian himself has no personal reason to protest against parental substance abuse, refraining from harmful substances fits with the ethos of the hard-core rock music that Ian's band plays. It also fits with his growing adherence to Buddhist philosophy and practice. Alex, on the other hand, does have a personal experience of alcoholism in his family. He has pledged to be alcohol and drug free through a peer leadership program in his school. As a peer leader, he visits elementary and middle school classes to speak to younger children about how to have a fun social life without using mood-altering substances.

Some Rejecters choose their style of dress to reflect their ideological commitments. Ian and Tim buy their clothes at thrift shops because they oppose materialism, consumerism, and exploitation by the advertising industry. They do not wear leather because it comes from animals, or certain name-brand athletic shoes known to be manufactured in sweat-shop conditions in third-world countries. Additionally, Tim mocks the attempt of the Catholic school to make him conform by the way he wears his school uniform of a dress shirt, necktie, conventional pants with a belt, and leather tie shoes. While he technically meets the requirements, the hole in Tim's shirt, his frayed pant cuffs, and his shiny patent leather shoes recycled from a tuxedo rental shop display his ridicule. While Alex's style of dress is less ideological, he did consciously break with his conservative image by dying his dark-brown hair blond over the Christmas break of his senior year. The most striking feature of Ian's appearance is his unnaturally colored yellow hair that spikes up from his head like the stiff bristles of a scrub brush. Rejecters display posttraditional self-mastery of outward appearance. They do not accept the imposition of consumerism, the standards of style, the codes of conformity, or even the endowments of nature to dictate how they appear.

The self-mastery that the posttraditional self exhibits can be interpreted as haughtiness, not competence. Ian is described by the church choir director as having an "arrogant" demeanor. Similarly, Alex is seen by one of his teachers as having "a patrician air" and being "cynical." While Alex is "capable," his teacher says, he is also "self-serving." "He asks to be nominated for honors."

What anchors security for Rejecters? What gives time, space, and the self in society its coherence and moral meaning? Having wrestled seriously with Christianity before abandoning it, Rejecters tend to substitute something in place of the Christian symbols and narratives—either a philosophy or what Giddens describes as "practical consciousness." In place of extrinsic sources of meaning, they look to the self as the arbiter of truth. The Rejecters in my sample struck me as some of the teens exhibiting a more highly developed level of critical thinking. Ian especially alludes to books and to more sophisticated media that have informed his thinking about a broad range of subjects.

Ian, the Buddhist/straightedge–hard-core-rock musician, understands God to be the self that he is aiming to be. His commitments give his life some coherence. He exhibits self-assurance as he moves amid the risks and routines of his daily life. He feels confident about his future plans to attend a small Quaker liberal arts college.

Alex, without a belief in anything in particular, yet still tethered to the church through his activity in the church youth group, seems more anxious than Ian about the future. At the Senior Mass, Alex stood up and told the assembly of parents and friends that the youth group had been "like a rock" for him, and he wondered how he would manage next year without his friends from youth group. Alex grounds his routines, relationships, and practical consciousness in the structures of Catholic life even if he has discarded the religion.

Tim, the protester against the Confederate flag emblem, appears to be the shakiest. He is clear about what he rejects, and he does that with zeal, but he is not as clear about what he positively accepts. There is no set of meanings that cohere to offer a firm sense of the world. Tim was suicidal twice in his life, once in sixth grade and once in tenth grade. He is still fragile. What drives him is getting into a good college, and perhaps entering a psychotherapeutic field. He admits that his story "has lots of holes in it." The contradiction most evident to me was that this boy who exposed his school's hypocrisy admitted to me that he inflated the number of hours he worked at his part-time job as he wrote his college applications in order to make his achievements look more impressive. Further, he voluntarily remains at the Catholic school he hates because he thinks that switching schools will hurt his record for college admission. Tim makes compromises to try to attain his goals, but he does not have a self-awareness of how that might put him on a par with others whom he scorns for doing so.

Rejecters are suspicious of the self-interest that corrupts big institutions like the American government and legal system, the entertainment industry, multinational corporations, and church bureaucracies. They seem to have a blind spot, however, when it comes to the American educational system. They seem unaware of how, by tracking students along certain paths, the educational system reinforces the class stratification that gives people unequal chances at opportunities. While Tim and Ian reject materialism and careerism, they aim their sights high, at the selective colleges that paradoxically will open those very paths to them.

For Rejecters, coming to a sense of peace about life and sustaining it for weeks or months at a time is a rite of passage to maturity. Ian is the Rejecter who has most achieved it through the coherence and stability evident in life. He affirms, "I love where I am and I finally don't hate myself or where I am. It's just great. Just where I am right now is fine with me." He enjoys writing humorous monologues from the perspective of a four-year-old about babysitters and "how your whole life is your front and back yard." Being grown up is being authentic; it is being your own author. It is being able to write an autobiography that explains how you chose to be who you are and what you can reliably expect to be in the future. The posttraditional self is the product of its autobiography.

Rejecters express derision for those who have given little thought to who they are, for those who conform uncritically to a religion or popular style. Ian dissociates himself from his older brother, a conservative Christian. He also distances himself from former friends in the church youth group "who may have good intentions but fall short on commitment." Ian affirms the role of religion in society, however. He wishes that more of his generation would "find a religion they believe in and study it and understand why." He sees religion as critical to the morality of society, and as "the foundation of everything" since ancient times, citing Plato's *Republic*.

Wary of large-scale institutions, but still committed to ideals like equality, respect for all, and honesty, Rejecters tend to involve themselves in local organizations that work on big ethical issues. Rejecters are involved in student government, their local chapter of Planned Parenthood, their school's Students against Drunk Driving club, and their city's Anytown, U.S.A., program, an ecumenical effort bringing together teens in the city to raise consciousness of racism, sexism, and religious intolerance.

In summary, while Rejecters report different reasons for opting out of the Christian tradition in which they were reared, they are similar in the way they conceive of their self-identity. Their reflexive selves have more posttraditional elements than the previously mentioned types, yet fewer than the type to follow. Rejecters conceive of intimacy through "pure relationships" built on shared commitments to common values. They strive for bodily self-mastery. They look to intrinsic sources to ground their sense of meaning and security. They seek authenticity as a mark of their maturity. They are concerned with global ethical issues, but work on them in smaller, local contexts.

In some respects, Rejecters are the most puzzling type to explain. They seem to have everything that would predict adherence to the Christian tradition. They have consistent nurture in their tradition, like Conventionals and Classics, but without the sheltering or heavy-handed patterning of the Conventionals. Further, they exhibit some values that seem compatible with Christian ethics, like showing compassion, seeking justice for the oppressed, and respect for the body. Unlike Marginalizers, Rejecters have high ideals that moderate their drive to follow a "career path." Unlike Customizers, they seem to respect the authority of a religious tradition to establish its integrity and boundaries. Unlike the Lost (the final group we will discuss), they come from stable environments, where the formative structures of identity did not shift from under them.

Could these Rejecters become tomorrow's Reclaimers? On the one hand, it seems unlikely, since their break with the tradition is lasting longer. Alternative understandings are providing some coherence and meaning in place of the Christian tradition. On the other hand, the college environment to which they go next may support a more critical appropriation of the Christian tradition.

Type Seven: The "Lost"

Trey's family attends church sporadically. They will go for a few weeks in a row, then be absent from church for several months. Trey's mother, nominally reared Protestant, had Trey baptized as an infant in a Presbyterian church. After a long period of nonattendance, they tried being Catholic, the tradition of Trey's father. Trey was rebaptized in a Catholic church when he was in seventh grade and sent through all the rites including Catholic confirmation. Not finding the Catholic church satisfying, the family settled on the evangelical megachurch three years ago. Trey was baptized there for a third time, this time by immersion. As Trey's mother says of her children, "They've been sprinkled, taken First Communion, and we've been submerged. . . . We've covered the bases."

All that exposure to mainline Protestantism, Catholicism, and evangelical Protestantism registers little in a measure of Trey's knowledge of the Christian tradition. He cannot repeat the Lord's Prayer from memory. He cannot distinguish a part of the worship service that he finds especially meaningful. He cannot name a religious song or hymn with which he is familiar. When asked about Bible stories, he mentions "Samson and Goliath" and "Joseph and the Technicolor Dreamcoat." He says he has no particular memories of church at all. When I asked him about the funeral of his friend Jason, which both of us attended in a Catholic church just the day before, he gave me a blank look and replied that he was not paying attention.

Despite his lack of knowledge, Trey says he is a religious person. "I believe in God, heaven, and everything. . . . I agree with everything they say at church." He makes no reference to the classic event, to Christ. Attending one of the Catholic high schools, he identifies himself as both a Catholic and a "regular" Christian. He says he prays every night, but he does not "confess." The fullest description he gives of his religious practice is of the prayer he has with the other football players before they start each game. Led by his coach, the team "takes a knee" and prays for safety and for the team to play to the best of its ability. Trey always holds hands with one of the other players during the prayer, and the two of them remain on their knees with their heads bowed a moment longer than the rest. "Kind of a solidarity thing?" I ask. "Uh-huh. Like closeness and being together and stuff."

In my research I encountered a type of church-related teen, like Trey, who displays only a superficial knowledge of the tradition and some fundamental misunderstandings of what the church's practices mean. These teens are underexposed to their religious tradition. They never had a chance to be formed in the religious identity and practices of their faith because their religious socialization was inadequate. Some of these teens come from families that switch from one tradition to another, sometimes switching more than once, like Trey's family. They never settle into one pattern of belief and practice that is sustained for a period of time. Other teens come from homes that are so chaotic the lack of a consistent religious upbringing is only one of many underdeveloped structures of their formative years.

Danielle is one who lacks a stable home life and whose religious development appears truncated as a result. In her freshman year of high school, Danielle's father abandoned her at a father-daughter dinner dance at her school to go to a bar. A week later, her father left home and Danielle developed stomach pains that medical tests eventually showed to be ulcers. Danielle thought at the time that she caused her father to leave because of the huge fight her parents had after her mother had to come to the dance to take Danielle home. Now Danielle sees her father only when she meets him at his office, sitting behind his desk. She estimates she has seen him for fifteen hours in the last four years. One Father's Day he declined her invitation to take him out to lunch because he was too sick to go out. She went over to his apartment to deliver a gift, but his car was not there. Danielle also feels abandoned by her mother. "We go our own ways," she says. Danielle reports that her mother considers her "already grown up." The mother goes out with her boyfriend after work and stays with him on the weekends. "Our only conversation is 'Where are you going?'" says Danielle.

The family stopped attending church long before Danielle's parents' marriage broke up. Most of Danielle's exposure to the Catholic tradition comes through her schooling. After her health problems began, Danielle says she realized "You have to believe in something." She's "not big on church," but she prays. God is there for her and she knows that through uncanny coincidences. For example, she prays about her boyfriend, and the telephone rings, and it is he. God is the cause behind everything. God "caused" Jason's death (a boy whose car swerved off the road, hitting a tree, while driving too fast) because "all those things happen for a reason which God had caused." Like some other teens of this type, Danielle says she intends to rear her own children in the church. "When I have kids I think I'll get back to going to church." For these teens, if church is worthwhile at all, it is good for giving young children "a foundation."

Striking among these teens is the absence of good relations with their parents, even when the family structure remains intact. Some of the Lost substitute family-like ties of commitment with nonfamilial adults even when their parents are present in the home. Trey says he is "not close" to his parents and looks instead to his football coach as a father figure. Similarly, Leigh looks to a man with whom she works at the zoo as "a dad." These teens do not reject their parents because they are overly strict or demanding; rather, it is the opposite. Trey says his parents are "lenient." Leigh says her parents should ask her more questions about her dates and her plans after the prom. There are "not many rules" or coordinated family activities in her home. They have "fix-it-yourself dinners," that is, "If you want it, you fix it," she explains.

Alan has lived with his grandparents since he was three years old. His mother, who lives in a separate apartment, gave up custody of her sons to her ex-husband's parents after she was diagnosed with schizophrenia and had to resign her job on disability. The father is "a deadbeat" and has never paid child support to his parents. The grandparents, in their seventies, struggle with poor health. They are incapable of forcing Alan to attend church, to help around the house, and to inform them of his comings and goings. They have a strong suspicion that Alan has joined a gang. Typically Alan comes in each night after they have gone to bed. He attends only three classes at school, the minimum he needs for graduation. He returns home from school each morning by 10:20 A.M., to fall back to bed. I only managed to interview Alan because his grandmother arranged an ambush. She asked me to come to the house at 10:20 A.M., before he could disappear into his room.

Alan's answers to questions about his friends were atypical. "What do you have to do to fit into your group of friends?" I asked. "Be trustworthy and loyal," he replied. "How can you tell when kids are not fitting in?" "They lie and steal from you." The answer I received consistently from other teens to the question about how to fit into your group was, "Be yourself." Typically, kids were seen not to fit in when they were "acting fake" or "trying too hard." Alan replaces the conventions of healthy teen friendship with the rules of gang membership.

Among other "Lost" teens not in gangs, there is a striking inconsistency in what they report about their friends. On the one hand, Danielle says she has a huge group of "fifty friends" who are very close and devoted to each other. On the other hand, she described how during their spring break trip to Panama City, Florida, she was the one friend who helped the girl who had to be rushed to the hospital because of alcohol poisoning. (See chap. 6.) Later, Danielle's friends drove home from Panama City without Danielle. Danielle did not appear to bear a grudge. "They're still my friends, and I love them to death."

Lost teens tend to report that they have difficulty with friendships. Ryan, a hip-looking guy who plays the saxophone in a band, says he does not have any "close friends." He is just part of "a group that hangs out."

Leigh finds it hard to make friends with anyone at school. She eats lunch at the room at school designated "Special Friends Club," for handicapped students. She says she and others who "don't fit in" go there. She says, "We don't really care about our clothes or the way our hair looks or something like that." Leigh does not smoke or drink because she does not want to ruin her conditioning for competitive swimming, but she describes hanging out on the weekends with a girl who does. She describes how this friend gets her to drive up and down the highway "looking for parties." Once her friend got her to stop at a hotel room where strangers who were drinking invited them to join in. Leigh managed to draw the line and refused to stay.

Leigh's desperate attempts to find friends are thwarted at church as well. Over spring break she went with the evangelical megachurch youth group to Florida. She accepted Christ and was baptized in the ocean. When I asked one of the youth leaders about Leigh's baptism, she shook her head, doubting the sincerity of it. "It was a friendship thing with Leigh," the youth leader said. "She just did it to fit in." Whether it was sincere or not, Leigh was one of the teens who always looked for me when I attended Vision. Because she was unable to make friends, she latched on to the friendly researcher. She often talked about her horse and her many pets. She tried to persuade me to take in a stray kitten, as she often was trying to find homes for strays.

For the Lost, styles tend to be extreme versions of what is worn by their reference group. Danielle dresses like a cheerleader, even though she is not one. Trey, the football player, wears athletic clothes all the time, except when he has to wear his school uniform. Leigh defiantly dresses for comfort, not fashion. She flaunts her inattention to grooming and style. Ryan is the most unkempt-looking one of this group. Like the members of his band, he looks grungy, sporting dark facial stubble and a tattoo on his arm, which shows when he wears a T-shirt with cut-off sleeves. Alan wears a T-shirt too, but his hair is cut so short, he looks almost like a skinhead, which is typical for certain gangs. Alan has enlisted in the Marines and already looks as if he is in boot camp.

Trey is one of the few teens in my sample who claims he loves going to the mall to shop for clothes. Going to the mall is a behavior most high school seniors say they enjoyed in middle school and perhaps even into their freshman and sophomore years. Trey, however, says he spends eight to sixteen hours a month at the mall, well over the two hours per month average for the high school seniors I surveyed. Most seniors report that they do not have the money to spend at the mall, or that they are saving their money. Trey is being recruited by the University of Michigan and other top football schools. He is on track for a lifestyle that promises high material rewards and consumer comforts. He seems to be enjoying them already.

With all this extreme conformity to different styles of dress, the Lost are uniform in their demeanor as well. They show a universal lack of training in the social conventions so prized by the Conventionals and Marginalizers, such as offering greetings and salutations, and remembering to say thank you.

Security for the Lost is not found in religious beliefs or in traditional frameworks of meaning that give value to work and motivation to serve society. Instead, like Marginalizers, these teens are on tracks structured by the market and government, channeling them toward a career after high school graduation. Trey the athlete and Alan the future Marine have well-defined tracks to follow after high school. Danielle, too, has decided, "I want to be really businesslike and I want to make a lot of money." She speaks of this choice with some regret because she loves children and cannot think of a way to turn that interest into a lucrative career. Leigh, an athlete, did not earn the swimming scholarship she had hoped to be awarded. Despite that disappointment, her other interests (her love of horses and record of volunteer work at the zoo) pointed clearly to a career working with animals. She plans to enroll in the state university to study zoology and equine sciences.

Unlike the other Lost teens, Ryan does not have a clear path to take after high school. He regrets not choosing to attend a Catholic high school like most of his childhood friends, because "going to Catholic school would shape a person," he says. He is glad he went to Catholic school at least through middle school. "Most of the people I know who go to public schools, they don't really believe anything, they're just, they are just kind of there, I guess. . . . The majority of, like, Catholic school people, they probably know what they're going to do a lot more than the majority of public school kids." By this, Ryan acknowledges a wish for something to "shape" him, for something to give him a direction, even for something to believe in.

While Ryan is grateful that his parents are not divorced like so many of his friends' parents, and while he appreciates the way his father, a doctor, comes home from work early so he will be there when Ryan and his sister return from school, Ryan's parents do not offer their children structure. Ryan does no homework unless he wants to. He watches three to three and a half hours of television a night and falls asleep in front of the television. When I showed up on a Sunday afternoon at his house for the interview (because he forgot the appointment that was supposed to be at the church), a whiff of pancakes and bacon escaped as he opened the door. Ryan was just getting around to eating breakfast at 2 P.M. He has complete freedom to wake and eat as he pleases. Growing up, the children were not forced to go to church, and no one in the family went except his mother, who is a paid church soloist. Members of the family usually eat separately and do their own laundry. Some of the laundry was strewn around the living room where we talked. His family's life is not well coordinated. Each person is on his or her own as an individual.

While some exaggeration is to be expected in what teens report, especially because much of what I was asking for was their subjective viewpoint, Lost teens are less reliable in what they say than teens of other types that I interviewed. What Ryan reported about his life was notably inconsistent with what his parents reported and with what I observed. For example, Ryan said he attended youth group "once in a while," yet the youth minister and I did not see him there the entire year. Ryan reported that he did not drink or do drugs. His parents told me that he had been arrested for possession of drugs once and had been required by a judge to go through a substance abuse awareness program. While it may be true that Ryan no longer drinks and does drugs, my conversation about his views normally would have elicited some comment about how his views about drinking and drugs had changed through personal experiences. Ryan also says he used to be "kind of bad in school . . . just little stuff, just talking back." Ryan's parents said he was so disruptive and defiant toward his teachers, they moved him to a small private school for one year. His family has seen a counselor off and on, focusing on the issue of establishing appropriate parental authority.

Danielle, like Ryan, brackets from practical consciousness things she cannot deal with, so she can get by in daily life. Danielle is glad she attends Catholic schools, because there she is sheltered from the violence she imagines to be rampant in the public schools. Yet she exposes herself willingly to greater dangers in the hours outside of school. She says one of her best friends is in the Crips gang. She claims to have other friends who are in Satanic cults and carry weapons. She claims to belong to a close group of friends, yet she tells stories of how unkind her friends are as they exclude her from parties and make her boyfriend feel unwelcome in their homes. She says she was not bothered when she woke up in the hotel room she shared with other girls on spring break to find a boy sleeping in her bed. "He's just someone I've known since childhood. He just passed out on the bed." She seems unconcerned about the risky behaviors in which she engages. She attends parties that are busted by the police, confident that her morals and values set her apart from those of her friends. She claims to have a special rapport with children, yet as we walked out of the interview together, her friendliness failed with a child who was in the building. She came on too aggressively, and the child shied away from her.

Just as Danielle and Ryan offer the interviewer a rosier picture of their lives than what other evidence suggests, there is an unreality to the way Leigh presents her life. The number of hours she reports that she spends in various activities adds up to more than is possible. She claims to have volunteered four thousand hours at the zoo during her high school years; she is a competitive swimmer, practicing an hour and a half before school each morning; she has a horse and spends weekends and some evenings at the stable; she holds down a part-time job at Dairy Queen; she goes out driving with a friend on weekend evenings for something to do. Besides the number of hours not adding up, she reports that she was sexually abused on at least two occasions, once at the zoo and once at the stable. Like Danielle, she keeps dangerous company and seems unconcerned about the risks she takes.

Other Lost teens seem out of touch with reality. Trey blanks out parts of his life, even something as recent as a funeral that happened the day before. It is hard to know what Alan really thinks, because he is so inarticulate. There is an illogicality in the way this member of a gang hopes one day to become a law enforcement officer. His long-term goal, after he finishes a tour with the Marines, is to become a state trooper.

Without a grounding in a religious tradition, and without the structures of a traditional home life, the Lost have no signposts telling them when they will reach adulthood. Alan is perhaps the one exception. He says he is joining the Marines "to become a man," as the saying goes. Danielle and Leigh are told by their mothers that they are already grown up. Danielle's mother symbolized this by buying a six-pack of beer for her daughter to take on spring break. Danielle portrays spring break as a test of your morals. "By the time you are seventeen or eighteen, your goals and morals and values are set," she explains. Danielle is already an adult in her work life. To earn money for any extras that she might enjoy, she works long hours at a YMCA and has no time to join clubs at school. "I go to school, come home, do homework, go to work, and by then I'm just so tired. I might talk to my boyfriend for like ten minutes, and then I go to sleep and I don't really have time for much of anything else."

What are the arenas of moral decision making identified by the Lost? The answers these teens give follow no pattern, just as the guides they use to make ethical decisions are not consistent or related to their religious tradition. Danielle mentions that she opposes abortion and has become more absolute in her position than ever before. She also opposes gossip. She favors tolerance of other people's choices, even the choice to do drugs. Alan's arena of ethical behavior relates to keeping the code of his gang. Leigh struggles with not being "two-faced." She says on the one hand she can decline pot when offered, but on the other hand, she can lose her temper and get in fights with people. Leigh admires a girl in the youth group who seems even-tempered and is unashamed to read her Bible in school. Trey and Ryan are unable to give examples of arenas where they are challenged to make difficult ethical choices.

In summary, the Lost are posttraditional, by and large unshaped by sources like a religious tradition or by other traditional structures usually patterned by families. The friendships that give many teens' lives a peer group of psychic support are largely absent for this type. The Lost conform rigidly in bodily presentation to their lifestyle option, the one that has evolved for them uncritically from the dispositions, practices, and routines that they have found to work. There is no consistent set of symbols or narratives to provide guidance for how to live a moral life, apart from what their lifestyle option offers as the way to actualize their personal goals. There is little coherence of meaning apart from the action that their life plan dictates. Unlike Rejecters, who are also posttraditional, the Lost exhibit little reflexivity, that is, the ability to revise their autobiographies based on new knowledge. The Lost display little of the self-mastery that Rejecters exhibit in their quest for authenticity through self-actualization.

⚜⚜⚜⚜⚜⚜⚜

In conclusion, while Giddens's posttraditional self does characterize the teens in my sample to greater and lesser degrees, my data analysis suggests that Giddens's assumption that all traditions, including religious traditions, can no longer function with authority to shape persons' identities is not supported. Giddens underestimates the strength and the variety of ways that teens do shape their self-identity in relation to their religious tradition. The fact that the teens in my sample did not perfectly fit Giddens's constructs is noted, for example, in the analysis of how Robin and Brynne, both of whom I categorize as Conventionals (the most traditional type), exhibited some posttraditional qualities. Likewise Ian, whom I call a Rejecter (a posttraditional type), affirms the value and positive role of religious traditions in undergirding the morality of the society. More significantly, my analysis shows that the two constructs of a traditional self and a posttraditional self prove woefully inadequate to represent how teens in my sample constructed self-identity. (Table 7 summarizes the patterns of self-identity that emerged in my sample of church-related teens.) The fact that I could find at least seven distinct and overlapping patterns of self-identity, not just two, indicates that there are different ways that people hold their beliefs in the late twentieth century.

It is not just *what* people believe, but *how* people believe that has adapted to late modern times. There is a genuine sense of choice, borne out in a voluntary and selective religiosity that one can see within social relations, practical activities, and institutional frameworks. Held in this way, religious traditions still function as a source for self-identity, even in what Giddens calls "late modernity."

There are some positive benefits for the religious tradition when believing in God, practicing faith, and belonging to religious institutions are not regarded as obligations. The majority of teens in my sample who choose to embrace their faith tradition are deliberate in their practices and creative in contributing toward new Christian expression in changing conditions. Most of these teens are remaking their religious traditions as they emphasize elements that are noninstitutional, democratic, and oriented to practices more than doctrines. In some public settings such as the school, many teens show respect for the role of religion as a meaning-making system that addresses the big moral and existential questions of their lives.

The next part of this book focuses on the parents of the teens I interviewed. Their stories will lead us back to a discussion of what fosters religious loyalty in teens.

Table 7. Five Elements of Self-Identity by Seven Religious Styles

	Intimacy	Bodily Presentation	Grounding of Ontological Security	Rites of Passage to Adulthood	Moral Dilemmas, How Resolved
Conventionals Rebecca, the home-schooled teen whose church youth group is the most secular group she attends	Family is inner circle; church family is second circle	Modest; traditional gender presentation; attention to grooming; deference to authority	The assurance of heaven and being saved in Christ	Marriage in the church	Sexual purity; pro-life; antievolution; antigay; no drinking or drugs; guided by Ten Commandments, Bible, WWJD, parents
Classics Graham, who both studies the Bible diligently and storms out of Christian book stores	Respect for parents; keen interest in friendships with peers	Relaxed self-presentation, no extremes	God grounds reality and gives vocation and motivation for service	Fulfilling commitments to parents, school, self; the blessing of parents as one leaves home	Injustice; religious intolerance; guided by Bible, Golden Rule, WWJD, parents
Reclaimers Paul, who is shifting from his circle of drug-taking friends to being known as the leader of the church youth group rock band	Problematic relations with parents; identify with loners among peers	A wounded body; boys wear earrings; girls dress sloppily; styles can be extreme	God forgives; staying close to God protects self from danger	Have experienced precocious adulthood; little left to mark crossing over	Staying drug and alcohol free; limits on sexual activity; anti-abortion; right/wrong is difficult to know, God sees your heart
Marginalizers Megan, a leader in the church youth group who claims, "God, I'm not really religious."	Cooperate with parents but not close; "core group" of friends at school	Attentive to health and outward appearance; style of dress like chosen reference group except without extremes	On the basis of talents and luck, personal assets are maximized; protection in accumulated assets	College acceptances, senior prom, school awards ceremony, church recognition of seniors marking the end of high school, not adulthood	Pollution of environment; the plight of the disadvantaged; sexism; racism; dilemmas resolved by cost/benefit analysis: who can I best help with what I have?

Table 7. Five Elements of Self-Identity by Seven Religious Styles (continued)

	Intimacy	Bodily Presentation	Grounding of Ontological Security	Rites of Passage to Adulthood	Moral Dilemmas, How Resolved
Customizers Michelle, who sees God as "the Man in the Moon" and lobbies against abortion in Washington as a Catholic youth representative	Intimacy is a driving need; quest for experience of being deeply loved and understood; often close to parents; intense romantic relationships and many "best friends"	Dress for comfort and sensuality	Angels; signs in nature; heaven for all after death; dependable relationships of commitment give protection	Increased levels of commitment in relationships, symbolized by gifts; personalized rituals sometimes with religious symbols	Hypocrisy; neglect of children, elderly, poor; dilemmas resolved by showing unexpected compassion for others and offering service
Rejecters Ian the former Methodist, currently Buddhist, the straightedge-hard-core rock musician	Achieved in shared commitment to common values; intimates are not determined by family ties of obligation; small circle of intimacy	Consistent with ideological commitment, clothes purchased from Good Will; no substance abuse, vegetarian; natural features altered to exhibit self-mastery; demeanor of arrogance	Chosen philosophy; practical consciousness evolving from routines of daily life and given structures, sometimes religious	A sustained feeling of serenity and authenticity; or the adoption of a personal practice or style that differentiates self from traditional authority	Racism, sexism, homophobia, capitalism, Western Christian hegemony; right and wrong action guided by "do no harm" or Golden Rule; global ethical problems addressed in local action
The Lost Trey, who "has been sprinkled, taken First Communion, and been dunked," but does not know the Lord's Prayer; he prays before his football games	Chaotic family life; socially inept with peers	Extreme dress and/or conformity to reference group codes of appearance; lack of knowledge of social conventions	Practical consciousness evolving from routines; no coherent set of meanings; inappropriate risk-taking; choices made in the moment	None; teens already considered grown up; career track offers some benchmarks	Betraying your group, telling lies, stealing, avoiding harm from drugs and alcohol, violence; avoiding Satanic cults; common sense shows right/ wrong

Part IV

Nurturing Teen Religious Loyalty in the Family

Chapter Nine

How Parents Influence Teen Faith

S ome parents feel that their job of religious nurture is finished by the time their teens are high school seniors, or even before that. "A teen is like a rocket that's already launched off the pad," one father said. "If the guidance system isn't in there, it's too late now." They point to the voluntary decision of their child to be baptized and/or confirmed in the church, and take it as a sign that the child has made the religious choice.[1] It is now up to the teens to continue with what they have chosen, because religion cannot be imposed on them.

My research findings contradict that assumption and show that it still matters what kind of religious nurture parents provide in the later years of high school. I feature here the voices of teens commenting on what matters most to them as they consider whether to choose the faith of their parents. Both teens and parents acknowledge that parents are the primary influence on their teen's choice. Yet it is not as simple and straightforward as that. Chapter 10 tells the stories of three similar families who reared their teens in the church, yet produced different outcomes of teen religious loyalty.[2] What elements of family life really matter in the religious nurture of teens? The four chapters in Part IV will help shape an answer.

What Teens and Parents Say about How Parents Influence Teen Faith

The majority of the teens in my interview sample said that their parents influence their religious beliefs and practices more than anyone or anything else. In response to the question "Who or what most influences you in your beliefs about God and how you practice your faith?" just over half of them named family members, generally their parents, as those who most shaped and continue to shape their religious lives.[3] As one boy expressed it:

> **Graham:** And I think God shows himself to you by people's love of you. Like, I think God working in my life is the fact that my parents love me so much, you know. Like agape, that sort of thing, you know?
>
> **Interviewer:** Kind of an unconditional, selfless kind of love.
>
> **Graham:** Yeah, so that would be a big thing. That influences me a lot.

A majority also named parents and grandparents as those they held up as a model of mature Christian faith.[4]

Another one-fourth of the teens in my interview sample said that they select for themselves what they believe and how they practice their faith. Some of these teens who emphasize their own agency said that when they were younger, their parents and church gave them "a foundation" of values and morals, including a religious ethic. As older teens, they choose whether to use these standards. Typical was Danielle's comment:

> Just because I don't go to church doesn't mean I don't have values and morals. I think my parents set those in me from going to church and the things they taught me when I was younger. . . . I believe by the time you're about, I'd say, seventeen you have your goals and your morals and your values set. I may go back to church later.

The remaining one-fourth of teens answered the question about influences on their faith in several different ways. Some named people outside their family; a few named same-age friends; some said God influenced them directly. Of those who named adults outside the family, they tended to name as their mentors and guarantors specific youth leaders, ministers, and choir directors in their church, religious brothers and nuns who teach at their school, athletic coaches, teachers, a young mother for whom a teen baby-sat, and other adults such as their friends' parents.[5] One boy described how the religious brothers at his Catholic school impacted him:

> It's just kind of weird like whenever a tragedy happens, like freshman year a teacher died at St. Peter, and the school came together as a com-

munity, but even more, just the brothers. When my grandfather died, my teachers that were brothers came, and it was just kind of like they were just a community within the community. It was just really neat.

Others named same-age friends as those who influenced them most, and showed how this worked both to encourage and discourage religious loyalty. Some teens had a circle of close friends at school with whom they could talk openly about their faith.[6] They supported, challenged, and held one another accountable to what they professed. Others said their friends were the ones who validated their doubts about God. Friends' examples of rebelling against their parents' pressure to continue attending church emboldened them to do likewise.

A few others said God directly influenced their belief.[7] Caroline had an experience of God through intense feelings of being loved and accepted. One girl felt God comforting her after she was raped. Another girl felt God saving her from committing suicide. Another girl experienced God giving her strength to endure a painful medical treatment. One boy experienced God as God called him to go to Bible college. Others experienced God as God answered prayers. For Emily, it was a very direct experience.

> **Emily:** Most of my understanding of God came through insights that he gave me. That's pretty much true of everything in my life. People think that I'm such a deep thinker, but it's not really true. God just allows me to understand more than most people, I think maybe because I listen to him more than a lot of people do, and so a lot of what I come to understand is because he tells me.
>
> **Interviewer:** How does he tell you?
>
> **Emily:** I'm not sure. Basically it's just thoughts that come to me, and I know that they're not something that I could think of myself if I shot around for a hundred years.

In all, the answers of the teens in my sample were consistent with national survey data that show the primacy of the parental influence.[8] It was striking that even teens who felt hurt or betrayed by a parent, like Robin, whose father committed adultery, or Danielle, whose father abandoned her at a father-daughter dance, still named their parents as those who gave them "the foundation."[9]

The majority of parents in my interview sample also said that parents exerted a primary influence on their teens' faith, despite the documented public perception that fewer families today are teaching religion and values to their teens.[10] Parents emphasized how teens have grown up watching their example of religious faith and practice, for better or worse.[11] "On a daily basis you can't lie to a kid," one father said. "You can't hide from him. . . . They see right through." Another mother said, "I've heard Bill West [the megachurch pastor] say this so often: 'Talk your walk and walk your talk.' Kids learn as much by observing as they do by what comes out of our mouths."

Besides striving to set an example, a few parents employed other strategies to rear children in their religious faith. Certainly Rebecca's parents, who home-schooled her and her younger siblings, went well beyond just setting an example. They were sheltering her from secular influences until they felt she could handle living "out in the world."

Mitch's parents also had a strategy—what could be called "a saturation approach." They explained: "Our parenting philosophy has been to saturate our children with as much as we could that was of the Lord. If you saturate them with it, maybe they'll absorb a half of it or more." Mitch's parents achieved "saturation" through the Christian people, symbols, and practices they brought into their home, as well as through the churches and schools they selected for their family. As Mitch and his older brother were growing up, the parents "exposed the boys to those who would be a good example of faith." They said, "We chose our own friends with that in mind." They conducted a "share group" in their home for parents who had children the same ages as their own. "It made it fun for the kids to play with other kids while we had a Bible study." As a family, they said bedtime prayers and read Bible stories, prayed for the sick, cared for dying friends, lighted Advent wreath candles before Christmas, and handed out religious tracts with candy at Halloween. They sent their son to a Christian school through the fourth grade, and then continued him in public schools after they felt Mitch could hold his own there. This family switched their church membership four times while raising their boys; each time "the move was for the children," to belong to a church that "gave them opportunities."

Saturation extended to the summer months and will continue beyond the high school years. Each summer they sent Mitch to a Billy Graham camp in North Carolina, where he eventually rose to the rank of counselor. After graduation they plan to send Mitch to a Christian college. Mitch's parents explained, "We met each other at a Christian college, and we want to increase the chances that our sons will marry Christians." I asked, "What are your hopes for Mitch in a religious sense?" With tears in her eyes, Mitch's mother said, "I want to meet my grandchildren in heaven someday."

One of the two questions that elicited tears most often from parents was this one, asking parents about their hopes for their teen religiously.[12] A high percentage (almost 43 percent) of parents mentioned (like Mitch's mother) that seeing their teen eventually marry someone of their faith, and/or rear their children in the church, would be a mark of their success in meeting their religious goals for their children.[13] As another mother said of her son, "I want him to work through his doubts, marry a Catholic, and remain Catholic." This mother represented a minority of Catholic parents I interviewed, who regarded being Catholic as "an ethnic identity . . . like being Jewish."

More often parents, both Catholic and Protestant, wanted their teens to marry within their faith in order to share a common religious commitment and to pass on Christian faith to the next generation. Catholic parents would sometimes distinguish their views from those of their own parents by saying that they were not as strict about their children marrying Catholics, or even remaining Catholics themselves. Typical was one comment made by a father in a family where both he and his wife were weekly church-attending Catholics: "I hope Andrea is involved in organized religion as an adult, preferably Catholic, but not necessarily." Similarly, evangelical and mainline Protestant parents expressed the concern that their children remain Christians and marry Christians; denomination was unimportant. Typical was this father's general summary of his hope for this son: "I want him to continue on the track he's taken and to marry a Christian girl."

Some parents hope marriage and/or having children will help their teens return to their faith if they seem to be drifting in their teen years. "I hope he'll go back to church when he's married," one mother said, recalling the religious doubts she had when she was her son's age. Another parent said, "I expect Tara will be active in the church someday, especially when she has kids."

Some parents hope that when their children become parents they will be better at religious nurture than they were. One father, a Methodist, said, "I want God to be important in my son's life, and for him to do a better job of raising his children in the faith than I've been able to do." Another father, an evangelical, said, "Attending church is a family thing, but we haven't followed through. We're a very small, closed religious family that doesn't go to church." His wife underscored the irony: "We're a nonpracticing religious family."

Some parents did not express their goals for their children in institutional religious terms at all, even when asked about them directly. As one mother said, "I want inner peace for my son, a life of putting others first." Some parents were disillusioned with the institutional church and did not cherish hopes that their children will be involved in a church. A former professional church educator, who is "burned out," said he and his wife are "more and more moving away from the church." They want their daughter to "have a relationship with God, but the church is not critical." Reared in an overstrict Lutheran home, another mother described her current religious orientation as "Science of the Mind," an individual spiritual practice, not an institutionalized religion. She spends time each morning reading and meditating on literature she receives by mail. Her husband says the burden rests with him to "sell" their son on Catholicism.

When parents were not united in holding similar religious goals for their teen, marital tension was sometimes evident. One father half joked and half baited his wife as he characterized a difference between them: "She wants Emily to marry a missionary. I want her to marry a banker."

I discovered that many parents coast toward their teens' high school graduation, especially after their teens get their driver's licenses.[14] They cease asking or expecting their teen to attend church. They ease up on their own religious practices as well. They believe their teens are "set." As one mother affirms:

> I think the influence really is when they're very young. I think at a certain age a parent is not going to influence their child. I mean, . . . you can make them go to church and I don't think that's right either. But I think you have to reach them when they're young. And, yet, maybe had we been more involved. . . . At one time we were involved with the school and the church. . . . You know, like I said, I think even though my kids stopped going to church, which I think is a stage, I think they will go back.

Sometimes parents, like this mother quoted above, ease up out of a conviction that their potential influence has waned; other parents are just worn out. By the time their teens are seniors, some relationships between parents and teens are riddled with conflict. They argue over many issues, especially grades, curfew, at-risk behaviors, and friends. "We're sort of walking on eggshells right now with Tara," said her mother. "She feels we're pulling her away from this guy. I wouldn't put it past her to turn up pregnant, to run away and get married. So we're in a real delicate spot."

Religion may be very important to parents, but with scarier problems consuming their attention, little energy is left for insisting that teens attend church. Many parents who ease off on their expectations of their teens' religious participation do so with a sense of resignation.

Some parents accent the church and the parochial school as the religious influences that matter or should matter more to their teen's religious formation than they themselves do. Some parents feel the church and parochial school have succeeded with their teen. Evangelical parents feel particularly indebted to junior high school youth advisors who helped their teens accept Christ and who sometimes also performed their baptisms. Catholic parents cite the positive impact of the retreat program at the Catholic schools even more than they praise the classroom religious instruction. On the other hand, some parents blame the church and/or parochial school for failing with their children. Speaking of the instruction offered by the teachers at their son's Catholic high school, one mother said angrily, "They have made it Mickey Mouse. It is not working."

Many parents denounced the insidious role of the popular media for undermining the religious perspective and Christian moral behavior they wish to foster. A typical comment was: "Sex, drinking, and drugs. We talk very openly about it. We tell the kids, and Michelle's friends . . . we will tell them we know what's on television and that our beliefs are totally different and we're going to tell them our beliefs." Few parents, however, actually exerted control over what their teen viewed. Even conservative evangelicals tended not to impose restrictions on the movies their older teens watched. One family put a restriction on their daughter's video card to keep her from renting an R-rated video without their permission. They removed the restriction when she turned eighteen, however. They try to instill in her a critical stance toward mass-marketed media. "We'll be watching something together and there'll be some violence or sex-related scene, or the obscenities and profanity. And I've said to the kids so many times, 'Why does that have to be in there? The movie would be just as effective and just as good if it was not in there.'"

Parents also commented on the influence of their teens' peers. "When you focus on teenagers, the peer group is everything," said Andrea's father. Parents are in "the fall-back position," he explained. "The difference in a Christian upbringing is that the kids can always come back home." The saying, "Show me your friends and I will show you who you will become," was quoted often by teens and their parents to underscore the importance of peer influence. This saying even appeared in big letters on a wall in one of the high school classrooms I visited. As important as peers are, few parents said they tried to influence who their teens selected as friends. Some steered their teens away from teens known to be involved in at-risk behaviors, but none tried to shield them from exposure to people of other religious faiths.

Clearly, peer pressure was regarded by parents as mostly negative. Bob Rhodes described the pressure his son and his girlfriend experienced: "They get teased, and on the football team they're always saying, 'Hey, Chad. How is she? Is she pretty good in bed?' And he was open about it. 'No, Tiffany and I are going to wait until we get married.'"

Parents also noted how peer pressure could be positive. Bob says Tiffany has made his son "a better person, and I'm hoping that he has done the same for her." Mitch's father quoted their pastor, Bill West, on the subject of peers as West affirmed a gathering of teens: "'You are the peer pressure,' Bill West said to them, and I think that's what Mitch has done. He is the [positive] peer pressure in his high school."

While many parents do ease up on their religious socialization as their children approach high school graduation, and while some regard the influence of the church, school, media, and peers as so great as to eclipse any influence they might try to exert during the later teen years, my research shows otherwise. It does seem to matter what parents do in the later years of high school to continue nurturing faith. In the next three chapters, I will show how this is so.

Chapter Ten

Three Families, Three Outcomes

A review of the literature and research about families and faith transmission suggested that certain parent variables are associated to greater and lesser degrees with teen religious loyalty. I tested many of these and found significant associations with the following:

1. Parent church attendance
2. A warm family climate
3. A parent/teen social network
4. Christian symbols, rituals, and practices in the home
5. Family participation in the same congregation
6. A nonchaotic parenting style
7. Intact marriage of parents
8. Adequate family income
9. Proximity to extended family and parents' hometown
10. Parents of same religious background

What parents do to nurture faith in their teens, however, is more than just checking items off a list. What follows here is a discussion of the nuances and complexities of what I discovered, especially by interviewing in depth a sample of the parents and teens. I begin by telling the stories of three particular families. While I selected them to illustrate the importance of the four demographic variables (7–10), it will be shown that the nondemographic variables are associated more significantly with teen religious loyalty. The three stories also illustrate the interactive effects of all ten variables.

Brynne's Family

Brynne planted a kiss on each parent's cheek as she left home to attend a meeting at the church, allowing me to be alone with her parents to conduct an interview. I started by remarking about the vase of fresh daisies on the kitchen table, something that struck me as unseasonal during the Christmas holiday, when we were meeting. They explained that it was a tradition in their family to mark the December 28 birthday of their infant who died, stillborn, twelve years ago. Thus, even before I began my questions, the daughter's affectionate gesture and the daisies tipped me off to two of the many important things I was to learn about the Watsons: this family's climate was warm and its culture was thick with symbols that strengthened their distinctive identity as a family.

"We are a churchgoing family," Ken and Anna Mae Watson explained, "but we are not in the business of 'raising Christians.'" These parents stressed that they understood faith to be the choice of each of their three children. Being a Christian was not an identity to be bred into children. "We are not a Christian family," Ken said emphatically. Being a Christian is having a relationship with God that depends on the decision of each individual when they reach an "age of discernment." Ken and Anna Mae themselves each made a decision "to become a Christian" in their college years. Ken, reared a Catholic, and Anna Mae, reared "Protestant," criticize their own religious upbringings as nominal. Anna Mae described their goal as Christian parents:

> I just want my children to be growing Christians. I want them to have a vibrant relationship with Christ. I don't want it to be, you know, go to church because they've always gone to church or because that's what you're supposed to do. You brush your teeth. You go to the doctor. You go to church. I don't want that. I want them to have a vibrant, growing, real relationship with Christ.

To reach that goal, Ken and Anna Mae witness to their own faith "as it flows." Anna Mae says, "They see us study. They hear us talk. They see our values. And we talk about the Lord, but we don't do a lot of official things. . . . Those 'Focus on the Family' books can become real plastic." Quoting their pastor Bill West, Ken repeated a saying that guides them: "'I'd rather see a sermon than hear one.'" Anna Mae expanded, "With kids, the moment is everything. You just have to listen so carefully to when they're ready to hear what you want to say, and then you say it in as few words as you can." While Ken and Anna Mae do nurture faith in their children through well-timed conversation and by their example, they also establish some basic rules for their children—rules like truth telling, showing respect for others, and attending church. They strive to minimize the number of rules, however, and keep things "negotiable" as much as possible.

Like almost all the parents of high school seniors that I interviewed, Ken and Anna Mae displayed more humility than pride in their parenting, even though they had every reason to be pleased with the oldest product of their parenting. Brynne exhibited what her parents most wanted for her: a vital relationship with God that she could talk about with a sense of naturalness. Living with a child for seventeen or eighteen years, adapting to the varied and sometimes tumultuous phases of a child's development, tends to engender modesty in parents' assessments of their performance. Most parents said they learned to do what worked through trial and error, more than through any formal parenting strategy, religious or otherwise. The Watsons tell Brynne, "We're just figuring this out as we go. You have to give us some time and be patient with us while we're trying to figure out what to do with you."

Brynne's parents may be just "figuring it out as they go," but they exhibit characteristics and patterns of religious nurture that are common to other parents of religiously loyal teens in my sample. First, they have cultivated a warm climate in their family that secures voluntary cooperation and willing adherence to family rules and expectations. The affection they show one another was evident in Brynne's parting gesture. The parents' comments also display respect for their children's autonomy. They accept their children's different inborn personality traits. They admire Brynne's talent for leadership, a talent for which they take no credit. "God made her who she is," they marvel. They allow Brynne to date someone they are "not crazy about," a boy from a Catholic background who does not attend church. They mention that Brynne has confided to them some doubts that trouble her about her faith, especially how to understand the absolute truth of God in Christ and still be respectful of other faiths. Brynne struggles with the biblical imperative to evangelize, and her parents respect her questioning stance. Because of this kind of sensitive listening and loving acceptance that these parents have shown their daughter over the years, they have won her affection and love.

The warmth of this family extends beyond its family members. Ken and Anna Mae try to know their children's friends. They even included Brynne's best friend on their last family vacation. Like many of the middle-class parents in my study,[1] the Watsons remodeled the basement of their home so their teens would have a comfortable place to socialize with their friends. The parents get to know Brynne's friends as they come over to hang out, and also through school and church functions. Active not just in church, but also in the parent-teacher association at their children's schools, the Watsons know many of the parents of their children's church and school peers. They and their children are part of a large web of inter-generational relationships that link families, schools, and their church. Thus they exhibit a second characteristic associated with teen loyalty, having a parent/teen social network.[2]

Third, this family has a relatively thick culture, one that is built in large part from religious symbols, stories, and practices. The vase of daisies on the kitchen table is their witness to God's providence and their affirmation of eternal life after death. A framed plaque by the front door tells who they are: "As for me and my house, we shall serve the Lord" (a quote from Joshua 24:15). They have a well-established practice of attending church. The rule in the family that "we attend church," is not experienced as coercive by teenage children, because they have been reared all their lives to attend church. They may go on Saturday night instead of Sunday, the traditional Sabbath, but attending church is taken for granted in this family.

Part of what it means to be in this family is to eat together. "Mealtime is family time," said Ken. "I think that's something that our children value immensely, because a lot of their friends have families who never eat together." As for many busy families, the evening meal is the one regular time when the Watson family gathers. It is also the regular time that is linked with the practice of prayer. The Watsons no longer have family devotions at bedtime as they did when the children were younger.

The family's attitude toward their church is very positive. The parents admitted that they have some theological disagreements with the church over baptism, but for the most part they love Riverland Heights. They got "burned out" at a megachurch in a previous city, so when they moved to Louisville they joined a small church. They switched to Riverland Heights at Brynne's urging, persuaded by her argument: "If I'm going to date Christian young men, I have to go where there are Christian boys." Both parents find their heavy involvement in church activities very gratifying. Ken is part of a men's accountability group that meets every Saturday morning. Anna Mae devotes twenty hours a week to preparing and leading a women's Bible study.[3]

For all their success with Brynne, Ken and Anna Mae Watson experience parenting and the task of Christian nurture as a very demanding learning experience.[4] It has been made all the more challenging for them because it has coincided with other difficult twists and turns of personal circumstance, the challenges that often characterize this stage of adult life: the declining health and death of parents, adjustments in the marital relationship, job changes, and relocation. Another set of parents I interviewed, Judy and Greg Marlboro, faced even more trying circumstances during their parenting years.

Parker's Family

When their seventeen-year-old son Parker was five years old, Judy Marlboro suffered a miscarriage late into a pregnancy. Her husband, Greg, had just changed jobs, and the new insurance plan had not taken effect to cover any of her medical bills. At the same time, Greg developed cancer. The debt the two of them incurred because of medical bills was one from which they never fully recovered. Later they gave birth to a second son, but the baby's serious health problems necessitated three brain surgeries, and years later the family still must spend time each day in therapy to help the child compensate for his learning disabilities.

In addition, Greg lost some key contracts in his business and had to fold it and start again from scratch several years ago. At the time I met this family, Greg was starting another new job and earning only $25,000 a year as a salary. With just two years of college, Judy could find work only off and on at low-paying jobs. Their low income qualifies Parker for a scholarship to the Catholic high school he chose. "Some people say we live under a black cloud," Judy relates. Their most recent sadness was the death of Maureen, Parker's best friend and a beloved frequent visitor in their home. Judy cried as she shared her grief over Maureen.

Given the tragedies this family has faced, their record of compassionate service to others is remarkable. Since before Parker was born, Judy and Greg have been involved in a relationship with a poor inner-city family with thirteen children, some of whom suffer mental retardation. "I've kind of been their birthday dinner, their Thanksgiving, and their Christmas," Judy said. "Or they'll call me from the hospital or in jail." The Marlboros say that their own troubles are put in perspective as they know this disadvantaged family. "God gave me [the inner-city family] to prepare me for our difficulties with a learning disabled child," Judy says. "I think that Parker has learned to respect that, and he really cares about them too."

Like the Watsons, the Marlboros exhibit a high degree of warmth in their family. Judy pointed to a vase containing several roses that sat on their living room coffee table. She explained that the flowers were left over from a bouquet she bought at the grocery store to make a corsage for Parker to give his prom date that past weekend. Judy worked hard to find creative ways to enable Parker to enjoy the prom and amenities that this family might not otherwise afford.

Also like the Watsons, this family has a parent/teen social network that connects parents and teens across the different contexts of home, church, and school. Judy volunteered her time and talents at the youth group at Transfiguration that Parker attends, even though it is not her church. She wants to pay in kind a pledge to Transfiguration, since they cannot afford to give financially to her husband's church. Even more, she wants to know her son's friends and be involved in his life. Judy's tears and Greg's tender comments about Maureen reflected the grief they shared with their son over Maureen's death. It was evident that both Judy and Greg knew the important people in Parker's life.

After I concluded my formal interview questions with the parents, Judy asked me my opinion of Parker. "Do you feel he has a strong faith?" she asked me with an edge of concern in her voice. Judy and Greg have slightly different hopes for Parker in his religious faith. Judy wants her son to "continue to search God [*sic*] and the Lord in the Scriptures . . . to marry somebody that is religious [so] they have the same values and the same convictions . . . [so] they're not struggling with two different backgrounds . . . like we did, or like I did." Greg's hopes for Parker's religious life are more vague. He says, "I want Parker to follow his heart . . . because, like I said, God only knows how many times we've been tested."

Like Ken and Anna Mae Watson, Greg and Judy Marlboro were reared in different Christian traditions. In both cases, the husbands were reared Catholic and the wives Protestant. While Ken and Anna Mae chose a single religious tradition and church for their family, Greg and Judy have remained members of their own traditions during their marriage. Judy's evangelical church became primary in the family, because church involvement is more important to her than to her husband. Greg also prefers to attend Judy's church when they go. He explains, "I think people that go to Riverland Heights get something out of the service rather than the boring, the staid-type sermon, you know, at any Catholic church basically."

For the Marlboros, attending church is a family activity, yet Judy regrets that their family's attendance at church has dwindled to just once or twice a year in the last few years. "My kids just started rebelling about wanting to go to church, and I just basically got really tired of fighting and pushing." Greg will attend church with the family as long as Judy initiates it. Judy criticized her husband for not setting a better example for her sons as the head of the family by leading them in regular church attendance.

Considering the home and religious nurture that Judy and Greg Marlboro have provided Parker, it is not surprising that he is a conditional loyalist, someone who predicts he will be active in the church if he finds a church he likes. The Marlboros exhibit some of the family characteristics that are associated with teen religious loyalty: a warm family climate and a parent/teen social network generated from relationships in the church. These are offset by some other characteristics less favorable to nurturing religious loyalty.

One of these less favorable family characteristics is the division they experience in church membership. Maintaining membership in two churches has been a compromise for Judy and Greg. Judy alluded to that circumstance as something that made her job as a parent "a struggle." She hoped her son would marry someone who shared the same religious tradition to avoid having a similar struggle. In my sample, greater degrees of loyalty were associated with teens coming from families in which the parents belonged to the same church.

The Marlboros differed from the families that tended to produce teen loyalists in another way—in the parenting style they displayed. The "open" style of parenting that the Marlboros exhibited correlates negatively with teen religious loyalty. (This "open" style of parenting, characterized by a random pattern of family decision making, is defined in the next chapter, in contrast to five other styles.) Like other families in my research who were overwhelmed by financial problems, poor health, and other difficult circumstances, the Marlboro parents lacked the energy to establish structures and rules in their family. During my interview in the Marlboro home, I was struck with the high frenetic energy of the household. There were telephone interruptions, visits from neighborhood children and dogs, and frantic snatches of conversation about different commitments they had to squeeze in later that day. Judy and Greg both wished for greater order in the family, even just to share a regular mealtime. Greg spoke wistfully of what he remembers of his childhood: "It's really sad, because I know when we grew up we had dinner at six thirty—meat, two vegetables, salad, and dessert every day." Parker eats his dinner by himself in front of the television. Their younger son also eats by himself at an earlier time. Judy waits to eat with her husband when he gets home later.

Some of the Marlboros' inability to establish order in the family was related to the parents' genuine disagreement over parental authority and gender roles. Like 40 percent of the evangelicals in my sample, Judy expected the man to be the head of the family, and specifically the "spiritual head." Greg had a traditional view of gender roles, but it was not loaded with religious meaning for him. He was not motivated to assume leadership of the family, much less to share the household work. Judy grudgingly shouldered most of the parenting responsibilities, something she was unable to execute alone with consistency.

One of the casualties of the parents' inability to establish order in the household was the family's practice of attending church. As it will be shown, the parents' ability to hold their child in the church throughout the teen years, especially by attending corporate worship regularly, is the variable that correlated most with teen religious loyalty. Despite all the positive family factors that the Marlboros had going for them, other factors (belonging to different churches, an open family style, and an inability to maintain the practice of church attendance) worked against them in fostering strong religious loyalty in their son.

Alex's Family

Like Greg and Judy Marlboro and Ken and Anna Mae Watson, a third couple, Phil and Linda O'Day, were reared Catholic and Protestant respectively. The O'Days, like the Watsons, felt that it was important for parents with different religious backgrounds to choose one church and rear their own children in a single religious faith. Linda O'Day converted to Catholicism from her Episcopalian tradition. She was confirmed at the Church of the Transfiguration on the same day their two-year-old son was baptized. Phil was less willing than Linda to switch denominations. "Louisville is a Catholic town," Phil explained, "the sense of [Catholic] community is very good." Louisville was Phil's hometown, not Linda's. He could envision his children attending the same parochial schools he attended as a child.

As a couple, the O'Days were not involved in any church until they were expecting a second child. When Alex was nearly two and another child was coming, Linda realized that she "missed church," and "felt it was important to establish that habit with the family and a routine." The O'Days agreed on having a Catholic "structure" of both the church and the parochial school, to give their children "a religious framework." Phil remembers, "My primary religious instruction was school, supplemented by family. And basically I think that's what we have done here, as opposed to some families who are the primary instructional force for religious structure."

As mentioned above, parents belonging to the same church is a variable that correlates positively with teen religious loyalty. Of the three couples, two of them, the Watsons and the O'Days, chose to belong to the same church and to rear their children in a single religious tradition. Therefore, one predicts that, like Brynne Watson, Alex O'Day would be loyal to his religious tradition. Yet that is not the case. (See table 8.) Alex calls himself an agnostic. He is even less loyal than Parker Marlboro, who is divided between his parents' two traditions. Alex is alienated from his religious tradition. With several key factors favoring Alex's religious loyalty, especially his parents belonging to the same church, what accounts for his alienation?

Like many people at Transfiguration, the O'Days voiced the opinion that church life at Transfiguration revolved around the parish school. Like other parents, they felt that when their children moved up to the Catholic high schools, which are not parish-based, there was little to keep them engaged in the parish. Linda criticized the parish mass, especially the sermons, because she wished for a message that was "more spiritual." Phil longed for more of "the magic show" that he remembered from his childhood, the "pomp and circumstance" that is hard to achieve with "guitar music."[6] Like many Catholic parents I interviewed, the O'Days talked about the possibility of switching to the cathedral downtown, where the newly renovated Gothic building is majestic and the priest is known for his inspiring messages.

The O'Days' weekly church attendance dropped off dramatically after Alex graduated from the parish school and entered Thomas Merton High School. Like the Marlboros, the O'Days did not maintain the practice of attending church, specifically the practice of corporate worship. Alex became active in youth group instead.

Table 8. Parents' Church Membership and Teen Religious Outcome in Three Families in Sample

	Parents Belong to the Same Church	Teen Outcome: Level of Loyalty/Nonloyalty[5]
Watson	Yes	Brynne: loyalist
Marlboro	No	Parker: provisional loyalist
O'Day	Yes	Alex: unlikely loyalist

At the time I interviewed the O'Days, their "church" was their Alco-holics Anonymous meeting. Phil and Linda took control of their addic-tion and successfully began their recovery three years earlier. Unlike their parish mass, Linda says of AA meetings: "I'm getting something out of it. I am closer to God than I have ever been in my life." Growing up, God was "just out there, Santa Claus God." Hitting bottom was "just what it took" for Linda "to get it," and to experience "God with me."

Linda and Phil see religion and faith as two different things. Religion is the structure and community chosen for you by your family; faith is the spirituality that an individual chooses.

> **Phil:** I identify myself as Catholic, and I can't see identifying myself as anything else. That's the religion, but the faith is an indi-vidual [thing], that's a choice.

> **Interviewer:** So you see a difference between religion and faith?

> **Phil:** Yes. I think faith is more important for living.

> **Linda:** I do too.

> **Phil:** I think that religion is the structure in the community that we feel worked well in our family situation and in our parenting in Louisville. But that could be different in different areas.

> **Interviewer:** So religion is the structure; faith is what?

> **Phil:** The beliefs and principles and values that they live day to day, the spiritual aspect, the spirituality of living. Faith is spiritual-ity. Religion is community and structure and a whole bunch of other things.

The O'Days have given Alex the "structure" of Catholic life, something he will always have in his background. Even if he has rejected Catholic beliefs for now, he has faith as they define it. "He's got a sense of himself and friends and respect of other people that is very strong." Phil contin-ues, "I would hope that he would use a structure if he is a parent. . . . He's had enough background that he can come back and remember what he had." Unlike the Watsons and the Marlboros, the O'Days express little concern about how their child has chosen to relate to his church and reli-gious tradition.

The O'Days hold a religious perspective that embraces spirituality more than a religious tradition. In splitting "structure" and "faith," they make nonessential the structure, the formal aspects of the tradition, the church and its practices. They claim faith is having a relationship with God that meets their personal needs. They represent a growing number of people of their generation, the baby boomers, who value having a relationship with God apart from the institution of the church.[7] Faith, according to this perspective, is an individual choice. Both O'Day parents may belong to the same church, a factor that does favor faith transmission, but their current religious practice is noninstitutional. If they return to the church, as they indicate that they might, Phil and Linda are likely to be the kind of returnees who emphasize spirituality more than tradition.[8]

Individualism is a cherished value in the O'Days' family culture. The individuality and autonomy of each family member appears to be valued more than their shared identity. I happened to arrive at the O'Day home for the interview just before they performed a nightly family ritual that dramatized their reverence for individuality. I got there just as they were rearranging their cars in the driveway in preparation for the next morning. The four members of the O'Day family have their own cars that they must line up in the driveway each night in a certain order to allow them to depart one by one from the house the next day on their separate schedules, taking their separate paths to the places where they would spend most of their day separate from each other.

Despite their overriding individualism, the O'Day family did have dinner together on an average of three times a week. They said a Catholic blessing before the meal as well. Other than that, there was no evidence in our general conversation or in the appointments of their home of any symbol, ritual, or practice that identified the family as Christian or Catholic. In fact, none of the Catholic families in my sample, even the more pious ones, exhibited crucifixes in their entryways, living rooms, dens, or kitchens that I observed, or the religious statues that are sometimes displayed outdoors by devout Catholics. The O'Days did gather with Phil's Catholic relatives on holidays, but the uncle that Alex enjoyed most, the one he chose as his confirmation sponsor, was the person who authorized for him that it was all right to choose not to have a religion. The religious elements of the family culture were thin as well as individualistic.

The O'Days' democratic style of parenting was consistent with their individualism. The parents respected the right of their children to participate in establishing the rules that affected them. Phil O'Day described the "contract" he had drawn up with Alex to spell out the agreements they negotiated about curfew, the use of the car, and other understandings. The consequences for breaking agreements, the revocation of car privileges in particular, were negotiated in advance. In this family, the children were treated as near equals with their parents.

The distinctiveness of the O'Days' democratic parenting style is more evident when contrasted with the hierarchical parenting style of the Watsons. Ken and Anna Mae Watson always preserved their parental authority to make decisions regarding their children and to establish the rules for them, as much as they tried to resist exercising that authority. A question I asked all parents, whether children were equal with their parents, shocked the Watsons. After my tape recorder was turned off and I was preparing to leave, Ken Watson asked me why I asked that question. The Watsons assumed that the inequality of children with parents was taken for granted by all responsible Christian parents. Yet as different as the O'Days' assumptions were from the Watsons, both sets of parents seemed to achieve order and elicit cooperation from their children through their chosen styles.

I was struck with how often families I interviewed had built a fire in the fireplace for the occasion of my visit, almost as if to illustrate the topic we were discussing: home and hearth. Judging from the hospitality I received from Phil and Linda O'Day, sitting in their cozy den before their crackling fire, I assumed that this family's climate was similarly warm. They mentioned that they knew a fair number of Alex's friends, as they made their home available to them as a place to hang out.

Phil and Linda seemed to have established a good parent/teen social network as well. When I accidentally used their street address on a letter I wrote to a different set of parents at Transfiguration, Linda hand-delivered it to the other parents. The families saw each other regularly at various Catholic school functions.

The O'Days may have a good parent/teen social network, but in my interview with Alex I got a different sense than I did from his parents about the family climate. Alex's references to his parents were notably brief:

Interviewer: How would you describe your relationship with your parents?

Alex: Not much to it. I can tell them whatever I need to and expect support.

After that, Alex moved on quickly to the topic of college applications. Alex never mentioned his parents' alcoholism. He may have been unsure if he had his parents' permission to talk about it with me. Alex's assessment of the amount of warmth in the family appeared to differ somewhat from what his parents experienced.[9]

In all, I chose to showcase these three sets of parents because, like the churches I chose, they initially seemed to represent the "best-case scenario" in the family. The Watsons, Marlboros, and O'Days are intact families, with mother and father still married and living together with their teens under the same roof. Divorce and fragmentation of the family are cited regularly as one of the biggest factors working against intrafamilial transmission of values.[10]

These three sets of parents also had in common a mixed religious background. Like 32 percent of the parents in my sample, they came into their marriage from different religious traditions, with one as a Catholic and the other as a Protestant. While a mixed religious background is associated negatively with faith transmission in children,[11] I wanted to show, by keeping this variable constant across the three cases, how parental religious background is less significant to teen religious loyalty than the choices parents make as they rear their children. More important, for example, are the decisions these three couples made about rearing their children in one church or in both. The Watson case, especially in contrast to the Marlboro case, shows how parents belonging to the same church reduces "the struggle," and is positively associated with nurturing teen religious loyalty. The O'Day case illustrates how parents belonging to the same church is not the fail-safe formula for producing religious loyalty in teens. Their infrequent church attendance offsets its positive effect. (See table 9.)

The picture of how parents rear their teens in their religious tradition is complex.[12] I have highlighted ten different variables that are associated with faith transmission in these three families. (See table 10.) These cases also show how these variables interact with each other. The positive effect of some are offset by the negative effect of others.

Table 9.   Parent Variables by Teen Loyalty for Three Families

	Family Structure Intact	Parents Belong to Same Church	Weekly Church Attendance by Entire Family
Brynne Watson: Loyalist	Yes	Yes	Yes
Parker Marlboro: Conditional loyalist	Yes	No	No
Alex O'Day: Unlikely loyalist	Yes	Yes	No

Table 10. Ten Parent Variables Associated with Teen Religious Loyalty by Family Type

	(1) Attend Church Weekly	(2) Warm Climate	(3) Parent/ Teen Social Network	(4) Thick, Religion-infused Culture	(5) Belong to Same Church	(6) Non-permissive Style Parenting	(7) Intact Family Structure	(8) Higher Income	(9) Close Proximity to Place of Origin	(10) Same Religious Background
Watson: Family Attender	yes	yes	yes	yes	yes	yes	yes	yes	no	no
Marlboro: Religious Individualist	no	yes	yes	yes	no	no	yes	no	yes	no
O'Day Religious Individualist	no	probably	yes	no	yes	yes	yes	yes	yes	no

Demographic Considerations

Throughout the study, it was important to look at demographic factors such as family structure, income, distance from parents' point of origin, and whether parents shared a common religious background. Of all of these, only the latter exhibited a higher correlation with teen religious loyalty than the nondemographic variables. (See table 12 in chapter 11.) Despite the lower statistical correlation of the demographic variable in general, there is certain logic evident in the qualitative data between the demographic variables and the tendency of teens to predict that they would stay in the church over time. I will illustrate these logics as I nuance and qualify the importance of each demographic variable.

The variable "intact family structure" is defined for the purpose of this research as parents of the teen being married to each other and living in the same house with the teen. Of the teens I interviewed, 80 percent of the teens' parents were married to each other and lived together in the same house. When stepparents are included, 83 percent of teens lived in two-parent households, 15 percent lived in single-parent households, and 2 percent (one teen) was reared in the grandparents' home instead of a parent's.

The decline of the intact family is often linked to lower levels of religious socialization of children. While empirical studies support this correlation,[13] the changed structure of the family is perhaps just the most visible of many changes in family and work that affect the religious socialization of children in families. Other dramatic changes are the greater presence of mothers in the paid work force and the longer hours that both parents work.[14] According to Wuthnow, fewer families today are centered on child rearing.[15]

Having a "higher income" is defined for the purposes of this analysis as an income of $50,000 or more. As noted in the Introduction, I attempted to keep socioeconomic and class variables constant by selecting my sample from three middle-class congregations. Despite this attempt, notable differences in families' economic resources surfaced in the interview sample. Parents made reference to economic resources as a factor that significantly affected family life, particularly the struggle of some parents to provide income for their families and still have time, energy, and attention to give to their teens.

Especially poignant was the Rhodes family. Several years ago the father, Bob, lost his job as supervisor of student dormitory facilities at a local college and started a business supplying vending machines. His wife,

Jan, who expected to be a stay-at-home mother for a few more years, suddenly had to generate some income for the family. These parents said that the quality of their parenting suffered when Jan started to work full-time as a secretary and stopped making family meals and performing other household chores that had made their home a relaxed, comfortable environment for rearing their children.

Bob and Jan try to compensate. Bob gets involved with son Chad's sports teams at the church, serving as timekeeper at many of his games. Bob has a late-night talk with Chad every evening after he returns home from work. Bob also hires his son to help him load and unload his truck on the weekends. Bob admits he would like to stay in bed on Sunday mornings, his only time to catch up on his sleep, but he knows Chad is counting on him to set an example by attending church at Riverland Heights. Bob's efforts to spend time with his son and to set an example as a churchgoer appear to be paying off. Chad says he admires his father's honesty in his work and names him as a model of mature Christian faith. Bob and Jan think that Chad may one day become a minister. They worry about his younger sister, however. Without a regular meal schedule in the home, she snacks instead of eating meals, keeps late hours, and appears to be getting in with a bad crowd of friends. Working the long hours they do, Bob and Jan cannot seem to compensate for their absence when it comes to their other child.

I also observed instances where a family's high income reached the point of diminishing returns for the children. Caroline resented the long hours her parents worked, even if they brought home a high income ($350,000 per year), which allowed her to attend a private Christian school and to drive her own car. Caroline described how she scrupulously obeyed her parents' rules and performed her chores, but also looked for chances to stage her secret protests. She managed to linger in bed all Thanksgiving morning instead of helping to cook and set the table with the china, crystal, silver, and linens that represent to her a misguided preoccupation with show and luxury on the part of her parents. Some families that had an income that was high enough to make long work hours unnecessary still did not spend much time with their teens.[16]

The third demographic variable, parents' living in close proximity to their place of origin, was defined for this research as living within an hour's drive of at least one parent's place of origin. While the aggregated data does not show that this correlation with teen religious loyalty is significant, my cases demonstrate a connection between the variable and the outcome. There is a tendency for parents remaining in their hometown to rear their children in the same institutions they know from their own childhood. This is illustrated in the O'Days' case by the fact that Alex O'Day attends the Catholic alma mater of his father, the parent who remains in his hometown. Especially if the parents' extended family remains in the area, their parents, aunts, uncles, and siblings exert overt or subtle pressure on the parents to replicate the socialization of their childhood, including their religious upbringing.

When parents had moved from their place of origin, the lack of ties to home church and extended family sometimes had a negative effect on the religious upbringing of their children. Fred Noire moved from Oregon to Louisville to work at the air hub of United Parcel Service. He described fond memories of the Catholic church of his childhood, located in a small town where Catholics were a distinct religious minority. Fred cannot seem to re-create for his son the same warm ties to the Catholic tradition without the tight enclave of Catholic neighbors that he remembers from his youth.

The Noires also illustrate the effect of the fourth demographic variable: parents having the same religious background. In their case its significance to religious loyalty in the teen is notable because of its absence. Fred's wife is a nonpracticing Lutheran, not a Catholic. Fred is unable alone, without the help of a spouse or his old neighborhood, to convey to his son a sense of being Catholic.

For this research I determined that parents came from the "same" background when they were either both Catholics or both Protestants. In actuality, some parents had to negotiate the differences between two different Protestant traditions as well. The decision about infant versus believer baptism is a major concern that confronts new parents when one of them comes from an Anabaptist heritage and the other embraces the Reformed tradition. A still greater set of differences, however, faced Catholics and Protestants when they reared children in a mixed marriage. Some parents from these backgrounds reported that they agreed before they were married how they would rear their children, especially whether the non-Catholic parent would sign papers promising to rear their children as Catholics.

Of all the demographic factors, parents having the same religious background proved the most significant of the variables that positively correlates with teen religious loyalty. (See table 12 in chapter 11.) The demographic variables as a group, however, proved less significant to teen religious loyalty than the variables to be discussed in the next chapter.

Chapter Eleven

How Families Influence
Religious Loyalty in Teens

Remember the ten factors listed at the beginning of chapter 10? This research shows that the first six are particularly significant in determining the degree to which teens expect to be active in a church after they leave home. This chapter explores each of those factors in more detail, in ascending order of influence.

Parenting Style

Parenting style is a different kind of family factor that relates to religious nurture. Unlike the demographic family factors, it is a choice parents make about current behavior. In speaking to parents, I asked four questions and then looked for patterns among their responses. The questions are:

1. What does the phrase "traditional family values" mean to you?
2. How do you view gender roles?
3. What is your family's decision-making style?
4. Are children equal with their parents?

Parental responses clustered into five parenting styles, which I call hierarchical, traditional, democratic, peer, and open. These parenting styles reflect the parents' understandings of the relationship between parent and child, and they can be placed on a spectrum by the degree of structure and control maintained by the parents as compared to permissiveness. (See fig. 8.)

Parents who exhibit the *hierarchical style* describe "traditional family

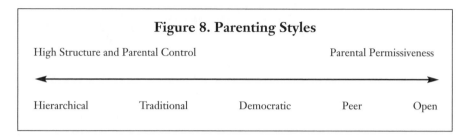

Figure 8. Parenting Styles

High Structure and Parental Control   Parental Permissiveness

⟵―――――――――――――――――――――――――――――――――――――――⟶

Hierarchical   Traditional   Democratic   Peer   Open

values" as denoting an ideal family structure: heterosexual parents living in a household with their children. To them it also means that adult children care for their infirm parents and other extended family. Holding traditional family values means preserving endangered Christian values in tension with the dominant secular culture. Gender roles are differentiated, with the man in the household acting as the head and primary breadwinner. The ideal is for the wife/mother to be a full-time homemaker, especially when the children are young. The husband is the ultimate decision maker; the wife handles day-to-day situations. Children are not viewed as equal in authority with parents. Children, including teenaged children, obey their parents as the Bible instructs. Adult children revere their parents and other elders.

In the hierarchical-style families I interviewed, half the wives are full-time homemakers. One homemaker, in addition, acts as her children's home-school teacher. I noticed that in a few cases the wife conspired with the children to disobey the father's wishes—for example, to sneak off to the mall together to spend the father/breadwinner's money. One mother said, "Dad's the boss when he's here and I'm the boss when he's not, and sometimes when he is [she laughs] . . . if I can get away with it." When there is a positive feeling prevailing in the family, as there was in many, teens tend to praise this parenting style as one that makes them feel secure in its structure and rules. When there is a predominantly negative feeling in the family—as there was for Caroline, whose high-income parents were seldom at their house—teens might obey the rules or "keep the letter of the law," but they confide their resentment to their friends. Female teens growing up in this family style tended to express greater fear than other teens about how they would manage at college the following year, on their own away from home.

Not surprisingly, the different parenting styles show a certain correlation with religious affiliation. (See table 11.) For example, the hierarchical style resonates with the conservative Christian views of family, gender

Table 11.   Frequency of Denominational Type by Parenting Style and by Teen Religious Loyalty

N = 39

Teen Loyalty Type	Hierarchical	Traditional	Democratic	Peer	Open
Unshakables (Loyalists)	5 evangelical 1 mainline	2 evangelical 2 mainline	1 evangelical 1 mainline	2 evangelical	
Tentatives (Loyalists)	2 evangelical	4 Catholic 2 mainline	1 Catholic 3 mainline		1 mainline
Conditionals (Provisional Loyalists)		2 Catholic		1 evangelical	2 evangelical
Postponed (Unlikely Loyalists)		1 Catholic			2 Catholic 1 evangelical 1 mainline
Alienated (Unlikely Loyalist)			2 Catholic		
Totals	7 evangelical 1 mainline	7 Catholic 2 evangelical 4 mainline	3 Catholic 1 evangelical 4 mainline	3 evangelical	2 Catholic 3 evangelical 2 mainline

roles, and hierarchical authority taught by church leaders at Riverland Heights. Notable, however, is the fact that *only* just over 40 percent of the evangelical parents in my interview sample exhibited this style. Clearly other cultural perspectives were informing evangelicals in their parenting styles in addition to church teaching.[1]

A second style of parenting, a *traditional style*, has much in common with the hierarchical style. Both see "traditional family values" as a particular family structure and a bulwark against secular humanism. Both understand family roles to be differentiated along gender lines. Where traditional-style parents differ from hierarchical-style parents is in their decision-making patterns. Fathers and mothers said they share equally the responsibility for making family decisions, and they aim to reach agreement between themselves about rules for their teens. They also more readily dispensed with the rules when teens demonstrated their trustworthiness to act responsibly without regulation. Traditional-style parents viewed children as unequal with parents; yet with maturity demonstrated over time, this inequality can level out.

A traditional style of parenting characterized just over half the Catholic families, almost one-fourth of mainline Protestant families, and only 12 percent of the evangelical families. In three cases of traditional-style parents, one member of the couple was disappointed that the other did not wholeheartedly share her/his traditional views. Two wives, in particular, were disappointed that their husbands did not exercise their role as head of the family. They regretfully found themselves acting by default as "the spiritual leader."

Tight economic circumstances that make it necessary for both husband and wife to contribute to the family income prevent some couples from differentiating their roles as breadwinner/husband/father and home-maker/wife/mother. As one man joked, "I wish I could be a '50s dad. I want to throw my dirty laundry down the chute and find it clean and folded in my drawer."

A third type, the *democratic style* of parenting, rejects the political over-tones and structural definitions that hierarchical and traditional-style parents associate with the phrase "traditional family values." These parents define traditional family values as "having morality," and, specifically for them, having Christian moral values. For these parents, roles are not determined by gender. If the wife/mother is a full-time homemaker, it is by her choice. Parental decision making affecting teens involves negotiation with the teen. Sometimes these families even draw up written "contracts" that specify understandings about the use of the car, who can ride as passengers, and the circumstances under which car privileges would be revoked. Democratic-style parents see children as gradually growing equal with parents as they demonstrate maturity. In some cases no formal rules remained in the family, because the teen's maturity made them unnecessary. The democratic parenting style characterized one-third of the mainline Protestants, one-fourth of the Catholics, and just 6 percent of the evangelicals.

A *peer style* of parenting characterized a small, distinct segment of the interview sample. There were three families comprised of mothers who were divorced in their late teens and left to rear their infant sons without the involvement of the fathers. In each case, the mother returned to the home of her parents, relying heavily on them for guidance and material support until she could attain the education and income to establish an independent home for herself and her son. Mother and teenage son act as near-equal parties in decision making, especially as trust is earned by the teen (which it was in all three cases in my sample). Near equality between parent and child is the lived reality.[2]

Not all single parents exhibit peer-style parenting. Some single parents do not have the support of their own parents, and their parenting becomes chaotic. Others remarry quickly, and their parenting styles are diverse. Others are widowed or divorced when their children are older, after they are already established in one of the other parenting styles.

All three of the peer-style families I interviewed were evangelical. I attribute no significance to that coincidence except to note that the evangelical tendency to preserve family structure goes along with the strong support that the grandparents gave these young mothers, which enabled them to establish a measure of stability and structure in the family. All three of the teenage sons reared in this style displayed an extreme seriousness about their responsibilities and future plans, one that exceeded that of most other teens in my study. Their precocious adulthood appears to be linked to the circumstances of their upbringing, which required them to take responsibility early in life. One of the three teens, the only one whose mother eventually remarried, seemed slightly less burdened by adult concerns than the other two boys.

Nearly 18 percent of the parents in my sample were either unable or unwilling to establish structures and rules in their families. This fifth type, the *open style* of parenting,[3] equally characterized Catholics, evangelicals, and mainline Protestants in my sample. A few open-style parents defined "traditional family values" and gender roles in the same way as hierarchical and traditional-style parents, but they were not able to realize these ideals in their own families. What open-style parents shared most in common that distinguished them from other parents' styles was a random pattern of family decision making. Clear patterns of who made the decisions that affected the teen were not established. When these parents did try to set rules for teens, they said they had difficulty getting teens to adhere to them. They also struggled with implementing consequences for rule breaking. In this style, parent and child were equal by default, because the parents were de facto permissive.

In most cases, the open-style parents were too distracted by their personal problems (such as being divorced, suffering from poor health, and/or having financial difficulties) to give sustained attention to their parenting role. Teens growing up in these households sometimes expressed the wish that their parents showed more concern for them. These teens were those who most often exhibited at-risk behaviors, such as drug use, gang membership, and sexual activity. Teens in these families spent the least amount of time in their homes.

As one might expect, there is a correlation between parenting styles and teen religious loyalty. Of those teens who predicted they would be active in the church after they leave home, only one had parents who exhibited the open style. The clear majority of teens who expect to stay "churched" had parents who used the hierarchical, traditional, democratic, and peer styles, with the largest group coming from the traditional style. (See table 20 in Appendix Q.)

As important as is the correlation between parenting style and teen religious loyalty, there are other factors that count even more. These are: a warm family climate, a parent/teen social network, a religion-infused family culture, and parents belonging to the same church. These variables correlate even more significantly with teen religious loyalty than the four demographic family variables and the parenting style variable. (See table 23 in Appendix Q.)

Parent/Teen Social Network

Along with parenting style, having a parent/teen social network helps hold teens in their religious tradition. The presence of a parent/teen social network in the family was determined by the teen's answer to the question "Do your parents know your friends and your friends' parents?" If they indicated that they knew more than one or two parents of their teen's current friends, I judged that there was a parent/teen social network. I confirmed their responses by the parents' answers to a similar question.

Some research indicates that with changing configurations of work and family, there is less of a parent/teen social network available to adolescents than there was thirty years ago. Mothers and fathers are less likely to know the parents of their children's friends than they used to be.[4] "Parents used to rely heavily on each other for answers, trading bits of strategy and inspiration over cups of coffee."[5] The change in social infrastructure over the last thirty years is especially dramatic in the suburbs.[6] Parents do not find the help they used to in church, school, media, and neighbors. The ecology of family supports has declined.[7] The family itself is more porous as a social institution. The connections among biologically related family members is less binding; loosely related individuals such as stepparents and adopted aunts are tenuously incorporated within permeable family boundaries.[8]

Some parents in my sample made more of an effort than others to know the parents of their teens' friends. One Catholic mother planned social occasions with other parents around their teens' activities. She invited parents to come to her house before the prom for a photographing session of their teens dressed in their prom-night finery. After the teens left for the prom, the parents went out for pizza at their teens' hangout. "Do you suppose we could drive over and peek in?" they joked. This mother also arranged an informal meeting with other parents to discuss plans for their teens' spring-break trip. Knowing many of them already from church and Catholic school functions, they bolstered one another in their expectations of appropriate behavior and limits that parents should set. The parent/teen social network they built allowed them to reinforce in their teens the religious values they shared.

The nature of a parent/teen social network differs by religious tradition because of the different institutional configurations associated with each tradition, and because of the different sizes of churches. For Catholics, the network of parochial schools across the city yields thick webs of relationships that proliferate widely. A significant group of teens in my sample bonded in the parish grade school, and they continue the friendships through the church youth group even though they now attend six different high schools.

When Jason Grant, a marginal member of the youth group, died in a car accident, hundreds of teens, parents, and school personnel gathered at his funeral to mourn. Even Alex O'Day, who attended a different high school, took the school day off to attend the service held at a neighboring Catholic parish. I was surprised to notice that Alex, an agnostic, took his place in the long line up to the altar to receive the sacrament. He could have discreetly remained in the pew, as a few people did. With his friends, his friends' parents, and his teachers gathered in this moving communal ritual, he fell into line, doing what was expected by his community. His web of relationships forged across the network of Catholic churches and parochial schools held him in his tradition, if only for an hour.

Among the evangelicals I interviewed, the nature of parent/teen social networks holding teens in the church is slightly different because of the enormous size of Riverland Heights. Parents of teens attending church youth activities tend not to know the parents of their teens' friends, even though they go to the same church. During the middle school years, when parents were needed to run car pools and chaperone events, some parents got acquainted. In the high school years, however, parents are unlikely to meet their children's friends' parents in a megachurch. They might know their teen's best friends' parents. They might know some parents in the church who also have children in the same school. Megachurch teens, however, are unlikely to have a parent/teen social network as it is usually defined, with their parents having face-to-face knowledge of their teens' friends' parents. Instead, megachurch teens tend to have a more general sense that a lot of people in their lives go to their church, even if their families do not know each other. The web of relationships may not be as thick as that of the Catholic network, and it may not integrate the parental relationship into it, but it reaches out farther to encompass many more people who interact with teens in different segments of their lives as teachers, school principals, coaches, employers, and community leaders. The sheer proliferation in the city of eleven thousand people affiliated with Riverland Heights increases the chances that teens will run into Riverland Heights people in various contexts, and connect with them in their evangelical beliefs and practices, even if there is no connection with the parents.

Methodist teens were part of a smaller church, but one that afforded them a tighter parent/teen social network. At First United Methodist, each teen (active or not) is known personally by the choir directors. The director of Christian education also remembers them coming up through the confirmation program in seventh grade. Teens are known individually and as part of their families. The web of relationships that holds them in the church tends to be less age-segmented than it is for the Catholic and evangelical teens. Church youth activities are not as segregated from the general activities of the church, especially in comparison to those held at Riverland Heights, where teens meet on a separate church campus a quarter of a mile away from the "big church" campus.

Methodist teens often had important friendships with younger teens in the choir and youth group. They also named other teens' parents as those who represented to them a model of mature Christian faith. In this church they had opportunities to get to know who-was-related-to-whom through different churchwide activities. For example, Graham was asked by one of his friend's parents to have a talk with their middle-school-age son about the dangers of drugs after they caught him with marijuana in his room. A parent/teen social network is an important resource for parents as well as teens.

Climate

A youth leader at the megachurch tipped me off to the importance of family climate when she once complained, "Some families are so cold."[9] Critical to fostering teen cooperation with parents' values is the emotional climate parents maintain in the home. Having a warm climate engenders teen acceptance of parental views affirming education, hard work, wholesome lifestyle, and other values, including loyalty to a religious tradition.[10]

A negotiation of independence and togetherness characterizes the relationship between parents and fifteen- to nineteen-year-olds. Adolescents may seek independence from the parent-child bond in order to interact with an ever-widening radius of individuals and institutions, but they generally do not abandon the relationship.[11]

By the time teens reach their senior year, it is nearly impossible for parents to impose their will on their children. By then, most children have grown to their adult height. Parents are speaking with their children eye to eye, or in some cases looking up to them. With the older teens' ability to drive, and with approximately 80 percent of them having a car at their disposal, they have freedom to come and go—especially to go.[12] Many earn money in part-time jobs and experience the freedom that purchasing power brings.[13] The only leverage over teens remaining for most parents is their willingness to pay or to help pay for college, and most would not withhold that from their teens to control their behavior. If parents want to exercise control of a high school senior, generally they can do that only through persuasion. That is facilitated by building a warm relationship between the teen and parent.

In particular, by the senior year parents can no longer force their teens to attend church.[14] Having a warm climate in the home, in which teens want to please their parents, motivates teens to fulfill their parents' goals for them, including their religious ones. The youth group leader at Transfiguration often thanks the parents with humor, "Thank you for not nagging your teenagers about picking up their rooms. I know their rooms are a mess." She considers parents invaluable as they use what positive emotional energy there is in the family to encourage their teens to attend youth group instead of dissipating it through arguments about doing unessential household chores.

Same-Church Families

Parents belonging to the same church is the third-highest factor associated with teen religious loyalty. When a teen is reared in a single religious tradition, with no dissonance generated from a parent who either belongs to another church or does not belong to a church at all, the teen tends to have a greater sense of belonging to his or her church. When no other option is endorsed by a figure as powerful as a parent, the teen more strongly identifies with the single tradition of the family. One father I met, who was disaffected from his Baptist upbringing and did not belong to any church, feared that his negative views about religion would be transmitted to his children. He avoided discussing religion with them out of respect for his Catholic wife. Despite his efforts, not one of the three teenage and young adult children was active in the church at the time I met this family. His silent nonbelonging communicated a powerful message to his children.

Usually parents who belong to different churches opt to rear the child in one parent's tradition. For the O'Days, it was Phil's Catholic faith. For the Marlboros, it was Judy's evangelical church—that is, until they decided to send Parker to a Catholic high school. There were some other parents, however, who opted to rear their children in two traditions. Jessica's parents are an example of those who opted for the second alternative. Jessica's mother, a Methodist, took classes to learn about her husband's Catholic beliefs so she could take charge of rearing their four children in both traditions. Because Catholicism is stricter about membership and more exclusive in its sacraments, Jessica's mother ensured that her children "made all the sacraments" through confirmation in the stricter tradition. She reasoned that if any of them later decided to marry a Catholic, there would be fewer obstacles for them to overcome. At the time of my research, Jessica was more active in the Methodist church than in the Catholic church. She had more friends from her public high school who were active in the choir and youth group at First United Methodist. Jessica intends to be active in a church after she leaves home, but there is some tentativeness about it. She is a loyalist, but she is keeping her options open about which tradition she will choose. She says her choice of a church will depend on "what is out there" near the college she attends, and on what religion her future husband wants to choose.

Religion in the Home

Another family factor, the culture of a family, is an even more difficult variable to measure. The culture of a family has a density or thickness built from shared symbols, rituals, and practices. It also can have a quality of religiousness depending on the type of symbols, rituals, and practices that the family chooses.[15]

I discovered that some families are inventive and intentional in symbolizing important events and values that have meaning for the family, such as the Watsons, who symbolized the loss of their infant by a vase of daisies. On the whole, there were very few artifacts in the homes that I observed that had obvious religious symbolism, like the plaque with a Bible verse in the Watson home. Likewise, few families considered any of their traditions, rituals, or practices to be religious per se. Explicitly religious rituals such as the lighting of Advent wreath candles, and practices such as reading Bible stories, may have been a part of their family life when the children were young, but much of it had petered out as the teen got older, even in the more religious families.[16] The family religious practice that persisted most often into the late teen years was that of saying grace before the evening meal.

Saying grace, having meals together, and weekly church attendance are three behaviors that tend to go together in families. If a family still prays together, it is usually at mealtime. Yet only eighteen (or nearly 44 percent) of the families in my interview sample eat dinner together three times a week or more. When families do eat together, this associates with weekly worship attendance. A high percentage of those eighteen families, 89 percent, have a teen who attends worship every week. One family gets its son to attend church by establishing the ritual of eating out after the 11:00 A.M. service. He will go because he enjoys the meal afterward.

Mitch's family, mentioned above, had one of the thicker religious cultures of any family I interviewed or observed. "Saturation in the things of the Lord" became so natural to his parents, there were times they were not even aware that their activities fit into their strategy. For example, the parents mentioned in their interview that they had just held their annual New Year's Eve party, and both their sons had attended with their girlfriends. The boys had planned to go out to other parties, but they had gotten swept up in the fun of the parents' preparations, and ended up staying. Without consciously teaching their sons—in this instance, anyway—that church people can have fun and that parties without alcohol can be enjoyable, Mitch's parents incorporated their sons and their girlfriends into their evangelical culture.

My research suggests that the more a family brings religion into the home through symbols, rituals, and practice, the more likely is the teen to show religious loyalty. In fact, this factor ranks high in the statistics. (See table 12.)

Weekly Church Attendance

The final factor, parents' weekly church attendance, also exhibited a high correlation with teen religious loyalty. (See table 12.) If parents living in the teen's household both attended church weekly, teens tended to predict that they would be active in the church after they left home. If just one of the parents attended less than weekly, teen religious loyalty plummeted.

Why is parental church attendance so influential to teens? Part of the answer is sheer logistics. Before the age of sixteen and a half, when Kentucky teens get their driver's licenses, they are dependent on their parents to take them to church. In suburban Louisville, few people live close enough to their church to walk. Taking public transportation to church is not feasible either. As long as a child is driver-dependent, a child cannot be more regular in church attendance than his or her parents. Occasionally grandparents take the child to church with them, but that is the exception. In almost all cases in my interview sample, it was the parents who were responsible for getting children to church before they were old enough to drive. If parents tapered off in attending church while their children were still driver-dependent, their children's link with the church was weakened as well.

Even after teens are old enough to drive to church themselves, parental nonattendance still has a negative effect on teen church attendance. Parents set an example, and parental church attendance patterns were mirrored by their teens. (See table 25 in Appendix Q.) There were no cases in my interview sample of a teen attending church when neither parent did. However, more than 19 percent of older teens were more active in the church than their parents when participation in youth group and other church activities were considered. If parental church attendance patterns differed, the teen usually mirrored the pattern of the less active parent.

One of the critical things parents do that is associated with teen religious loyalty is to choose a church that is attractive not only to their teen, but also to themselves. If they want their child to attend, they must be willing to attend themselves. That is what the O'Days failed to take seriously enough—the impact of their own dissatisfaction with the worship at their parish that made it a chore for them to continue attending after their children graduated from the parish school. When they stopped going, their driver-dependent children had no choice but to stop as well. Later, when as older teens they could drive, they perpetuated the pattern of nonattendance that they learned from their parents.[17]

"In Our Family, We Attend Church"

The parents' regular attendance at church becomes even more influential when the entire family is expected to go along. Indeed, if regular and required family attendance at church is counted as an eleventh factor, it assumes the number-one correlation to teen religious loyalty. (See table

12.) Over half the families in my interview sample maintained a rule—"In our family, we attend church"—and all but one of the teens from these families indicated the intention to stay connected to church. (See table 26 in Appendix Q.)

"I'm glad we stuck to the grind of, you know, our family goes to church every Sunday . . . ," said Mitch's mother. "The consistency pays off."

The best results were from families where church attendance is considered a family activity from which no immediate family member is exempt. In families where church attendance is left to each individual as a matter of choice, either because parents prefer this or because they feel unable to enforce more regular attendance, teens tend to drift away in later years. They do not seem to have the desire and/or maturity to continue with their commitment to the church if their parents do not help them. Brittany's story illustrates how this typically happens.

Brittany's parents were regular attenders at First United Methodist during the years she and her older brother were in elementary school and junior high. Brittany went through the confirmation program in seventh grade and chose to profess her faith. Never having been baptized as an infant, she was the only one in her confirmation class also to be baptized during the confirmation ceremony. Brittany said she felt unpressured as she made the choice to be baptized and confirmed. Her older brother had already set the family precedent of not joining.

Brittany said that after she was confirmed, her parents became less active in the church. They stopped going every Sunday, and gradually stopped going at all unless Brittany suggested it. At the time I met Brittany, their attendance had evolved into the following pattern: Brittany would suggest to her mother the night before that they go to church, and the two of them would go alone, roughly once a month.

Another key piece in this story is what happened to Brittany's youth group participation. Brittany was the only teen in her church who attended her elite private high school. She found that after confirmation she got busier at her school with field hockey and drama, and it became harder for her to make the time to come to youth group. She also felt that her peers at her church were cliquish. The majority attended one particular high school, and it took a lot of effort for her to feel included when she did attend youth group. After a few months, she stopped going altogether.

Table 12. Eleven Family Variables by Teen Religious Loyalty

	Family Attender	Parents Attend Church Weekly	Religious Family Culture	Parents Belong to Same Church	Warm Family Climate	Parent/ Teen Social Network	Non-permissive Parent Style	Parents Same Religious Background	Higher Income	Intact Family Structure of Origin	Close to Parents' Family
Loyalist	95%	92%	83%	81%	80%	78%	78%	87%	72%	71%	71%
Provisional Loyalist	5%	8%	13%	10%	13%	11%	9%	8.7%	10%	12%	9%
Unlikely Loyalist	0%	0%	3%	10%	7%	11%	13%	4.3%	17%	18%	20%
Totals	100%	100%	99% *	101% *	100%	100%	100%	100.%	99% *	101% *	100%

*Total exceeds or falls short of 100 percent due to rounding.

When I met Brittany near the end of her senior year, she struck me as an unhappy girl. On the positive side, she was an accomplished musician and athlete. She was the lead in the play at her school in her senior year. She had plans in place to attend college the following year. These positives, however, did not counterbalance her heavy worries about her family. Her father's mental illness complicated by alcoholism precipitated an early retirement from his medical practice on disability. Her parents' marriage was falling apart. Brittany often cried in her room alone at night. She also worried that she did not know what she wanted to do with her life. She felt unmotivated, and lately she and her friends got drunk on the weekends for something to do.

I asked her, "Do you get a sense that God might have a vocation for you?" She asked me what I meant. I reminded her of her athletic, musical, and dramatic talents, and of her interest in children. I asked if she ever thought God gave her those talents, interests, and the privilege of a good education for a reason—to have a part in what God was doing in the world. Brittany's face brightened up at that idea. She said that it had never occurred to her. "My friends and I never talk about God, but I'd like to know more about how to understand vocation. I think that's something I really need in my life."

What was happening with Brittany? She hungered to be a part of something bigger—bigger than herself and a life of maximizing her personal self-interest. She wanted her life to have a larger meaning and direction from God. She also felt very alone in coping with her family problems, even though she had a therapist with whom she counseled. Brittany said that she usually prayed by herself at night, but did not expect God to answer prayer. "God just listens," she said, "God doesn't answer."

Brittany was left stranded after she was confirmed in the church. She needed her parents to continue coming to church and to encourage her to go to youth group. She wanted to stay connected to her church, but she needed help to get past the hard parts, like the times when she felt excluded in youth group. Her parents, because of their problems, could not offer that help to her. Teens, in and of themselves, cannot be expected to have the inner strength to keep participating in church on their own unless their parents urge them to do so. After young teens are confirmed and/or baptized and become active members of the church, they still are not mature enough to be committed to their community of faith. If they are going to continue in their religious tradition in the late teen years, they benefit from the help of their parents or other adults who are close to them.[18] They need their parents to choose regular religious participation for the family in order to help them make the same choice for themselves as an emerging adult.

At the same time, there needs to be some degree of flexibility. Maintaining a rule that "in our family, we attend church" was experienced by most teens in family-attender families as a supportive push rather than as a dreaded requirement. Within the general rule there was a wide variation in how it was interpreted by different families. One evangelical boy was allowed to skip the worship service as long as he attended Sunday school. Another girl could choose either her mother's Methodist church or her father's Catholic mass. Another boy opted to join a different Methodist church from his parents', one that his high school friends attended. He drove to his church alone every week.

Teens found the rule requiring weekly church attendance more acceptable when there was allowance for some kind of choice. Among Catholic teens especially, there was a lot of "church hopping" on the weekends. On any given weekend, one can find teens from Transfiguration's parish attending different masses all over the city. Transfiguration teens said they sought out alternatives at other churches because the masses were shorter, the pews were less uncomfortable, the priest was more appealing to them, and/or the time of mass better suited their schedule.

There were also variations in what "attending church as a family" means. For some, it means families should sit together. In other families, teens and parents were dispersed around the sanctuary. A point of hot contention between one evangelical teen and her parents was their requirement that she sit with her family instead of with her friends. Other teens reported that they enjoyed churchgoing in part because they sat with their families. They viewed churchgoing as one of the things they liked doing as a family.[19]

Sometimes family members take separate cars to church to accommodate individual commitments to choir, Sunday school, and committee meetings before and after Sunday worship. Other families take multiple cars to church because they view church participation more individually, and family members hardly see each other during the time they are at church. In some families where teens are expected to go to church, no effort is made to coordinate family schedules to attend the same service together. One family of four reports that they drive four cars to church each Sunday. There is allowance for personal autonomy even when the family church attendance rule is maintained.

Of the twenty-two teens in my interview sample who are expected to attend church every week, 82 percent of them say they would attend each week anyway. As one teen affirmed, "Church is important to me because I see it as voluntary."[20] Another teen said,

> When I was little, I would say, "Oh, do I have to go to church today?" and my mom would say, "Get up" and "You have to go to church," and it was just something I did. . . . Now I want to go to church and I want to go to camp and I want to go on choir tour and it's because I want to. I think I understand more like why—why we do what we do in choir and why I have these friends at church.

Families who cultivate the collective understanding that "our family attends church" tend to produce teens who believe they should be there.

Maintaining a family church attendance rule is something that clusters naturally with the other ten family factors favoring religious loyalty mentioned above and in chapter 10. For example, for any family attendance rule to "work," the parents themselves must attend church weekly. Any such rule also must be supported by all parents in the household, since teens tend to mirror the attendance patterns of the less active parent (as mentioned above). Having a warm climate in the home engenders cooperation with the church attendance rule. When there is a parent/teen social network connecting family and church relationships, teens feel that they belong in the church, and all the more so when both of the teen's parents belong to the same church. Teens who see continuity between the culture of their home and their church already know the language, rhythms, dispositions, and values of their tradition. They eventually understand attending church as a practice with intrinsic value, not just as a requirement imposed from outside themselves. In the times when a teen's motivation flags, if their family has some structure, order, and accountability, the family can hold them to the discipline of attending church.

While the practice of maintaining a church attendance rule associates most with the six factors mentioned above, it also clusters with the four demographic family variables favoring teen religious loyalty. When teens lived in a parent's hometown, and especially when their parents came from the same hometown and same religious background, the extended family that gathered periodically, especially on religious holidays, reinforced the taken-for-grantedness of the religious tradition. I observed this most often in the Catholic teens in my sample because of the high concentration of Catholics in the Louisville area. Some Catholic teens' families had a relationship with the parish that extended over a generation, and that included several families of aunts, uncles, and cousins in the current generation.

The importance of other demographic variables, such as intact family structure and higher family income, were better understood in their absence. I observed several teens who experienced disruption in their church attendance because of their parents' divorce and shared custody arrangement. On alternate weekends Courtney was bounced between her mother's church, First United Methodist, and her father's church, Riverland Heights. She struggled to develop friendships at either church until finally she found a way to attend exclusively at First United Methodist. She told her father she was expected to sing in the choir there each Sunday, and he began to drop her off there on his way to Riverland Heights. He did not know that the high school choir sang only intermittently.

When there are fewer economic resources in the family, parents like the Rhodeses, who work long hours at low-wage jobs, are tempted to catch up on much-needed sleep on Sunday, their only day off. Lower- and middle-income families have fewer resources to spend on church ski trips and church camps, as much as churches try to keep all activities affordable. Having to miss church activities for any reason, including working at a part-time job, weakens the teen's church-based social network. If the teen participates in the full range of church youth activities, worship attendance tends to rise.

In summary, regular family church attendance appears to be the most significant of all the factors contributing to teen religious loyalty, yet it interacts with other family factors and depends on them for its effect. The high significance of regular family attendance suggests that parents still influence their children during the teen years by what they do. When parents hold youth in their church a little longer, through all the years of high school, teens tend to predict they will be active in the church even after they leave home.

Chapter Twelve

Parenting in Particular Religious Traditions

Before concluding my analysis of data related to the influence of parents on teen religious loyalty, some attention must be given to how particular religious traditions instill different styles and attitudes toward parenting through their distinctive beliefs and within the pieties of their particular traditions.

As noted earlier, the hierarchical style of parenting is prevalent among evangelicals, with over 41 percent of the evangelical parents in my interview sample manifesting that style. Even more so, the traditional style of parenting strongly associates with Catholics, with over 58 percent of Catholic parents exhibiting that style. Over half the mainline Protestant parents weigh in as either traditional or democratic, with over 36 percent of them in each of these two parenting styles.

In addition, parents within these traditions manifest different pieties and "temperaments"[1] that loosely correlate with three types historian Philip Greven identifies as rooted in seventeenth- and eighteenth-century American Protestantism: the evangelical, the genteel, and the moderate. Evangelical parents in my sample are like early American evangelicals in their hierarchical view of authority within the family and in their Calvinist emphasis on the view of the self as the source of sin. While few evangelicals in my modern-day sample would go so far as to affirm the dictum "Break their wills that you may save their souls," evangelicals do tend to view the child's willfulness as something that must be denied and regenerated. Catholic parents in my sample have much in common with the "genteel" type that Greven describes—those who tend to take a state of grace for granted and exhibit confidence that the church and sacraments suffice to ensure their personal salvation. Catholic parents tend to assume

184

that as they school their children in the sacramental life they will naturally grow in faith, becoming "good Catholics" and "good people" in society. Mainline Protestant parents in my sample are most like Greven's "moderates." They are "caught between the poles of duty and desire," preoccupied but not obsessed with morality, more interested in self-control than self-suppression.[2] Many mainline Protestant parents in my sample also noted the active role they took in nurturing faith in their children from a very young age.[3]

What did this look like in three cases I described in chapter 10? The Watson family illustrates how parents from the evangelical megachurch find the hierarchical style of parenting and Greven's "evangelical" temperament compatible with their religious tradition. The Watson parents are pleased that their daughter Brynne has been baptized as a believer and manifests a strong religious commitment. Her parents have worked hard to foster that in her through their gentle and sensitive exercise of parental authority. While they have succeeded with Brynne, they struggle more with her younger brother, who has "more horsepower." With him they fight to assert parental authority to enforce the structures, boundaries, and rules that will hold him within the fold until he makes the choice they hope he will make: to commit his life to Christ.

Andrea's family illustrates how the Catholic tradition tends to go along with a traditional style of parenting and a "genteel" temperament. Her father told the familiar story of how he "wandered" from the faith in his college years and came back to church when he met Andrea's mother because he realized that if he was going to date her he had to attend church. Andrea's parents hope that Andrea will do the same when she marries.

For Catholics, attending mass is a solemn obligation. It is a sacrament; it is participating in the mystical body of Christ. The distinctive religious goal of Catholic parents centers on teaching children to participate in the sacramental life. Like all the Catholic parents in my study, Andrea's parents steered their children toward the religious training that enabled them to make the sacraments of First Communion and confirmation. Even so, Andrea's parents have suspended the rule about attending mass in Andrea's last year of high school with the hope that easing up on it will help her to view it as less onerous. Attending mass is Andrea's choice as long as she continues to attend youth group. Their traditional style of parenting seeks to bend the will rather than break it.

Like other traditional-style parents, they are willing to dispense with rules if they think they can win the voluntary cooperation of their teen by other means. They know that Andrea is influenced by their example.[4] Not only are they regular mass attenders, Andrea's father started the social justice committee at the parish, which resettled a Somalian refugee family and participates in various ecumenical community ministries like Habitat for Humanity. Even if now Andrea exhibits only tentative religious loyalty and chooses not to attend mass, Andrea's parents say that she is "not gone from faith. She's practicing it in her way." They see life as "a journey." They exhibit the "genteel" assumption that in time Andrea's journey will take her back "to organized religion," especially when she marries. In the meantime they are comfortable with her values and integrity and her focused pursuit of high educational goals at a prestigious Catholic university leading to some kind of professional career.

Graham's Methodist parents exemplify the active style of religious nurture that characterizes Greven's "moderates." "What drives so much of the involvement of the kids [in the church] is the parents' getting involved," Graham's father explained. They have been very involved in church throughout Graham's childhood as copresidents of their Sunday school class, as officers on the church boards, and as volunteer leaders in important positions, for example, as chairman of the building campaign and as moderator of United Methodist Women. Even during the earliest years of Graham's life, Graham's father would arrange his business travel so that he would be home on Wednesday nights so the family could attend the weekly church dinner together.

Consistent with Greven's description of the "moderates," mainline Protestant parents expect their children to question their faith, even to rebel, as they become teens, and therefore they mold their children's religious experiences from the earliest years into patterns of piety that might endure. This assumption of the child's eventual independence and choice is also compatible with a democratic style of parenting that gives over to the teen ever greater freedom for self-regulation and treats teens as equals when they demonstrate maturity.

Graham's parents' style of religious nurture has produced an outcome that has exceeded their highest expectations. Graham's father calls it "reverse modeling." He and his wife say they are challenged by their son's good example of attending a rigorous weekly Bible study that is reading through the entire Bible over the course of a year. They speak with pride of Graham's service as class president and of his close friendships with classmates of different races, religions, and social classes. They support his plans to pursue a career as a high school teacher, even though the projected financial reward would be small compared to the $150,000 per year salary that his father earns as a business consultant.

Each of these three religious traditions—evangelical, Catholic, and mainline Protestant—resonates with particular parenting styles and temperaments. Within the congregations of each tradition, parents not only develop their own religious faith, but they are shaped themselves as parents to rear their children in particular ways.

So how do parents influence their teen's religious loyalty? *First, teens are influenced in the most lasting way by how their parents connected them (or not) to the church from a young age.* This was evident most in what the teens themselves said about the importance of having a "religious foundation" given to them from early childhood. While my research did not test this process in young children,[5] my data point to the power of early socialization in childhood to shape the lasting dispositions of how people relate to their religious tradition. If teens are given the symbols, stories, and practices to interpret their experiences as experiences of God, they move forward with a religious outlook in their lives.

The impact of early religious socialization, especially through parents in the home (the most important childhood environment), continues in a secondary way as teens choose their social networks in their high schools and in the wider community. Older teens may be disengaging from their families, but they expand their social networks from where their parents started them, from the matrix of their childhood relationships, and from the various institutions to which parents have steered them: their church, parochial school, public high school, or private school. When there is a moral and religious coherence among home, church, and school, there is more coherence in the social network of the teen. This coherence may be perpetuated by the teen's choices, even as actual face-to-face relations in the parent/teen network become looser. Teens from religious families tend to choose a religious social network; those from less religious families do so less often.[6]

Second, parents influence teens in what they believe and how they practice their faith by maintaining a church attendance rule even into the teen years. By doing so, they maintain the teen's link with the church. The family is too small an institution to bear the whole burden of the task of religious nurture. As influential as parents are, as important as religious practice in the home is, religious faith is taught, caught, and lived in powerful ways in congregations. Congregations, not families, are the basic unit of religious life.

The church and parochial school together with the family offer religious instruction and formation in Christian practices.[7] It has also been shown that parents themselves are shaped by the distinctive beliefs and patterns of piety of their congregations, which convey particular religious traditions. There is an interactive effect between the church and home as each shapes the teen's religious sensibility.

Since it is generally no longer possible to coerce teens to attend church by the time they are high school seniors, parents must persuade teens of the value of the "rule" about church attendance. They do this by setting an example of attending church, by fostering a warm family climate and a thick, religion-infused culture in the home, and by maximizing other family factors mentioned above. The "rule" works because it has been internalized more than because parents enforce it.

Third, parents influence teen religious loyalty by choosing carefully the church to which they will link the teen. A high percentage of parents (41 percent) switched churches during their child's growing-up years because of personal preference, not because of a change in residence. Church mattered so much to some parents that they went to the trouble of uprooting their family from their church rather than being dissatisfied and unmotivated to attend.[8] A church that offers corporate worship that is attractive both to parents and to teens tends to foster loyalty best. A church may have a vital youth program, and/or the teen may attend an effective religious school, but those involvements appear to be secondary in importance to the teen's engagement in the church's weekly gathering for worship.

Increased personal autonomy remains the thread running throughout this study, even in how parents nurture their teens in their religious traditions. Besides demonstrating readiness to switch church membership out of personal preference, parents exercised religious autonomy in an even more basic way. Most parents say they choose their faith more than receive it as a tradition that is passed down; they choose what to believe. Likewise, parents expect their teens to choose what they believe, to "claim" their faith tradition as their own. Many hope that their teen someday will marry within their faith so that their grown child would share the same faith with a spouse for the sake of mutual support in the marriage.

Modern teens are more like their baby boomer parents than different from them.[9] For both parents and teens today, church affiliation and participation have less to do with social background and family loyalty, and more to do with personal needs and individual choice. In the culture of the home, teens learn to make choices and to act on them—and they learn this from their parents.

The awareness and power of choice can be a positive force that enables teens to make a responsible religious commitment. When teens today receive significant support from parents and other adults, they may choose to become personally committed to religious beliefs and practices and find the "vibrant, growing, real relationship with Christ" that Anna Mae Watson described. Another mother's comment summarizes the positive outcome of such heightened personal autonomy that can result for the next generation:

> When I was my daughter's age, we didn't question things. I'm glad that her faith has been presented in a more meaningful, thorough way than what I had. . . . I really feel like she's embraced her faith instead of just, you know. Sometimes I feel we were just Catholics just because we were born that way, and we were brought up that way, and that's the way it was supposed to be. Now Catholics are brought up that way, and they also choose to claim it.

Choosing Faith across Generations

Since colonial times, Americans have tended to view religion as a matter of individual conviction and voluntary adherence. If Americans choose to be religious it is because they are free not to be.[1] While this has always been more characteristic of Protestants than Catholics, in recent decades individual autonomy in religion has escalated and decisively altered how Catholics view religion as well. The basic tension that exists between the givenness of one's religious community with its authoritative tradition and the freedom of the individual to choose what and how to believe has reached new heights for both Protestants and Catholics.[2]

Sheila Larson's articulation of her belief in "just my own little voice" was startling enough to many in 1985.[3] Today, however, a generation of teenagers has grown up knowing real people who are just like Sheila Larson. They live next door to "Sheila Larson" and see her mowing her grass on Easter morning. They baby-sit for her and discover that her children have not been taught who Moses is. Some know "Sheila Larson" as the nurse who comes to their high school to conduct an assembly before the prom and show them gory slides of what happens to teens who drink and drive. They also hear her advocating the practice of safe sex. Teens today grow up with authoritative adults in their communities who exemplify and teach teens to make choices "for themselves," without the knowledge or influence of moral and religious traditions. As Giddens expressed it, "The signposts of tradition [appear] . . . blank."[4]

190

Teens and the Power of Choice

The thread running through my study of the religious lives of church-related high school seniors is the heightened sense of personal autonomy that alters how teens today view their religious tradition. Teens experience an enlarged arena of voluntary choice and greater freedom from restraint in many areas, including religion. This is true even for the church-related teens in my study. In fact, they are a second generation of choosers.[5] Their cultural broadening did not occur in college, as it tended to for their baby boomer parents. It began in the crib. The implications of this escalation and expansion of individual choice for the religious lives of teens was evident in some of the following illustrations introduced in the earlier chapters of this study.

Megan is relied on by the youth minister at her Catholic parish as a leader. She volunteers to mentor eighth-graders on their confirmation retreat. Yet Megan asserts, "God, I'm not really religious. . . . Religion is just not a big part of my life."[6] Instead, Megan's life appears to be guided more by utilitarian individualist calculations of how to achieve career goals defined by the marketplace. *The church-reared teen's belief and allegiance to the religious tradition—even that of the ones most active in the church—cannot be assumed.*

"We're a very small, closed religious family that doesn't go to church," a father at the evangelical megachurch explained. His wife affirmed, "We're a nonpracticing religious family."[7] Even families listed on the rolls of a church may not rear their children in the church.[8] *Some church-affiliated teens are reared to view religion as a mode of individual self-expression and as a means to achieve one's own ends.*

Michelle is so convinced of the rightness of the Catholic view of the sanctity of life that she travels to Washington, D.C., as an advocate for the Right to Life organization. Michelle also says she dislikes doctrine and liturgy, and is more comfortable referring to God as "the Man in the Moon." She attends mass each week and also practices a "cleansing ceremony" of her own devising. Like many teens, Michelle makes substitutions for elements of her church life that she views as routinized—even essential elements of her tradition like liturgy.[9] *Adherence to a religious tradition may be selective and interwoven with elements appropriated from popular culture and other sources.*

Trey has been exposed to mainline Protestantism, Catholicism, and evangelicalism. He "has been sprinkled, taken First Communion, and been dunked." He is seen by others as exceptionally devout as he and a friend pray longer on their knees than most players on the football field during the pregame invocation. Trey does not know the Lord's Prayer or the basic stories of the Bible, however, since his family kept switching churches in their spurts of church attendance between longer stretches of nonattendance.[10] *The second generation of choosers tends to be shortchanged on religious socialization—i.e., exposure to the symbols, rituals, and practices of their religious tradition in ways that help the teens appropriate these things as part of their daily life.*

While these illustrations might suggest that the prospects for church-oriented religious belief and practice are dim, some other outcomes linked to heightened personal autonomy bode well for the vitality and persistence of religious traditions among this generation. Some of the following illustrations suggest how this is so.

As one mother put it, "Sometimes I feel like we were just Catholics because we were born that way. . . . Now Catholics are brought up that way, and they also choose to claim it."[11] Paul is a good example of one who comes back to his Catholic faith by choice. Having dabbled in drugs until the previous year, Paul was wooed by Angie into youth group and asked to revive the youth group rock band. He also deepened his religious commitment through the senior retreat at his Catholic high school. While Angie describes him as "still fragile," Paul affirms that the church is meaningful to him as never before because he has come to it himself.[12] *Teens today who embrace the religious tradition of their nurture do so more freely and less out of a sense of obligation.*

Even Rebecca, who was sheltered in a Christian subculture because she was home-schooled, asserts that she is not a Christian because she was brought up that way. She says believing is her choice.[13] Beth describes how her parents used to make her attend church and how she now comes because she wants to.[14] *The teens who were most heavily socialized in their tradition and grew up with the understanding "in our family we attend church" are also the ones who say emphatically that their church participation is something they would choose even if it were not a family requirement.*

Graham is a deeply committed Christian and attends a weekly Bible study. He also storms out of Christian bookstores that sell books describing Muslims and Hindus as heathens.[15] Ian finds greater serenity in the meditation practices of Zen Buddhism than he does in the Methodist tradition of his upbringing. He has strong views favoring the importance of religion, whatever religion a person chooses. He says he wishes his peers at his high school would get more serious about understanding religion and about putting it into practice.[16] While religious pluralism posed a difficult problem for many youth, challenging their view of the absolute and universal truth of their religion, increased pluralism also prompted lively and respectful conversation about religious differences. *With greater religious pluralism and tolerance for diverse religious expression has come increased respect for religion as a source of personal meaning among teens.*

Teens described how they felt comfortable enacting their religious faith in public settings. While they did not always link their volunteer service to "religious" motivations, many took it for granted that they should give some time to helping others in community centers, nursing homes, and inner-city schools. When they introduced their religious views into high school classroom discussions, their views were honored when they were presented intelligently.[17] Religious clubs on high school campuses often had more members than any other student organization. This was true at Grinstead High School, for example, where Fellowship of Christian Athletes was the largest club on campus.[18] *For teens today, acting on and speaking about religion is not a taboo.*

In addition to the heightened sense of personal choice, some related structural changes in American society contribute to an altered religious climate for these teens. As noted above, one of the biggest changes that this generation experiences in comparison to the baby boomer generation is the decreased consistency and intensity of their religious socialization. While part of this can be attributed to parents who exercise their option to switch churches or to not attend church at all, another part can be linked to the increased levels of family restructuring. Today's youth are more often reared in single-parent families than were their baby boomer parents.[19] Courtney's unhappy experience of being shuttled back and forth between the evangelical megachurch of her father and the Methodist church of her mother is a mild example of the disruption in religious socialization attributable to divorce.[20] Many teens did not attend church at all when their parents ended their marriage. Coping with the strain of solo parenting is all that some can bear. Many single parents say they are unable to take on the added challenge of cajoling a teen to attend church.

Second, the nature of community is radically altered for this generation. More than ever before, they do not live in a unitary society with overlapping social relationships.[21] Thirty years ago, the adults in teens' lives, especially their parents, tended to know one another and exchange ideas on parenting strategies, religion, and other shared values.

Today, parent/teen social networks are looser. Thick webs of relationships yielded by multiplex relations—the overlapping face-to-face relationships among key people in the teen's life—no longer tie home, school, and church into a coherent moral and religious community. There are fewer adults who might mentor teens in Christian faith across institutional settings. C.J., who lives in three distinct social worlds of his church, school, and 4-H Club, typifies this change in how teens experience their social lives as segmented or even as fragmented.[22]

Without parent/teen social networks linking relationships across settings, some teens develop modal personalities that shift according to the social world in which they find themselves at the moment. Whitney was able to switch off her religious identity in a nonreligious context. She switched it back on for church choir rehearsal.[23] There was no social group that overlapped her institutional spheres to keep her accountable to her religious self in a nonreligous setting. Her sense of being a Christian became a secondary identity, something she could shrug off in certain contexts.

Third, hyped consumerism and the pervasive influence of commercial advertising have gradually changed the environment in which teens have grown up since World War II. More than ever before, teens are viewed as a market, a viable consumer group with opinions, tastes, and buying habits worth cultivating for the billions of dollars that teens have at their disposal. Teens also are courted as a cheap labor force by fast-food restaurants, retailers, and parents of young children seeking child care. While some teens' own parents actively counter these overtures, other teens are left open to exploitation by the market. Their moral and religious formation tends to be eclipsed by a strongly promoted ideal of the self as an expressive consumer. Irresistible cues beckon them to purchase goods and earn spending money. The value of personal choice is underscored as consumer choice.

Congregations Adapting to a Culture of Choice

Not only has the religious sensibility of teens changed in this milieu, religious institutions have to negotiate this climate of heightened religious autonomy. Part of why these particular congregations—Transfiguration (Catholic), Riverland Heights (evangelical Protestant), and First United Methodist (mainline Protestant)—attracted large numbers of teens to their worship and programs was because they did adapt to the new climate of personal choice. *Each of these three traditions adapted in its own way to large societal change and to the culture of choice, and that is why they are effective.*

Transfiguration offered Catholic teens a way to participate in institutional religious life apart from the established activities and worship style of the main congregation. The segmentation of the teenagers from the congregation as "a youth group"[24] gave the teens greater autonomy to shape their own programming, their own worship, their own service projects, and their own physical space. The youth minister herself encouraged teens to take ownership of their group. She focused her efforts on teaching leadership skills to younger teens, so that by the time they were seniors they were capable of running the youth group. At Transfiguration, the high school seniors were the leaders.

The personalistic style of youth ministry at Transfiguration appealed to the teens' sense of personal autonomy. Teens became known as individuals. They were celebrated for the talents they offered the group. They also were mourned when they died. As Angie said, her goal was to offer teens a way to see their church as "relational."[25] She wanted to "touch their hearts" in ways that complemented the "head learning" of their Catholic schooling. Transfiguration achieved personalism in the intimacy of their group. Youth group offered thick, tight affective bonds to offset the thinness and looseness that increasingly characterizes teens' social networks.

Riverland Heights offered evangelical teens a wide array of options compatible with a culture of choice. At the megachurch teens could focus on their particular interests, such as music, sports, drama, audiovisual technology, Bible study, small groups, large-scale worship, mission trips, spring break trips, and camps. Their program offered teens the option to stay at the entry level with its low commitment and anonymity or to make progressively higher commitments through graduated levels of involvement. There was a close institutional similarity between the megachurch with choices and tracks and the other social institutions in suburban/metropolitan teens' lives, such as the shopping mall with its many consumer options and the large high school with its specialized educational/vocational tracks.

Additionally, the megachurch offered a large plausibility structure: it shored up belief because of its sheer size. As Jeff, who belongs to a small fundamentalist church, explains why he attends the midweek Vision meetings at Riverland Heights: "I just like being with so many Christian kids."[26] It is hard not to believe when you are surrounded by four hundred teens who appear to be persuaded.

The evangelical megachurch deemphasizes institutional elements of church life and the routinized religious symbols and rites that many teens (and adults) find unappealing. For example, they do not take time in the worship service to install church officers. Instead of singing traditional hymns accompanied by the organ, the music at Riverland Heights sounds like what teens listen to on the radio. The worship leaders do not speak about "sin"; instead the youth minister prays in the language of everyday life, "God, you must laugh when you see how stupid we are. . . ."

The megachurch uses the looseness of teens' social connections and the porousness of their community to their advantage. At the entry level, the loose weave of relationships at Riverland Heights offers plenty of openings for newcomers. The boundaries are exceptionally permeable. It feels all right to be a stranger in the hallways of the church or a newcomer in a Bible study—there are always so many. Over time, however, the looseness proves to be a disadvantage as the novelty wears off, and older teens tend to fall away. Only the proportionally few older teens who move on to high commitment small groups form the tight bonds that hold them in.

The mainline Protestant church in my sample keenly felt the threat of competition posed by the rapid growth of Riverland Heights. Having lost many of the evangelical-leaning families to Riverland Heights, First United Methodist was galvanized to "find their niche," and "to be ourselves."[27] They chose not to imitate the contemporary style of music of Riverland Heights. Instead, they excelled at traditional church music and incorporated some contemporary pieces that met the standard for "quality." They also dedicated a large percentage of their resources—an amount in their budget out of proportion to the size of the teen population in their church—to the hiring of staff to run the junior high and senior high youth programs, to adding dedicated space for the youth, and to underwriting part of the costs of the ski trips and other activities of the youth ministry. Finding a youth minister with the right qualities[28] was also competitive. The pool of candidates for this very difficult and poorly compensated job is small. It also proved difficult to keep a youth minister after one was painstakingly secured.

First United Methodist adapted to this competitive religious environment by doing especially well what mainline Protestants do. In worship, they selected the best of the aesthetically rich and emotionally accessible music of their Methodist tradition and augmented it with equally fine new music. In Sunday school, they affirmed the intellectual capacities of teens, assuming their ability to reason, criticize, see both sides of an argument, and appreciate ambiguity. In church life, they integrated teens into their democratic style of community life and decision making. On mission trips, they introduced teens to "their neighbors" in need. For a proportionally smaller number of teens, the mainline Protestant tradition offers a depth and complexity that has appeal. In a culture of choice, this is the preference of some teens, especially those who have been reared to appreciate its aesthetic style and historical tradition.

First United Methodist also offered teens a certain kind of tightness in its social network that held them in its community in a particular way. It fostered an intergenerational social network that assisted teens, parents, and different generations of families to know one another. Instead of segmenting teens and focusing on peer networks, they incorporated teens into the whole life of the church, especially as they valued teens' music leadership in corporate worship.

The thread of heightened personal autonomy was not something I set out to find as I investigated the religious lives of high school seniors and their religious congregations. It appeared in regular ways often enough, however, to get my attention as I investigated the stated themes of my research: religious identity and religious loyalty. I turn next to these two themes, summarizing the findings that resulted from the questions I brought to my research.

Religious Identity

The research questions that related to religious identity were as follows. What are the different ways that teens hold their religious beliefs and adhere to their religious tradition when they do? Specifically, are they as "posttraditional" as Anthony Giddens posits, no longer shaped in their identities by the traditions of society—and specifically the religious traditions of their churches? *What I found is that religious traditions still function with authority to shape basic elements of teens' identities.* Teens do not simply accept or reject their religious tradition, however. Because they do exercise choice and action in religious life, they exhibit identities that are more varied and complex than expected. I discovered seven distinct styles of how teens in my sample shaped their sense of who they are in relation to their religious tradition: conventional, classic, reclaimer, marginalizer, customizer, rejecter, and the lost. I based these categories on how teens viewed the authority of their religious tradition and on how much certainty they expressed about their religious belief. (See figs. 6 and 7.)

Within the seven religious identity styles that resulted, I sought to understand how the religious tradition shaped particular elements of the teens' self-identity: intimacy, bodily presentation, ontological security, rites of passage to adulthood, and the resolution of moral dilemmas. (See table 7.) I took these five elements from Giddens's analysis of the posttraditional self so I could assess how posttraditional the teens in my sample might be.

I found that while some teens conceive of self-identity as a "reflexive project," as Giddens describes—as having a sense of self that is sustained by coherent yet continually revised biographical narratives in a context of multiple choice, filtered through abstract systems—the signposts of tradition are not blank for most church-related teens in my sample. The tradition guides them in powerful ways to shape a distinct sense of self as Christian. A Christian identity is a "reflexive project" in itself. Teens in my sample freely and constantly rewrote their biographies in a constitutive relationship with God and their communities.

Religious Loyalty

I focused on a second theme that organized the questions of my research, religious loyalty. It was operationalized as a dependent variable by asking teens if they intended to be active in the church after they left home. From their responses I developed a fivefold typology that allowed me to distinguish different types of religious loyalty that I named: unshakable, tentatively yes, conditional, postponed, and alienated. (See table 4.) As expected, this fivefold typology overlaps somewhat with the sevenfold typology of religious identity. Both religious identity and religious loyalty measure the teens' stance toward their religious tradition. Religious identity is a larger category, however; it includes religious stances unrelated to the institutional church.

The questions I brought to the research about religious loyalty were as follows: Given that people today, especially teens, are less attracted to institutional expressions of religious belief and practice, how are the congregations that are attracting large numbers of teens accomplishing that? And if they are attracting large numbers of teens, are they also securing their religious commitment to a church-oriented sense of faith rooted in the religious tradition? And if so, how are they securing religious commitment?

Briefly, my analysis suggests the following about religious loyalty. *Congregations that attract large numbers of youth do so by offering teens a sense of belonging that ties them into the fellowship of their church, a sense of the comprehensive meaning of the whole of life that is based in religious truth, and opportunities to develop various competencies that assist them as they cross the threshold into adult roles and institutions.* It is these fundamental conditions of human nature—belonging, believing, and achieving competence—that are addressed when the teen's attention is "grabbed"[29] by a religious institution. Other factors are secondary, such as the material resources of the congregation, adult leaders with continuity and certain personal qualities, facilities dedicated to youth, the size of the congregation, programs and structures of youth ministry, and social networks—including social networks outside the congregation. (See fig. 4.) The gender of the youth minister, the array of fun activities that a church might offer, and the style of music are less significant as factors that capture teens' attention in the sustained way that will yield religious commitment.

When a teen is attracted to participate in his or her church over time, religious commitment (or loyalty) is fostered in a circular process by which socialization and religious experience mutually build on one another. (See fig. 5.) Because youth have the symbols, stories, and practices to use to interpret their experiences as religious, they are enabled to name experiences of God as such. Congregations that both socialize youth into religious traditions and create conditions where teens feel they experience God also tend to have teens who exhibit religious commitment.

The particular time of life in which a high school senior finds himself or herself lends itself in a particular way to religious experience. At the boundary between childhood and adulthood, teens yearn for rites of passage to define a new, more mature status. When congregations encourage teens to use the symbols, stories, and rites of the religious tradition to structure their passage into adulthood, they offer teens resources that shape their self-identity in powerful ways as "Christian." On the other hand, when they do so, congregations must also respond to teenagers' novel religious expressions of the religious tradition. As teens in my study used Christian symbols to order and assist their passage out of home and high school, they incorporated new symbols, such as butterflies, and new practices, such as the giving of colored ribbons. Church practices such as baptism were amended to allow for its celebration by nonclergy and for its repetition as rebaptism.

Faith transmission proves to be a negotiation, more than just a "passing on of the baton." Faith transmission is a two-way process, where teens are given the faith tradition by parents and churches, and the faith tradition itself is regenerated by the new ways in which teens appropriate it. (See fig. 9.) The innovations that teens offer sometimes disturb established understandings and practices. Yet because they prompt a renegotiation of what forms the essence of the religious tradition, they can be a dynamic force that keeps it vital for a new generation.

What Parents Can Do

This study has practical implications as well as theoretical ones. It responds to a question that church leaders ask about intergenerational faith transmission: What most influences what teens believe about God and how they practice their faith? I asked teens about the relative influence of various people and shaping forces in their lives. (See fig. 3.) I found that teens usually name their parents as those who most influenced how they viewed God and their religious participation.

I sorted the various family factors that might make a difference—such as demographic variables, styles of parenting, and religious practices of parents. As I tested these variables and assessed the findings, I found that a cluster of factors correlated most with religious loyalty in the teen, a cluster that I called the "family attender variable," which includes the maintenance of a shared family understanding: "In our family, we attend church." (See table 12.)

In affirming that parents are the most influential factor in faith transmission, my study shows that they are so because of how they link teens to their churches, the primary place where they develop religious commitment through socialization and religious experience. (See fig. 2.)

First, the early religious nurture of parents in linking the child to the church and teaching the child the stories, symbols, and practices of their faith is the source for many of the enduring traits of identity, religious experience, and patterns of thought and action. While it was beyond the scope of this study to investigate early childhood religious nurture, the teens themselves described how the early role of their parents mattered, even if the churchgoing practice in their families petered out in their teen years. In addition, there is evidence of a polarization effect. The teens who were heavily socialized as youngsters tended to be closely allied with the tradition as they got older. Conversely, those who were inconsistently socialized in their tradition tended not to be. Teens who are given a strong religious background are able to interpret their experiences as religious because they have the symbols, stories, and practices to use to interpret their experiences in religious categories.

Second, the parents' role of linking the child to the church continues to be important in the teen years. It matters to religious loyalty that teens are held in the church to the end of their high school years, because it is during these years that they make some choices of vocation and attachment that set them on the trajectories that take them into adulthood. Like "a rocket that is already launched," by the time the teen is a high school senior "if the guidance system isn't there, it's too late now."[30] It is generally not possible to introduce a "church attendance rule" at this time, but if there is one in place, it matters that parents maintain it. By attending church themselves, by fostering a warm climate of cooperation in the home, and by encouraging teens to stay in the web of relationships connected to the church, parents can persuade teens to continue in the church. They can encourage the development of an intrinsic motivation to be linked to their church after they leave home.

Most teens do not appear to be mature enough to sustain their religious commitment without parental encouragement. Brittany, for all the enthusiasm she displayed at her baptism and confirmation in seventh grade, was unable to maintain her resolve to participate in her church without the assistance of her parents.[31] The senior year is pivotal. By then, some teens may be "unshakable" in their religious loyalty, but most are more tentative or conditional.

Third, one of the most important things parents do is choose a church that is attractive to teens. Before teens are old enough to drive, they have no choice of which church to attend. Dependent on their parents to get them to church, they also rely on parents to choose a church. If parents choose a church that attracts teens by the sense of belonging, meaning, and competencies that it offers, parents facilitate the link between the teen and the church that is crucial for developing religious loyalty.

With these three logics noted, some caveats must be added to qualify what are outlined as the significant factors in faith transmission. Some parents would not say religious loyalty was their goal for their teen. Some, like the "burned out" professional church educator, said that he and his wife were themselves moving away from the institutional church, and they no longer viewed "organized religion" as desirable for their daughter.[32] Some parents from the beginning sought other religious outcomes for their children, such as attaining moral maturity as seen in the compassion they might show for others. These parents tended to substitute the word *spirituality* for *religion*, as they view religion in individual expressive terms.

The goals parents exhibit displayed some elective affinity with denominational type. Evangelical parents most often talked about conversion, salvation, and marriage to a Christian spouse. Catholic parents most often spoke of the moral qualities of their teens and the teens' continuing incorporation into the universal church. Mainline Protestant parents talked of moral maturity and of having a relationship with God—usually implying membership in a church of any denomination.

Few parents in my sample, including the ones who had religiously loyal teens, claimed credit for the outcomes. If they had produced a religious virtuoso, they could point to the teen's sibling as counterexample of their "successful" religious nurture. It is evident that even if parents do maintain the link to the church in early childhood and into the later teen years, and even if they choose a church that attracts their teen in the ways described above, much more is going on in faith transmission than can be expressed in a formula or a method. The larger cultural elements that exist in society—such as the heightened sense of personal autonomy, family attenuation, the segmentation and thinning out of the network of social relationships, and the pervasive commercialization of vocations and goods in society—are macrosocietal factors that are beyond the parents' and churches' control. Parents and churches may adapt to these changes, as I have shown they do, but still faith transmission is a complex process—and a mysterious work of the Spirit—that cannot be fully analyzed or predicted.

⚜⚜⚜⚜⚜⚜

So, can religious traditions still vitalize faith and practice in teens, helping them to choose church in later years? Definitely. Even with a heightened sense of personal autonomy, even in these times when "believing and belonging" for many Americans means something individual, expressive, and noninstitutional, religious traditions attract and hold teens in new and powerful ways. Teens tend to choose faith when they live in families that "talk the walk" and "walk the talk." Moreover, church-related teens are most likely to "grow up into Christ" when they belong to congregations that have learned to convey unchanging, eternal truths within a changing "culture of choice."

Part V

Appendixes

Validity, Reliability, and Generalization of the Findings

B abbie defines "validity" in social scientific research as whether some-thing actually measures what it is supposed to measure rather than something else.[1] To test the validity of my findings I looked for discon-firming evidence. I attempted to remain aware of my own biases, which I name as follows: my personal commitment to encouraging religious loy-alty in teens; my Presbyterian affiliation, which differs from that of my subjects; my identity as ordained clergy; my role as the mother of children who were ages nine and eleven at the time of my data gathering; and my liberal arts education and feminist commitments. Elements of my social location influenced some of my reactions to the people, situations, and views I encountered. I noted, for example, my negative reaction to a high school principal who confided that he hoped eventually to eliminate the teaching of evolution in his public high school. There was one sermon I heard preached in a Catholic church that I interpreted as supporting the ordination of women. When I attempted to confirm that with others, they claimed they did not hear that message. In that case, I suspended judg-ment on what was actually preached.

I attempted to enhance the credibility of the field data by minimizing the subjects' reactivity to my personal commitments and social location. I described myself to subjects as a researcher and a parent, but generally did not reveal, unless asked, that I was a minister, a Presbyterian, and had other personal identifications. I tried to be neither "Martian" nor "con-vert," just a nonthreatening, friendly, interested researcher.[2]

I was sensitive to the possibility that I was exploiting my subjects. I turned off the tape recorder during interviews if I was asked. I disguised identities of the particular teens and altered identifying details in their descriptions. I withheld their real names and the names of their churches and schools to minimize the risk of exposing any information that could harm an individual, particularly a teenager. My protocol was approved by the Review Board for the Protection of Human Subjects of the Graduate School of Arts and Sciences at Emory University. I followed all procedures they outlined for gaining prior written consent from parents for conducting interviews with minors and for storing data in a secured location. I obtained written approval from each of the three churches before I launched my fieldwork there.

I was keenly aware that there was no tangible reciprocity in the relationship between researcher and subject. I offered nothing to them in return for allowing me to interview them and to be in their midst to gather data. The Catholic and Methodist youth leaders seemed genuinely pleased to have me around and took my presence as an affirmation that what they were doing was worth studying. The evangelical megachurch youth leaders were friendly and tolerant of my presence. They conduct national leadership workshops for youth ministers and are used to public recognition of their work and skills. The help and cooperation of the church leaders in all three congregations proved crucial to the success of my data gathering. When I had difficulty getting some of the busy teens and parents to agree to meet me for interviews, a call from the youth leader on my behalf always produced a positive response. I am aware that church and community leaders are interested in my findings and eager to read this study.

Ethnographic data is not replicable. Even if I conducted the study again, I doubt I would get the same results.[3] The findings offered here are "second order constructs," what Geertz calls "second culture," observations apprehended in the light of my own first culture.[4] The reliability of my findings is maximized, however, by the multiple indicators I sought. I collected different kinds of data to verify something initially learned from one source. For example, one teen never told me about her previous drug use, but I heard a youth leader allude to it once. Her parents also volunteered this information. Knowing about that history with a risk behavior was a clue to understanding the religious life of that teen, and all the more so because she decided not to mention it in our interview at a time when it would have been appropriate to do so. The triangulation of multiple interviews, field observation, and nationally normed surveys enhances the reliability of my findings.

As Becker and Eiesland note, "Ethnography allows for the expression of emergent understandings, partial accounts, and contradiction."[5] By offering my findings in the form of direct quotations, fine-grained descriptions, and raw narratives that do not smooth out the inconsistencies and messiness of people's real lives, it is hoped that the reliability of my portrayals is demonstrated to a sufficient degree.

Finally, does this data apply more generally, to teens beyond Louisville and to high school seniors years later? I caution against generalizing my findings to youth in congregations self-defined as of a particular racial and ethnic membership other than Caucasian and European American, and to youth in rural and urban settings. Particular cultural traditions and institutional arrangements such as race, ethnicity, and community type do affect cultural transmission. Originally my research design included a black church, but in view of the different familial patterns and sociostructural issues, my study would have focused mostly on race if I had executed my original plan.[6]

Like Csikszentmihalyi and Larson, I conclude,

> In the last analysis, this . . . only claims to be an accurate map to the subjective experiences of the adolescents who were directly studied. With its help, the conscious experience of other teenagers in different places and different times also will be better understood.[7]

Criteria Used for Selecting Three Congregations and How My Sample Matched Them

Criterion # 1

Each congregation must have at least sixteen high school seniors on its membership roll to provide a large enough sample from which to interview youth of high, middle, and low commitment levels within the same congregation.

At Transfiguration, the Catholic church in my sample, there were 132 seniors on the mailing list used by the youth minister to publicize activities of the high school youth group. Many of those were members of other parishes who attended youth group at Transfiguration. While the mailing list did not indicate which teens were members of Transfiguration, the membership of the church was large enough to ensure that I could find at least sixteen seniors who were members at Transfiguration. The membership of the church was 3,307 (or 1,123 families). There were 377 members on the rolls who were ages thirteen to eighteen.

Riverland Heights, the evangelical church in my sample, had 260 seniors on its mailing list, assuring me of a surplus of teens to interview at different commitment levels.

First United Methodist, the mainline Protestant church in my sample, had 24 seniors on its rolls.

Criterion # 2

Each congregation must be representative of its type as Catholic, evangelical Protestant, or mainline Protestant.

"Catholic" is defined as belonging to the Archdiocese of Louisville of the Roman Catholic Church. "Evangelical Protestant," for the purposes of this research, is defined by two core theological propositions: (1) the divinity of Jesus and (2) the necessity of personal faith for salvation.[1] "Mainline Protestant" is defined, for the purposes of this research, as the liberal and moderate Protestant groups classified as Episcopalians, United Church of Christ, Presbyterians, Methodists, Lutherans, Christians (Disciples of Christ), Northern Baptists, and Reformed.[2] While *members* of mainline Protestant churches may agree with the theological propositions defining evangelical Protestants, *the churches themselves* are designated "mainline Protestant" if they represent the dominant, culturally established faiths held by the majority of Americans.[3]

Transfiguration was a parish in the Archdiocese of Louisville.

In a sermon on September 22, 1996, the senior minister at Riverland Heights described the theological stances of the church in conformity to the theological propositions that define evangelicalism. He also claimed the title "evangelical" (in contrast to Catholic and liberal) as descriptive of his church. Riverland Heights is affiliated with the loosely connected independent congregations who call themselves Christian Churches, a branch of the restorationist movement that emerged among Protestant and free church leaders in the early nineteenth century in Ohio, Pennsylvania, and Kentucky.[4]

First United Methodist is a congregation affiliated with one of the mainline Protestant denominations, The United Methodist Church.

Criterion # 3

The three congregations must be of a similar socioeconomic level and racial and ethnic composition. I hold constant these significant demographic variables so that other variables, such as religious tradition, can be more sharply contrasted.

A marketing research map produced by Urban and Associates, a local marketing research firm, delineates six socioeconomic zones of the city that are relatively homogeneous. I located within one of these zones the congregations that met the first two criteria. Racial composition of membership was determined by observation in the congregations. I was able to count those who appeared nonwhite. I disqualified congregations that self-identified themselves as of a particular ethnic membership.

The Catholic and Methodist churches I selected are located within three miles of each other, in the same socioeconomic zone. Because the evangelical megachurch drew members from the entire city and from southern Indiana, I treated it as transgeographical, offering a diverse socioeconomic membership. In the course of my interviews with parents, I confirmed that median family income levels in the three congregations were within a close range (varying by $22,500). The median income of the families in my interview sample was $70,000 per year. For Transfiguration families, the median was $80,000. For First United Methodist families, it was $67,500. For Riverland Heights, it was $57,500.

Each of the three congregations was 99 percent white. None of the congregations self-identified as representing a particular ethnic heritage.

Theoretical Models of Faith Transmission

The theoretical models used by sociologists to explain the process of faith transmission cluster in five categories. The social learning theory emphasizes socialization, modeling, and reinforcement through parents, teachers, and other important agents.[1] The subcultural theory assumes that religious identity is a voluntary choice resting primarily on the selection of social ties.[2] Rational choice theory views religious choice as guided by preferences that inform the actor's calculation of the relative costs and benefits of various cultural choices.[3]

The remaining two theories approach faith transmission from the opposite direction, explaining what counters the process of faith transmission. The cultural broadening theory explains the loss of religious commitment as a result of the intellectual growth and crosscultural learning.[4] Emancipation theory explains why adolescents reject their parents' religion. It is based on Erikson's description of the adolescent identity crisis and the need for the adolescent to differentiate from the parents.[5] In this study I investigate the different elements and emphases of all these theories to understand which one, if any, best explains how the subjects of this research appropriated or rejected their faith tradition.

Appendix D

Previous Studies, New Empirical Research, and My Analysis of Religious Loyalty

M ost studies on adolescents and religion fit into the following types: teenagers' ideas of God; other religious beliefs; religious attitudes; religious experience, especially conversion; religious behavior such as church participation; religion and morality; religious knowledge; personality traits; parental influence, especially as compared to that of peers and teachers; and the religious influence of parochial schools.[1] My study does not fit into one of these types because its two dependent variables, religious loyalty and religious identity, intersect with almost all the categories, especially beliefs, attitudes, religious experience, church participation, knowledge, and comparative influences. What I investigate comes close to "religious loyalty" as McNamara studied it among Catholic teens.[2] Another term, used by Ozorak,[3] "religious commitment," approximates what I investigate. Similarly, Olson studies the transmission and reinforcement of "religious identity" among evangelical adults.[4] This research does not replicate previous studies because no other study has investigated faith transmission to teens using qualitative research methods in the church setting.[5]

While abundant data exist on youth in school settings,[6] there is overall absence of research on organizations that provide structured leisure time activities for teenagers.[7] The absence of research on youth in church settings is noted by Dean.[8] Even quantitative data on church teenage youth programs is also scarce. D'Antonio notes that much of the research on youth and religious institutions that does exist focuses on the institution's role of exerting social control, not of giving social support.[9] This research investigated individuals and institutional settings simultaneously. An "interactive model" reveals how institutions shape individuals.[10] This study shows how the congregation imprints its particular characteristics on the individual's style of religious faith.

Other studies on religion and adolescents focus on social class,[11] educational level, ethnicity and race,[12] regional variables,[13] and age of subjects.[14] According to Wuthnow, it may have been true that "a generation ago social scientists often held the view that scientific generalizations could be made about the relationships between social factors and religious orientations. . . . [Now] attention has turned toward describing the rich and complex processes by which religious orientations and social environments intermingle."[15] My research holds constant the classic variables of class, ethnicity and race, regional subculture, and age. Instead, the only variable I vary in my cases is the theological tradition. By holding most variables constant, I compare and contrast the particular youth ministry strategies of three congregations, ones that differ most by theological orientation. Other variables that have been the focus of previous research on religion and adolescence are gender,[16] gender of parents,[17] at-risk behaviors,[18] and prosocial behaviors.[19] Since these other variables vary naturally within each of my three cases, I note how these other variables interact with my dependent variables as I conduct my analysis, keeping my focus on the dependent variables of religious loyalty and religious identity.

In 2001, Christian Smith and his colleagues at the University of North Carolina launched a new national study called National Study of Youth and Religion. Their preliminary analysis of three existing data sets is referenced in this work. It will be important to compare the findings of this research with their new data as it becomes available.

Adolescence

In 1904 G. Stanley Hall wrote a seminal book defining "adolescence," setting the terms that are still revisited in current analyses of this developmental period.[1] Hall described this as the period "when life pivots" from autocentric to heterocentric, as a time of "Sturm und Drang," and as a "second birth."[2] Hall links the term "second birth" with adolescence to establish it as the normal time for religious conversion, especially among Protestants.[3]

Since Hall, the concept of adolescence has come to mean the transition to adulthood. In each decade of the century, however, assumptions about the tasks of adolescence have changed, largely because of different social conditions. The most dramatic development has been the shift from the home- and work-centered experience of the early part of the century to the school- and peer-centered experience of more recent decades. Mirel, summarizing the changes since 1900, suggests that

> adolescents went economically from being producers to becoming consumers; psychologically from bearing the burdens of premature adulthood to confronting the problems of prolonged childhood; socially from easy integration into adult society to an ever-lengthening period of age segregation; and politically from being the object of campaigns to end child labor to being the focus of efforts to reduce teenage unemployment.[4]

Today, adolescence is an ambiguous category, one without even a fixed beginning or end point.[5] Out-of-date assumptions about its inherent characteristics linger beyond their usefulness. For example, James Coleman, on the basis of his research on the social networks of high school students in the late 1950s, coined the term "generation gap" to describe what he found and assumed to be inherent in adolescence: an alienation between generations, especially between parents and teenaged children.[6] Other prominent experts on adolescence at that time widely supported this idea.[7] Today much empirical research demonstrates that alienation between parents and teens is not inevitable. The majority of these intergenerational relationships are positively evaluated.[8]

In the same study of high school students, Coleman found evidence that youth "have their own small society, separate from adult society. It is a subculture."[9] Still today some attempt to delineate the distinct elements of "youth culture" in the 1990s.[10] Most researchers, however, find the idea of a monolithic youth subculture a fiction. Instead, there are multiple subcultures that include youth but are not defined primarily by age.[11] The social historian Grace Palladino argues that any such notion circulating today is the achievement of merchandisers who have much to gain by promoting clothing, music, food, and other consumer products as part of "youth culture" to make them more appealing to teens, who have a great deal of disposable income to spend, and to adults who want to appear youthful.[12] As an essay in the *New York Times* summarizes, "Youth is equated with hipness, and hipness with sales and success."[13]

While the concept of adolescence has changed with social conditions and cultural understandings, some more enduring generalizations can be made about teenagers. Robert Kegan and others have synthesized understandings of biological, psychological, moral, cognitive, social, and religious capacities defined by Piaget, Erikson, Selmen, Kohlberg, Mead, Fowler, and other social scientists.[14] These stage theories represent maturation as an ordered, sequential unfolding of basic capacities that are developed in familial interaction in childhood, and of specific skills or competencies developed later in various institutional contexts beyond the family.[15]

Most relevant of all these stage theories to this study is the faith development stage theory of James Fowler.[16] According to Fowler, 50 percent of youth ages thirteen to twenty are at a Synthetic Conventional Faith Stage, meaning that beliefs and values are connected to significant others and form a largely unexamined unity. Another 28.6 percent are in a stage higher, the Individuative-Reflective Faith Stage, exhibiting a sense of self that is regrounded in choices and exclusions. At this higher stage, the adolescent is able to convert the meanings of symbols and myths into conceptual formulations. The remaining adolescents are in earlier stages.[17]

For the purposes of my study, it will be assumed that my sample reflects the variation Fowler describes.

One of the more compelling recent challenges to developmental stage theorists comes from sociologists investigating the impact of new media and communications on identity formation. According to Joshua Meyrowitz, television interrupts the staging and sequencing of childhood development as generally understood.[18] The biological and cognitive stages are still in place, but the structure of the socialization process has been altered. Through television children see what goes on "backstage,"[19] that is, adult secrets and "the secret of secrecy." Children's innocence used to be prolonged by their inability to comprehend the print code of restricted materials. With television, however, it is as if the walls inside the home are removed, and children can view all that goes on. My study is attentive to the effects of mass media as it relates to the socialization of teenagers, and especially as it affects the transmission of religious faith.

In this study I focus on life cycle effects[20] in adolescence more than developmental stages, because these more directly reflect the influence of culture on the adolescent, including the influence of religious culture. I had not intended to focus on life cycle effects when I began my research. It became evident to me very quickly, however, that my subjects faced a life cycle transition that dominated their senior year of high school. The overwhelming majority of the teens I studied were preparing to move out of the family home to attend college the following fall, some to live on university campuses, and others to share apartments with classmates.[21] The anticipation of leaving home presented high school seniors with the expectation that they soon would negotiate outside the familiar perspectives of the meaning systems provided by family, church, and high school. This burden and opportunity to explore different structures affected youth in different ways. For some, this crisis prompted them to revisit their religious tradition and fortify themselves in familiar understandings. For others, more typically, it led to the loosening of their ties to the church in preparation for engagement in a new set of institutions in a different setting that is associated with adulthood.

Appendix F

Faith Tradition as Religious Culture

F aith tradition, for the purposes of this study, is taken to be religious "culture." Like all kinds of culture, religion represents patterns of meanings through symbols to convey knowledge and attitudes about life.[1] The content of religious culture is distinctive. It symbolizes transcendent truth, "a conception of a general order of existence."[2] It tunes human actions to cosmic order and projects images of it with "such an aura of factuality that the moods and motivations seem uniquely realistic."[3] Religious culture, further, conveys ethical ideas. "What is" shapes "what ought to be," and reciprocally, "what ought to be" reinforces "what is." Even if the circle of "is" and "ought" proves to have some gaps, for example where questions about death and undeserved suffering escape complete explanation, what matters is how religion's adherents account for the gaps. In this study I follow Max Weber to interpret religious culture substantively, looking for the coherence of meaning, more than Emile Durkheim, who explains religion functionally, as it addresses the human need for religious meaning.

Four levels of culture are used in this exploration of religious culture, the first being culture as something subjectively understood. At this level I examine what is internalized as the individual's beliefs, attitudes, opinions, and values. Second, culture is structural. There is a coherence in the pattern and relationship among various cultural elements. There are symbolic boundaries and mechanisms by which these boundaries are maintained or modified. Culture can be separated analytically from what is subjectively understood about it. It is observed in gestures, objects, acts, and events, and heard in discourse. It can be recorded and classified. At this level, culture is objective. Third, culture interacts with social structure. It is dramaturgical, expressive, and communicative. It is the symbols that articulate how social relations are arranged. It is rituals, ideologies, and other symbolic acts that communicate the moral nature of social relations. It may be implicit, "what is given off," as much as what is given. Finally, culture is institutional. It consists of actors and organizations with resources who are related to macroinstitutions such as the state and economy. Actors have special competencies to facilitate the production of culture. Organizations process resources for the purpose of ritualizing, codifying, and transmitting cultural products.[4]

The relationship between religious faith and culture has been framed in different ways. Paul Tillich understood Christ to be disclosed in culture.[5] H. Richard Niebuhr understood Christ in opposition to culture.[6] "Christ," for Niebuhr, is seen to be wholly different. In this study, normative theological understandings of God are not seen to be compromised or reduced by regarding them in sociological terms as culturally constructed symbols. My approach is hermeneutical; the goal is to interpret my subjects' understandings of God.

Cohort Effects

With Mannheim's conceptualization of a generational unit, or "cohort," the study of cohort effects developed as a specialization within research on adolescence.[1] Studies of cohort effects probe how attitudes and tendencies formed by the time of adolescence exercise an enduring appeal and binding force among contemporaries who are close in age and share common experiences. As Roof puts it, a generation develops a "consciousness" of its shared culture.[2] Cohort effects are to be distinguished from "period effects," that is, the impact of particular historical events, such as a war, an economic depression, or Vatican II.[3] "Age effects," a third phenomenon, are what can be linked to the age of the subjects in a comparative sample. For example, the character of the teen's peer network can be predicted by the teen's year in high school.[4] Cohort, period, and age effects can interact in ways that make it difficult to separate specific effects.[5]

Mannheim's theory that adolescence is the period during which persons are shaped in ways that forever impact their behavior and attitudes is proven to apply to the shaping of religious orientations. For example, Firebaugh and Harley show that cohorts entering adulthood during a period of particularly high or low religious practice tend to bear that mark through their lives.[6] Glen shows that lower loyalty to church in later generations of young adults is explained in an analysis of the "no religion" responses to national surveys of Americans between the 1950s and 1980s.[7] These data show that older generations tended to have higher levels of religious participation, even when they were young, than more recent generations. Similarly, Wade Clark Roof establishes a correlation between high involvement in the counterculture during adolescence and low levels of religious participation during adulthood.[8]

The assertion that cohort effects established by the end of adolescence predict future religiosity must be qualified by other research indicating that religious influence in the teenage and earlier years does not guarantee adult religiosity. Studying whether parental role models of religious practice are imitated by children in adulthood, Willits and Crider find that there are mixed effects. Overall this study finds that what matters more to adult religious practice than adolescent experience is the religious involvement of the spouse.[9] Hoge, Johnson, and Luidens also find that high school and pre–high school experiences are less important than adult experiences as predictors of adult religious participation. They find a weak correlation between high school youth group activity and adult church participation.[10] On balance, it can be concluded that while positive religious influence experienced during adolescence and earlier does not guarantee high levels of adult participation, low levels of youth religious activity and counterreligious influence does predict low adult religious participation. A study of the counterreligious influences on today's teenage generational cohort that catalogs what religious communities do best to diffuse the power of those influences while transmitting their faith traditions will suggest the best prospects for religious traditions to persist in the future.

Nearly all the parents in this research were baby boomers.[11] This cohort has been the subject of much research.[12] Their teenage children, specifically those born in 1979 or 1980, are part of a generation that is loosely named Generation X.[13] To date, no major qualitative research has been published on teens within five years of the age of those in my sample. McNamara's study, the one most similar to mine,[14] researches teens eight to twenty years older.[15] Myers's study, also similar to mine,[16] studies teens born at least ten years before those in my sample.[17] There is adequate quantitative research on Generation X, and it will be used in my analysis to complement my qualitative findings.[18] This study offers narrative accounts of this teenage cohort's assessment of their religious upbringing in order to sharpen the picture of them that is suggested in survey data. The result is a deeper understanding of how teens today appropriate the Christian tradition when they do.

A Telephone Survey of Teen Activity Levels

(Used with Catholic Parishes in the Archdiocese of Louisville)

1. What is the membership of your parish?
2. How many high school seniors do you have on your membership rolls?
3. What special programs do you have for high school youth? What is the attendance at these activities?
4. What are the parishes in Louisville that have the most active ministries with high school youth?
5. What is the goal of your parish's ministry with youth?

Appendix I

Regular Weekly Activities for High School Youth in Three Congregations

Table 13. Regular Weekly Activities for High School Youth in Three Congregations

	Transfiguration	Riverland Heights	First United Methodist
Sunday	Mass at 9:00 A.M. and 11:00 A.M. 7:00 P.M. Youth group	Morning worship at 8:30 A.M., 10:00 A.M., and 11:30 A.M. Insight (Sunday school) and Choir at 10:00 A.M. Focus meeting at 6:30 P.M.	Morning worship at 8:30 A.M. and 11:00 A.M. Sunday school at 9:30 A.M. Bell choir at 4:00 P.M. Choir at 5:00 P.M. Snack supper Senior high youth group at 6:30 P.M.
Monday			
Tuesday	Youth Center open in evening for dropping in		
Wednesday	Youth Center open in evening for dropping in	Vision at 7:00 P.M.	Churchwide supper followed by discussion class or project of senior highs
Thursday			
Friday			Fifth Quarter (unstructured social time) open to senior highs, but mostly attended by junior highs
Saturday	Mass at 5:00 P.M.	Worship at 5:00 P.M. and 6:30 P.M. Insight at 6:30 P.M.	

Agency and Religious Socialization

R eligious socialization is cultural transmission, but it is a two-way process of transmission that preserves human agency. On the one hand, congregations transmit religious traditions to individuals, including teens. On the other hand, teens remake the tradition as they appropriate it. Sometimes teens transmit back to the congregation their revised version of religious symbols, narratives, rituals, and practices.[1] (See fig. 9.)

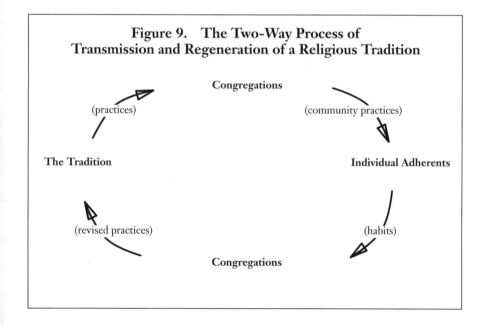

**Figure 9. The Two-Way Process of
Transmission and Regeneration of a Religious Tradition**

Congregations

(practices)

(community practices)

The Tradition

Individual Adherents

(revised practices)

(habits)

Congregations

As church historian Dorothy Bass points out, it is in the two-way process of transmission and revision that the religious tradition itself is renewed. There is a renegotiation of symbols and practices that takes place as new adherents revise the practices. That revision and dialogue keep the tradition dynamic.[2]

In the course of my research I observed that teens are not passive recipients of a religious tradition that is transmitted to them. Teens exhibit agency to select from within their options particular "strategies of action." They tend to select from Swidler's metaphorical tool kit the recipes for action that they have found to work.[3] Teens may have been predisposed to select some strategies by their religious socialization, class, gender, and other structures, but they still exhibited choice.

The diverse elements that structure choice are both concrete and invisible, conscious and nonconscious, small and large. They include the durable dispositions established by family and class from the time of birth, such as the inclination to attend church on the Sabbath.[4] They also include the macroinstitutions such as the state, economy, and educational institutions that both assist and constrain people's options. They are shaped by educational institutions and the market offer "tracks," or established courses of study or training, leading to careers. Career options are sorted by class, as New Institutionalist theorists describe.[5]

The teen's own social network is an example of a structure that influences a teen to choose whether to be church affiliated. It is a structure that is both given and chosen, as for example when churchgoing parents predispose their children to choose friends among those they know at church.

Whether it is from free choice or from false consciousness of it, teens themselves asserted emphatically that they did choose what they believed. There can be a disjuncture between actual states and how people perceive them, because people follow scripts and schemata that dictate to them how to view their circumstances. Actors may see themselves as sovereign and free, yet public institutions regulate them and track them along age-graded paths by performance. This is the argument of New Institutionalist theorist John Meyer.[6] In this case, teens may have little freedom as agents choosing their religious affiliation or nonaffiliation, but they are influenced by the institutions of society to believe that they have complete freedom to do so. It is beyond the scope of this study to assess how freely teens make religious choices, except to say that the wide variations I observed in teen religious loyalty in my sample indicate that they exhibit some measure of true agency within certain constraints.

Like Selznick, I conclude that human agents are societally constituted and self-determining, multilayered and voluble. In fact, teens said they believed they had greater freedom to choose their faith than they thought their parents and grandparents had at their same age.[7]

Two Poems Posted in the Youth Center at Transfiguration

I. (The text, typed on blue paper, is shaped inside the outline of a teardrop.)

This one's name just happened on Maureen
The tears that shed matched floodings of the Nile
Her hair had a fantastic golden sheen
But none could match her smile

She went to work as all good angels should
And there she was to lend a helping hand
No doubt she always did the best she could
No doubt as angel princess does she stand

But Lord, I must admit if you ask me
I'd have to say this world is sickly bent
I find it hard; could you please make me see
Why you save me and kill the innocent

I only knew Maureen for a short time
But yet these thoughts are all too much to bear
I'd like to know what stupid, mortal crime
Thought right to take the oxygen from air

See Lord, if you had asked me in advance
Or anyone who knew Maureen's fair face
We all would sacrifice our living chance
And gladly take her undeserving place

Do you cry, my Lord
When your sacred sword
Quickly cuts the cord
On a faithful and true

This choice we were given
This freedom of living
Through which we have thriven
In the hatred of you

How Lord, you should have gone and asked me first
For I would not take long to make you see
This choice you made was possibly your worst
You could have done much better choosing me
You would have done much better choosing me

II. (An unsigned poem placed near the grapevine wreath decorated with
butterflies, in honor of Maureen on the anniversary of her death)

Some birds aren't meant to be
     caged . . .
Their feathers
     are just too bright.
And when they fly away,
        the part of you
     that knows
        it was a sin to lock them
     does rejoice.
But still,
        the place you live in
     is that much more drab and empty
     that they are gone.

I miss you Maureen.

Interview Schedule for Teenager

Preliminaries

Be sure informed consent forms are signed by parents and youth.

Inform the individual about the circumstances of the study and receive permission to tape-record interview. All interviews will be confidential. If I plan to quote from an interview using an individual's name, I will seek permission first. The names of the churches and location will be used in the final document generated from the study.

Background information

Age?

Race?

Relationships

How would you describe your relationship with your parents (including stepparents, if applicable)?

Are your best friends from one particular part of your life—for example, school, church, sports?

Or do your best friends go to the same school and church, and attend the same outside activities?

Do your parents know your friends and your friends' parents?

Do your parents know the people in your life whom you consider most important to you?

Culture

How many hours a month are you at the mall?

What music do you like best? How many hours a day do you listen?
Do you watch MTV? Other programs you especially like? How
  many hours a day do you watch?
Is there a movie or type of movie you especially like?
Fill in the blank: "To fit into my group I must. . . ."
Fill in the blank: "You can tell someone isn't fitting in when they . . ."

School and other institutions

What type of school do you attend? Who made the decision?
What groups, institutions, or causes do you identify with? Why do
  you think that these are important?
Do you participate in church mission projects or other community
  service programs as a volunteer?
Do you work for pay? How many hours a week?

Church

Are you confirmed and/or baptized in your church? Tell me about
  your confirmation and/or baptism.
How often do you attend worship services at church [give range]? Do
  you take part in the mass [Catholics only]?
Is attendance at church or mass an individual choice, or is church a
  family activity?
Do you attend religious education or Sunday school, youth pro-
  grams, choir, or other church activities?
What is your role at church?
Describe worship at your church. How do you feel about it?
Do you have particular prayers, scriptures, stories, hymns, songs,
  church seasons that stand out for you?
Do you have particular memories of priests/ministers or members of
  the congregation?
Do you sometimes wish you attended another church? Or no church
  at all?
Do you expect to be active in church after you leave home?

Other religious practices

What, if any, other religious practices are important to you? Are
  these religious practices shared as a family or performed individually?
How often and where do you pray? Individually and/or as a family?
Do you read the Bible or religious literature at home? What literature?

Do you attend a Bible study or religious support group?

What season/saints' days/holidays are most important in your home?

Do you have conversations with your parents about religious faith and values? How often?

Beliefs

Do you consider yourself a religious person? What does that mean to you?

How do your religious views compare with those of your parents? Your church? Your friends? Others who are important to you?

Who most influences what you believe and value?

Has your image of God—your relation to God—changed over the years?

Are there events that stand out as especially important as you think of changes in what you think about God?

What is your image or model of a person of mature faith?

Do you think actions can be right or wrong? What actions are always right? Are there certain moral opinions that you think everyone should agree on?

How do you explain the presence of evil?

Interview Schedule for Joint or Individual Interview with Parents

Preliminaries

Inform the individual(s) about the circumstances of the study and receive permission to tape-record interview. All interviews will be confidential. If I plan to quote from an interview using an individual's name, I will seek permission first. The names of the churches and location will be used in the final document generated from the study.

Background information

Where are you from? If not Louisville, how far away is place of origin [offer ranges]?

When were you born [offer ranges of birth years]?

When were you married? divorced? previously married?

How many children do you have? Ages and genders? Are any living with a previous spouse?

What is (or was) your most recent employment? Do you each work for pay? How many hours?

What is your income [offer ranges]?

How much schooling have you had [give scale]?

What kind of schooling [offer types]?

What is your race?

Both members of the church? If not, is one affiliated elsewhere?

What is your level of church involvement [offer choices]?

What does the phrase "traditional family values" mean to you?

What is your view of appropriate roles for males and females?

What kinds of decisions do you make as a family? For your child?

Does one parent tend to make more decisions about your child?

Do you believe children are equal with parents? How?

Religious practices

How often do you attend worship services or mass at church [give range]?

What, if any, other religious practices are important to you?

How often and where do you pray? Before meals, and if so, how often?

Do you read the Bible or religious literature at home? What literature?

Do you attend a Bible study or religious support group?

What seasons/saints' days/holidays are most important in your home?

Is your child included in any religious practices in the home? (NOTE: Once the number of children and their genders are established, the word "child" will be replaced by "daughter," "son," "children," "teens," or something comparable.)

Do you pray with your child or as a family at any particular time during the day, and how often?

Do you talk about your religious faith with your child? How often?

Is attendance at church or mass an individual choice or is church a family activity?

Does your child attend religious education or Sunday school, youth programs, choir, or other church activities? Voluntarily or at parent's behest? Has your child ever rebelled against church?

What type of school does your child attend [offer types]? Whose decision was it? Did the choice have anything to do with your religious faith?

Does your child attend any religious camps, participate in church-related sports leagues or any other clubs or groups of a religious nature?

Do you encourage your child in any particular behavior or activity because it is the right thing for a Catholic [a Christian] to do?

How do you feel about your child coming into contact with religions or ways of living that contradict your religious beliefs and values? Do you limit your child's exposure to contradictory outlooks? How? Can you give some examples of types of people or particular instances when you have restricted your child's exposure?

Do you try to influence your child's choice of friends?

Does it matter to you what your child's friends' religious views are?

How many of your child's friends do you know personally? How many of their parents do you know? How many of your child's friends do you know about but have never met? Do you tend to know a set of friends and their parents from one area of your child's life, such as church, school, neighborhood, sports?

Reasons given for parenting practices

Tell me what you remember about your child's baptism. What does that event mean for you?

Have your views about giving your child a religious upbringing changed over time? What caused you to change your views or ways of doing things?

Do you have a particular hope for how your child will practice her/his faith as an adult?

In this family is faith a matter of individual choice or a family choice?

What is religious faith to you?

How do your beliefs and practices compare with those of your church?

Does your choice of a church have anything to do with what you feel would most meet the needs of your children?

Have you ever switched from a church? Why?

Tables Related to Loyalty Types

Table 14. Loyalty Types by Church Attendance

	Unshakable (Loyalists)		Tentative (Loyalists)		Conditional (Provisional Loyalists)		Postponed (Unlikely Loyalists)		Alienated (Unlikely Loyalists)	
	N	Percent	N	Percent	N	Percent	N	Percent	N	Percent
Every week	15	100%	7	54%	2	40%	0	0%	0	0%
Once a month	0	0%	4	31%	0	0%	1	20%	0	0%
1–2 times a year or rarely	0	0%	2	15%	3	60%	4	80%	3	100%
Total of all loyalty types	15	100%	13	100%	5	100%	5	100%	3	100%

Table 15. Frequency of Praying and Bible Reading of High School Seniors by Church

Practice	All Teens in Interview Sample		Transfiguration		Riverland Heights		First United Methodist	
	N	Percent	N	Percent	N	Percent	N	Percent
Prays[a] and reads Bible every day[b]	13	32%	0	0%	10	59%	3	25%
Prays every day	10	24%	4	33%	4	23%	2	17%
Prays at random times	13	32%	5	42%	3	18%	5	42%
Never prays individually	5	12%	3	25%	0	0%	2	17%
Totals	41	100%	12	100%	17	100%	12	101%

a. The figures for prayer exclude family prayer before or after the evening meal. Sixty-one percent of all teens reported that their family asked a blessing at dinner. Transfiguration teens reported the highest incidence (83 percent). Riverland Heights teens and First United Methodist teens reported 53 percent and 50 percent respectively. Family prayer before the meal is included in the variables considered in Part IV.

b. There were no cases reported of teens who read their Bibles who did not also pray daily. Daily prayer and Bible reading went together as a single practice for these teens.

Table 16.   Loyalty Types by Consistent Religious Socialization

Variable	Unshakable (Loyalists)	Tentative (Loyalists)	Conditional (Provisional Loyalists)	Postponed (Unlikely Loyalists)	Alienated (Unlikely Loyalists)
Socialization consistent?	Yes	Yes	No	No	No

Table 17.   Loyalty Types by Religious Experience

Variable	Unshakable (Loyalists)	Tentative (Loyalists)	Conditional (Provisional Loyalists)	Postponed (Unlikely Loyalists)	Alienated (Unlikely Loyalists)
Religious experience?	Yes	No	Yes	No	No

Table 18.   Loyalty Types by Religious Experience and Socialization

Variables	Unshakable (Loyalists)	Tentative (Loyalists)	Conditional (Provisional Loyalists)	Postponed (Unlikely Loyalists)	Alienated (Unlikely Loyalists)
Religious experience?	Yes	No	Yes	No	No
Socialization consistent?	Yes	Yes	No	No	No

Appendix O

Cases Where Socialization and Religious Experience Were Not Exhibited Together

While the variables of socialization and religious experience are interrelated, there were instances in my interview sample where teens exhibited one without the other. In the spring of her senior year, Danielle, a provisional loyalist, spent time alone in a chapel at a monastery during a retreat sponsored by her Catholic high school. She was wrestling with the decision of where to attend college. As she described to me the experience of sitting in the chapel thinking about it, I was struck with how she was missing the vocabulary to describe this as a Christian practice of discernment. She may have been taught to understand her lifework as ministry at some time during her Catholic schooling, but she was not using that term to interpret her present dilemma. Absent was the theological understanding of having a ministry from God and the experience of the faith community's assistance in "discerning one's gifts." She made no reference to a moral life shaped by an overarching "good" or a principle of what was "right."

Instead, Danielle arrived at what she called a "career choice" that was shaped by economic life and the tracks that were available to her through educational institutions. In the absence of theological constructs, a default vocabulary of the marketplace shaped her strategy of action. On the other hand, Danielle had sought out a religious place to do her thinking. She was seeking guidance from God for an important decision. Implied in her story was the sense that being in a chapel signified having an experience of God. Teens like Danielle who had religious experiences without consistent socialization tended to be provisional loyalists.

There also were teens who exhibited the opposite of Danielle's circumstance: they had plenty of religious socialization, but could not iden-

236

tify any experiences they had had as an encounter with God. To them, religion was "boring."[1] "It's just not a big part of my life," one girl (a tentative loyalist) explained. "I feel like I'm just going through the motions." Another tentative loyalist told me that she wished she could have an experience of God. She was reared in the church all her life but feels as if she is missing something that should be happening to her. "If I had had an experience of God, I think I'd know it," she said. Teens with consistent socialization and no religious experience tended to be tentative loyalists.

Tentative loyalists, like the two teens quoted above, say that they find the church "too bureaucratic" and "institutional."[2] Some said they grow weary of the church's requests for money. As Andrea (mentioned in the Introduction) put it in individual expressive terms, "You can have your own sense of faith without the rituals, without going to church." Even one of the young adult youth leaders who assisted Angie at Transfiguration said he hardly ever attended mass. "Religion was shoved down my throat," he said. "First I needed to discover myself. I'm a Catholic. Yes. Religion is what you make of it."

Appendix P

Comparing Loyalty among Churches and to National Sample

In all three congregations, socialization and religious experience worked together in different ways and to different degrees to engender the loyalty of teens to their faith traditions. There also were associations between degree of loyalty and religious tradition. Most notably, the Catholic congregation produced no teens in my interview sample who predicted that they would definitely continue attending church after they left home. They produced a high percentage in the next category (five of the twelve teens, or almost 42 percent, were tentative loyalists). Evangelicals produced the highest percentage of the most loyal "unshakable" loyalists (eleven out of seventeen or almost 65 percent). Mainline Protestants had the highest percentage of their teens in the top two loyalist categories combined (ten out of twelve, or over 83 percent). (See table 19.)

Table 19.   Religious Tradition by Loyalty Types

	Catholic		Evangelical Protestant		Mainline Protestant	
	N	Percent	N	Percent	N	Percent
Unshakable (Loyalists)	0	0.0%	11	64.7%	4	33.3%
Tentative (Loyalists)	5	41.7%	2	11.8%	6	50.0%
Conditional (Provisional Loyalists)	2	16.7%	3	17.6%	0	0.0%
Postponed (Unlikely Loyalists)	3	25.0%	1	5.9%	1	8.3%
Alienated (Unlikely Loyalists)	2	16.7%	0	0.0%	1	8.3%
Total of Loyalty Types	12	100.1%*	17	100%	12	99.9%*

*Total exceeds or falls short of 100 percent due to rounding.

I determined the relative differences among the distributions of loyalty types among religious traditions in my interview sample, not to make a case about numbers, but to compare how my sample matched national samples of teens sorted by religious tradition. My findings are generally consistent with them. A Gallup poll taken ten years earlier shows that Catholic teens find religion less important than Protestant teens do. According to Gallup and Castelli (1987), 37 percent of Catholic teenagers consider religious faith to be a very important quality as compared to 57 percent of Protestant teenagers. This poll also shows that Catholics are less likely than Protestant teens to give high priority to helping those in need. Forty-nine percent of Catholics, 64 percent of mainline Protestants, and 74 percent of evangelicals give a high rating to this moral idea.[1]

Data Related to Parenting Variables

There are three types of variables related to parental influence on teen religious loyalty: demographic, styles of parenting, and church attendance. Here I display the numbers and percentages that I find in my interview sample. These quantitative data are offered as illustrations of the logics argued in Part IV. The case for the relative influence of variables does not rest on the number in this small sample. They complement the evidence found in the qualitative data of the research and are helpful in a comparison with national surveys on parenting factors in the transmission of religious identity to offspring.

Finally, I display here the numbers and percentages of a fourth variable that is a composite of some of the others: family type. In Part IV I argue that this fourth variable is most significantly correlated with teen religious loyalty.

1. Data Related to Demographic Variables
(See table 21.)

2. Data Related to Parenting Styles
My research shows a correlation between parenting styles and teen religious loyalty. The hierarchical, traditional, democratic, and peer styles are more likely to lead teens to stay connected to the church after they leave home. The open style is less likely to engender this response. (See table 20.)

Table 20.   Parenting Style by Teen Religious Loyalty

	Hierarchical		Traditional		Democratic		Peer		Open	
	N	Percent	N	Percent	N	Percent	N	Percent	N	Percent
Loyalists	7	100%	10	77%	6	75%	2	67%	1	13%
Provisional Loyalists	0	0%	2	15%	0	0%	1	33%	2	25%
Unlikely Loyalists	0	0%	1	8%	2	25%	0	0%	5	63%
Totals	7	100%	13	100%	8	100%	3	100%	8	101%*

*Total exceeds 100 percent due to rounding.

Table 21. Percentages of Each Teen Religious Loyalty Type by Demographic Family Variables Favoring Loyalty

Loyalty Type	INTACT FAMILY STRUCTURE[a]				HIGHER INCOME[b]				CLOSE PROXIMITY TO AT LEAST ONE PARENT'S PLACE OF ORIGIN[c]				PARENTS HAVE SAME RELIGIOUS BACKGROUND[d]			
	Have Intact Family Structure		Lack Intact Family Structure		Have Higher Income		Lack Higher Income		Have Close Proximity to at Least One Parent's Place of Origin		Lack Close Proximity to at Least One Parent's Place of Origin		Have Parents with Same Religious Background		Have Parents with Different Religious Backgrounds	
	N	Percent	N	Percent	N	Percent	N	Percent	N	Percent	N	Percent	N	Percent	N	Percent
Loyalist	24	70.6%	4	57.1%	21	72.4%	5	62.5%	25	71.4%	3	60%	20	87%	6	42.9%
Provisional Loyalist	4	11.8%	1	14.3%	3	10.3%	2	25%	3	8.6%	2	40%	2	8.7%	2	14.3%
Unlikely Loyalist	6	17.6%	2	28.6%	5	17.2%	1	12.5%	7	20%	0	0%	1	4.3%	6	42.9%
Total	34	100%	7	100%	29	99.9%[e]	8	100%	35	100%	5	100%	23	100%	14	100.1%[e]

[a]"Intact" is defined as parents of the teen being married to each other and living in the same home with the teen.

[b]"Higher income" is defined as a yearly family income of $50,000 or more.

[c]"Close proximity" is defined as within a one-hour car ride.

[d]Having "the same" religious background means that the parents were both reared as Catholic or both reared as Protestant.

[e]Total exceeds or falls short of 100 percent due to rounding.

Hierarchical-style parenting correlates significantly with the highest loyalty type. All the teens in my interview sample who were reared by hierarchical-style parents are loyalists. This association is even more striking when looking separately at the two categories of loyalists, the unshakables and the tentatives. The hierarchical style is associated significantly with the most loyal loyalists, the "unshakables." Seventy-five percent of teens reared by hierarchical-style families are unshakables. (See table 11 in chapter 11.)

In all, the correlation between parenting style and teen religious loyalty type is not significant enough to warrant singling it out as the key factor predicting teen religious loyalty. While a high percentage, nearly 85 percent, reared in either hierarchical or traditional-style families were loyalists, a full one-third of all the loyalists were not reared in hierarchical or traditional-style families. Loyalty correlates generally with all four nonpermissive parenting styles, that is, with all the styles except the open style. (See table 22.)

**Table 22.   Nonpermissive and Permissive
Parent Variables by Teen Religious Loyalty**

Teen Loyalty Type	Parents Are Nonpermissive (Indicates a hierarchical, traditional, democratic or peer style)		Parents Are Permissive (Indicates an open style of parenting)	
	N	Percent	N	Percent
Loyalists	25	78%	1	14%
Provisional Loyalists	3	9%	2	29%
Unlikely Loyalists	4	13%	4	57%
Total	32	100%	7	100%

My research suggests that the more a family brings religion into the home through symbols, rituals, and practice, the more likely is the teen to show religious loyalty. In fact, this factor ranks high in the statistics. (See table 23.)

3. Data Related to Parental Church Attendance

Parents' weekly church attendance had the highest correlation with teen religious loyalty. (See table 24.)

Table 23. Four Family Variables by Teen Religious Loyalty

Loyalty Type	FAMILY CLIMATE[a]				NETWORK[b]				THICK, RELIGION-INFUSED FAMILY CULTURE[c]				PARENTS BELONG TO SAME CHURCH[d]			
	Have Warm Family Climate		Lack Warm Family Climate		Have Parent/Teen Social Network		Lack a Parent/Teen Social Network		Have Thick, Religion-Infused Family Culture		Lack Thick, Religion-Infused Family Culture		Parents Belong to Same Church		Parents Do Not Belong to Same Church	
	N	Percent	N	Percent	N	Percent	N	Percent	N	Percent	N	Percent	N	Percent	N	Percent
Loyalist	25	81%	3	30%	21	78%	7	50%	25	83%	3	27%	25	80%	3	30%
Provisional Loyalist	4	13%	1	10%	3	11%	2	14%	4	13%	1	9%	3	10%	2	20%
Unlikely Loyalist	2	7%	6	60%	3	11%	5	36%	1	3%	7	64%	3	10%	5	50%
Total	31	101%[e]	10	100%	27	100%	14	100%	30	99%[e]	11	100%	31	100%	10	100%

[a]This was determined by the teen's answer to the question, "How would you describe your relationship with your parents?"

[b]This was determined by the teen's answer to the question, "Do your parents know your friends and your friends' parents?"

[c]This was determined from comments made by both teens and parents about family symbols, rituals, or practices that had religious significance. I excluded the practice of church attending in this variable, since it was considered separately (below).

[d]If one parent was deceased, a "yes" determination was made. If one of the parents did not belong to a church, a "no" determination was made. In this sample, at least one parent of each teen belongs to a church.

[e]Total exceeds or falls short of 100 percent due to rounding.

Table 24.   Parents' Weekly Church Attendance
by Teen Religious Loyalty

Teen Loyalty Type	Parent(s) in Household Attend Church Weekly. If Two Parents, Both Attend Weekly		Less than Weekly Church Attendance by One or Both Parents in Household	
	N	Percent	N	Percent
Loyalist	23	92%	5	31%
Provisional Loyalist	2	8%	3	19%
Unlikely Loyalist	0	0%	8	50%
Total	25	100%	16	100%

Nearly 93 percent of all teens in my interview sample replicated attendance frequencies of one or both parents. (See table 25.)

Table 25.   Attendance Patterns of Parents and Teens
at Corporate Worship by Church

Parent(s) and teen attend each week, not necessarily together	Parent(s) and teen attend about once a month	Parent(s) and teen attend 1–2 times a year	Parent(s) attend each week, teen attends once a month	One parent attends regularly or once a month, other parent and teen attend 1–2 times a year	Parent(s) attend each week, teen attends 1–2 times a year
5 Catholics[a] 12 evangelicals[b] 7 mainliners[c]	0 Catholics 1 evangelical[d] 3 mainliners	2 Catholics 3 evangelicals 0 mainliners	0 Catholics 1 evangelical 0 mainliners	3 Catholics[e] 0 evangelicals 2 mainliners[f]	2 Catholics 0 evangelicals 0 mainliners
Total: 24	Total: 4	Total: 5	Total: 1	Total: 5	Total: 2

In no case did teens attend when parents did not. Sometimes teens were more active in church than parents when the full range of church activities was considered. Columns 1, 2, 3, and 5 represent cases where the teen replicated the attendance pattern of at least one parent, the parent who attended less frequently. These cases in columns 1, 2, 3, and 5 total 92.6 percent of the teen-parent(s) sets.

[a]In one case where the parents are divorced and custody is shared by alternating weeks, the teen goes when she is with her mother who attends each weekend, and slightly less often when she is with her father.
[b]In three cases, the parent is a single mother (two divorced, one widowed).
[c]In one family, the father attends Catholic mass, the mother and daughter attend Protestant worship.
[d]In this family, attendance ebbs and flows. They attend regularly for a few weeks and then not for months.
[e]In one case, the father attends. In the two other cases, the mothers attend. One mother (divorced) attends a Protestant church with her boyfriend. In the other case, the mother performs as a soloist at mass.
[f]In both cases, mothers attend alone. One is divorced; one is married.

4. Data Related to Composite Variable of Family Type: Family Church Attender or Religious Individualist

I determined that a teen came from a "family attender" family when the following three conditions were met:

1. Parents reported that weekly church attendance was a "family activity" or a "rule."[1]
2. Teens confirmed that church attendance was a family activity or rule.
3. I saw nothing to disconfirm the family's claim to attend church on a weekly basis.

All other families were designated "religious individualist." In the latter group, church attendance was left to the choice of each individual family member. (See table 26.)

Table 26.   Family Type (Family Attenders or Religious Individualists) by Teen Religious Loyalty

Teen Loyalty Type	Family Attender N	Percent	Religious Individualist N	Percent
Loyalist	21	95%	7	37%
Provisional Loyalist	1	5%	4	21%
Unlikely Loyalist	0	0%	8	42%
Total	22	100%	19	100%

In my interview sample, twenty-four teens attended church every week and only two of these were not family attenders. The two weekly-attender teens who came from religious individualist families went to church by their own choice in the absence of family pressure to attend. Most teens from religious individualist families were once expected to attend church, but expectations were relaxed as they grew older. In some cases, parents stopped insisting that their teens attend after they were confirmed in seventh grade. In other cases, parents gave their older teens a choice of whether to attend when they got their driver's licenses and had the option of getting there by themselves if they wished. Many parents admitted that they would have liked to continue the family rule about attending church, but they were simply unable to enforce it. They were religious individualist families by default.

Roof and Gesch, from whom I adapted the terms "family attender" and "religious individualist," demonstrate that assumptions about religious choice are tied in predictable ways to people's work and family experience. Family attenders' parents tend to be well established in careers and earn higher incomes. They tend to be professionals, managers, and full-time homemakers. They are generally more conservative politically and morally. Two-thirds are in two-parent families with children. Fewer are divorced or separated. These parents are more likely to be active in religious activities and socially involved. Their family ties are closer. In contrast, religious individualist parents tend to be those who work full time in clerical and service jobs and earn lower incomes. They remember being less close to their parents growing up, and were reared in permissive homes. Their parents were not strong church attenders, and they are less embedded in church and other social networks themselves.[2]

Roof and Gesch's descriptions are somewhat consistent with family characteristics I observed in families in my sample as they divided along family-attender and religious-individualist lines. In particular, family-attender families tended to experience closer family ties and be more active in religious activities. Religious-individualist families tended to be more permissive in parenting style and to exhibit mixed religious marriages and blended families.

Roof and Gesch note that religious individualism is on the ascendency with the baby boomer generation as a whole. Both inside and outside the church, more people favor an autonomous, personal approach to their religious views and more noninstitutional kinds of religious practice.[3] Levels of religious individualism vary by religious tradition, however. In their study of baby boomers, 44 percent of mainline Protestants, 42 percent of Catholics, and 35 percent of conservative Protestants were religious individualists. They attribute higher levels among liberal Protestants to "the logical working out" of the "Protestant Principle," in which the individual is bound only by responsible personal commitment, not by ascriptive loyalties. High religious individualism among Catholics is linked to the emphasis since Vatican II on the role of individual conscience over the given tradition of the church.[4]

Roof and Gesch also note that families who emphasize religious choice exhibit lower levels of religious training of children and lower levels of children's involvement in religious activities.[5] This too was evident in the families I studied. Religious individualist families tended not to hold their children in the church through the teen years.

Notes

Preface

1. Smith et al. (2002: 605–6) cite three national studies of American adolescents to show a steady decline in religious participation with age. Weekly attendance at a religious service drops 10 percent over the four years of high school. The percentage of youth who attend once or twice a month and those who never attend remains constant at 15 to 16 percent. While 50 percent of 13-year-olds participate in youth group, only 28.6 percent of 18-year-olds participate. This constitutes a 42.8 percent decline over the five-year span of the teens' years in the church. Gallup and Bezilla (1992) also report decline in worship participation with the age of the teen.
2. Roof (1981) identifies the 18- to 25-year-old range as the peak period for dropping out of church. Similarly, Barna (1991) documents that teens' religious participation, self-description as "religious," and "desire to know God" declines notably at age 18.
3. For more on this individuative-reflective stage, see Fowler (1981).
4. Excerpt from Field Notes, Transfiguration, Fall Retreat, September 5, 1996.
5. Lofland and Lofland (1995).
6. Gerth and Mills (1946: 55–56).
7. Excerpt from Field Notes, Transfiguration, Fall Retreat, September 5, 1996.
8. This is qualitative research as Wuthnow (1987: 11) defines it.
9. Excerpt from Field Notes, Transfiguration, Fall Retreat, September 5, 1996.
10. This experience occurred in the "liminal phase" of ambiguity that followed. Victor Turner builds on Van Genneps's construct of liminality (1969: 96–97). For a fuller explanation, see chap. 3.
11. Gender is an important variable in research on the religious life of high school age youth. Smith et al. (2003: 120) report that American adolescent girls, like American adult women, score higher than males on most measures of religiosity. Six percent more 8th through 12th grade girls than boys say that their faith is very important. Similarly for religious participation, Smith et al. (2002: 605) report that 6 percent more girls than boys attend church services weekly. Twenty-eight percent of 12th grade girls, compared to 22 percent of 12th grade boys, have been involved in a religious youth group for all four years of high school.
12. Like gender, race is an important variable in any research on American religion,

247

including research on teenagers. Smith et al. (2003: 123) report in a study of 8th–12th grade American youth that 50 percent of African American youth say that faith is "very important," as compared to 33 percent of "other race" youth (presumably nonwhite and nonblack) and to 27 percent of white youth. They report that the race effect is consistent with frequency of prayer. Smith et al. (2002: 607) report African American adolescents have the highest rates of church and youth group attendance, followed by whites. Youth of other racial and ethnic backgrounds are less likely to attend church frequently or attend a religious youth group. They report that 47.7 percent of African American youth are Baptist, 55.7 percent of Hispanic youth are Catholic, 35.5 percent of Asian youth are Catholic, while another 11 percent are Buddhist. White adolescents are 22.7 percent Catholic, 20.3 percent Baptist, 8.6 percent Church of Christ/Disciples of Christ, 7.1 percent Methodist, with the remainder distributed among different denominations, each with less than 5 percent of the total.

13. Burawoy (1991) describes the circular movement of empirical data leading to theory building as follows: A theory that explains data receives confirmation (or not) in further empirical data; the theory is revised on that basis; the revised theory is tested again by more empirical data.

14. Lofland and Lofland (1995: 194).

Introduction

1. All names and distinctive marks of identification have been altered to protect the confidentiality of the youth and parents in this study. Churches, high schools, and adult professionals have been given pseudonyms to add a further layer of protection for teen subjects. The place where the data was gathered, Louisville, Kentucky, has not been disguised.

2. Hammond (1992).

3. Roof (1978).

4. Dolan (1992).

5. D'Antonio et al. (1996).

6. Fischer (1982).

7. While very large Catholic cathedrals and some large Protestant churches have existed throughout history, since the 1970s the number of Protestant churches with two thousand or more worshipers in attendance has risen dramatically. This new type of religious organization, called a "megachurch," is now recognized as a distinct pattern of American religious life in the late twentieth century (Vaughan [1993], Thumma [1996], Trueheart [1996], Miller [1997]).

8. Gluckman (1967) cited by Coleman (1988:S109). See also note 30 in chapter 2.

9. In the analysis of my findings, I do not make a historical argument that personal autonomy has increased, because my data are not longitudinal. I rely on the established understandings of a host of theorists who have traced this phenomenon and articulated it in the body of literature produced by sociologists of religion. I accept heightened personal autonomy as an assumption that helps me to explain the patterns of religiosity that I observed among the church-related teens in my sample.

10. Bellah et al. (1991: 184).

11. Hammond (1992).

12. Berger (1979).

13. G. K. Chesterton [cited in Bellah (1998: 622)], McNamara (1992), Wuthnow (1993),

and Hammond (1998) are some who allude to the protestantization of all religious traditions in the United States. The theologian Paul Tillich (1963: 176) coined the term "Protestant Principle" to express the radical suspicion of any church's claim of hierarchical or doctrinal absolutism, a suspicion that is rooted in the sixteenth-century Protestant Reformation. Hammond (1998) traces some of the discussion about recent interpretations of the religious clauses in the American Constitution.

14. Lippy (1994) is one who discusses personalism in American religious life. Greeley (cited by McNamara [1992]) coined the term "communal Catholic."

15. Thomas Luckmann (1967) anticipated this shift away from adherence to a religious tradition when he predicted the diffusion of religion in society outside traditional religious institutions. Similarly, Robert Bellah (1970) understood religion as evolving to ever higher levels of freedom for personality and society relative to the environment. He anticipated that the symbolization of humanity's relation to the ultimate conditions of existence would exceed what is labeled "religious." He correctly predicted that religious action would be associated less and less exclusively with the church.

16. Herberg (1956).

17. This is noted, for example, by American religious historian Albanese (1996: 736). See Appendix F, "Faith Tradition as Religious Culture," for a discussion of what is meant by the term "religious tradition" in this study.

18. Wuthnow (1993: 30). Gallup (1992: 22) reported that in the fifty years they have been conducting surveys, the percent of people interviewed who say they believe in God has remained consistent. In a 1989 Gallup survey, 95 percent said they believe in God; 90 percent pray; 88 percent believe that God loves them; and only 3 percent believe this is not the case. In the same year, the percentage of Americans who identified themselves as members of a church or synagogue, 65 percent, was the lowest since the Gallup Poll began tracking such figures in 1937 (Gallup [1989: 29, 45]).

19. The terms "religion" and "spirituality" have been redefined in popular usage. In the past, and particularly in scholarship, "religion" has encompassed "spirituality" within it, as spirituality refers to one aspect of it, the personal experiences of the transcendent. In popular usage today, however, religiousness has been redefined as something narrower and institutional, while spirituality denotes all kinds of experiences of the transcendent, individual and institutional (Zinnbauer and Pargament [1997]). For this research, I use religion as a broad term, what Geertz uses to describe that which relates humans to the ultimate conditions of existence. I see the embrace of a "faith tradition" or "heritage" as one particular expression of religion. I understand "spirituality" as another broad category that overlaps with religion. It is personal transcendence, supraconsciousness, sensitivity, and meaningfulness. Spirituality may coincide with religious understandings of the transcendent (Zinnbauer and Pargament [1997]).

20. Roof (1993) finds that after the 1960s the deeply personal, subjective approach to "spirituality" characterizes American religious faith more than the outer, established institutional forms of religion. Roof popularized the seeking metaphor in *The Generation of Seekers* (1993). Wuthnow (1997) complements it with the dwelling metaphor.

21. Smith et al. (2003: 131) report that two-thirds of older adolescents are not alienated or hostile toward organized religion in America, yet a significant minority of them—about 15 percent—does appear to be. Another 15 percent appear to be disengaged in

attitudes toward religion. The percentage of this hostile or disengaged minority has not grown in recent decades.

22. Smith et al. (2002: 600–601). They surmise that the growth of the number of youth in the "other religion" or "no religion" category has some link to immigration patterns. In 1995, the following distributions of teens by religious affiliation existed: 24 percent Catholic; 23 percent Baptist; the remaining percentage are affiliated with a variety of Christian traditions, other religions, or no religion.

23. Roof and McKinney (1987), Hoge, Johnson, and Luidens (1994), Williams and Davidson (1996: 276).

24. Two recent studies illustrate dramatic changes in understandings of what it means to be Catholic. D'Antonio et al. (1996) find that about half of the "nuclear Catholics" they sampled said that one could be a "good Catholic" without going to mass weekly. This finding is surprising, because the nuclear Catholics are themselves the "regulars" (p. 139). McNamara (1992) describes how, in a Catholic high school he studied, teachers devised compromises to help students remain Catholic "in essentials." Teachers put into students' hands "the very broom some need to sweep their doctrinal and oral arsenals clean of everything but what they feel and believe makes sense to them" (p. 116). The complexity of institutional affiliation is exemplified by the paradoxical findings of D'Antonio et al. (1996). Women and persons with the most Catholic schooling are the most highly committed members of the post–Vatican II generation, but they also are more likely to disagree with church teaching than men and Catholics with less Catholic schooling. In my study I cite similar findings and show how this may be a sign of religious vitality.

25. Hoge, Johnson, and Luidens (1994).

26. Wheeler (1996: 295).

27. Berger (1967) and Smith (1998). Yet the teens in my sample do not quite fit the exaggerated picture that Smith portrays when he describes mainline Protestants as viewing religious identity as ascribed. I did not find Methodist teens and parents who viewed their faith as part of an inherited way of life or viewed their religious identity as "given," as Smith argues (1998: 148).

28. Smith et al. (2003: 117) report that youth in more theologically conservative denominations, Pentecostals, and sectarian traditions evidence higher levels of agreement with statements about the importance of faith than Jewish, Catholic, and mainline Protestant teens.

29. Hoge, Johnson, and Luidens (1994), Berger (1967), Smith (1998: 106).

30. Wuthnow cited by Foster (1994). Smith (1998: 49) finds that over 50 percent remain within the religion of their family of origin across different Christian traditions, with Catholics retaining the highest percentage (83 percent). This trend of switching and dropping out is somewhat moderated, however, by Roof's (1993) findings that the movement in and out of active involvement within religious institutions and across denominations is more fluid and difficult to sort. When individuals switch out of their denomination, they tend to switch into a church within the same denominational family, that is, to another evangelical church or to another mainline Protestant church. Hadaway (1990: 110) finds that "increasing numbers of Americans continue to maintain a religious identity but are no longer counted as members by their denomination of choice."

31. Warner (1993). The options that compete with traditional religion as sources of ulti-

mate meaning are very diverse. For example, religion-like understandings of career and work are promoted by the market. Chidester (1996) makes a case for including baseball, Coca-Cola, and rock 'n' roll in the ambit of religion. Berger (1983) argues that secularity itself competes for adherents in "the religious marketplace."

32. These percentages are taken from Roof's (1993) study of baby boomers, those born between 1946 and 1964. Those remaining within the tradition are both "loyalists" and "returnees" (those who dropped out for a period and then came back). The difficulty of measuring this phenomenon is illustrated by the discrepancy between Roof's findings and Smith's findings (1998: 49). Smith shows that Catholics retained more of their own (83 percent) than evangelicals (78 percent).

33. Most notable in this regard are Roof and McKinney (1987), who describe the loss of religion's ability to provide an integrative force in American culture. They call this religion's "third disestablishment" (pp. 33–39), a theme expanded by Hammond (1992). Coalter, Mulder, and Weeks (1992) describe a "shattered synthesis of religion and culture" (p. 41). Gilkey (1994) describes the decline of mainline Protestant congregations in many ways, but specifically their diminished ability to be "central nurturers and irreplaceable guardians of the nation's moral and spiritual health" (p. 104). Some scholars are more optimistic about the capacities of congregations to transform themselves in response to a changed environment, notably Ammerman (1997).

34. Csikszentmihalyi and Larson (1984).

35. I looked for five religious criteria of Christian faith. First, I investigated how the symbol of Jesus Christ is used to signify the uniquely "real" and provides answers to timeless human problems such as those of injustice, suffering, and death. I looked for evidence of reverence for Scripture, creeds, and Christian doctrine. Second, I looked for rituals and practices, such as prayer, the celebration of sacraments, and the reading of Scripture. Third, I looked for participation in the church, the "community of memory" (Bellah et al. [1985]) constituted by Christian symbols. Finally, I looked for how teens differentiated the Christian tradition from what lay outside of it.

36. James Coleman (1989), in his comparative assessment of the different generational cohorts of adolescents beginning in the late 1950s, observed that today's youth are less embedded in enclaves of adults. He attributes this to the decreased strength of institutions, particularly the family. Hersch (1998) documents the widespread lack of supervision of teens by parents and other adults in an affluent Washington, D.C., suburb.

37. Feldman (1990) represents the widely supported view that today's teens have less family stability in their lives as they confront divorce, unwed motherhood, and geographic mobility. Carroll and Roof (1998) find that today's young adults are less likely to be involved in religious institutions growing up than their parents were as they were growing up. They link this lower incidence of a religious upbringing to higher levels of family disruption. They find that 35 percent of "Xers," those born between 1964 and 1979, indicated religious involvement while growing up, compared with 45 percent of baby boomers, those born between 1946 and 1963, and 53 percent of pre-boomers, those born before 1946. Forty-five percent of Xers went through some sort of family disruption, such as the divorce or separation of their parents, or were raised by a single parent. That is compared to 27 percent of baby boomers and 23 percent of pre-boomers.

38. Gillis (1996) studies the change in "family cultures" that used to provide models to

youth from religion and communal cultures. Now the burden of producing family myths, rituals, and images falls on the individual family. Hadaway and Marler (1996), Stolzenberg et al. (1995), and others find that churches best serve conventional families, a form of family that is becoming less and less typical.
39. Hyde (1990).
40. Niebuhr (1929: 20).
41. Wuthnow (1993: 53).

Part I: How Churches Attract Teens

Chapter 1: Three Congregations

1. The Kentuckiana Interfaith Community (1993); U.S. Census Bureau (1990); Urban and Associates (1995). The Standard Metro Statistical Area of Louisville comprises seven counties, including three in Indiana.
2. In the years of my study, the population of Jefferson County (the county encompassing the city of Louisville) was 27 percent Catholic and 27 percent Baptist. Methodists, Presbyterians, Disciples of Christ, Episcopalians, and Lutherans are the best represented Protestant denominational traditions besides Baptists. The city has been the home of the headquarters of the Presbyterian Church (U.S.A.) since 1988, and Louisville Presbyterian Theological Seminary since 1893. Beyond mainline Protestants, there are two Orthodox congregations in Louisville. There has been a Jewish presence in the city since 1843, with the number of Jewish congregations at the time of this study totaling seven. There are three Islamic centers of worship in the city. The first Hindu temple was consecrated three years after the time of this research. There also are two Baha'i assemblies and three Mormon churches.
3. This is Southern Baptist Theological Seminary, whose shift toward conservative and fundamentalist stances since the late 1970s is documented in Ammerman (1990), and the film *Battle for the Mind* (1995).
4. Research on both adults and teens establishes that people from the South exhibit higher levels of religiosity and participation than those in other regions of the United States. Nelson and Potvin (1980) describe regional variations in religious norms in adults. Smith et al. (2002, 2003) analyze youth data sets to validate similar norms.
5. Two of these are predominantly white, and both are independent Christian churches, loosely linked in the Christian Church restorationist movement. Two are predominantly African American, and both are affiliated with the National Baptist denomination.
6. Public schools are closed on the last Friday of the first week of May, the day before the Kentucky Derby. Local residents, including many school teachers, attend "Oaks Day" at the racetrack, held on this day, or busy themselves with elaborate preparations for the celebrations the next day. Local residents say, "Louisville has two Christmases," one in December and another in May.
7. Gallup Poll surveys over the past fifty years show consistently that approximately one-third of the American adult population report that they attend a church or synagogue each week. In the *Courier-Journal*'s Bluegrass State Poll of 1997 adults, 34 percent reported they attend church or synagogue every week (the *Courier-Journal*, June 15, 1997).
8. New Orleans is the other exception.

9. See Appendix B, "Criteria Used for Selecting Three Congregations and How My Sample Matched Them."

10. As I visited various youth ministers in their church offices, I viewed their bookshelves containing youth ministry resources. Most popular were resources by Group, Youth Specialties, and Rick Warren, as well as denominational resources for youth ministry. Interestingly, the Catholic youth minister said she found most of her resources at the local Baptist bookstore. I noted that the evangelicals and the Methodists used the same Bible study curriculum with their high school teens.

11. See Appendix H, "A Telephone Survey of Teen Activity Levels."

12. Later I learned that the majority of youth ministers in the Catholic Church are either middle-aged women or young men. The pay scale for youth ministry is too low to attract people who must support a family on their salary. (Information conveyed in personal communication with Robert McCarty of the National Federation of Catholic Youth.)

13. I will illustrate in Part II how teens at Transfiguration developed rituals, especially as they struggled to cope with their experiences of death.

14. Founded in 1962, Riverland Heights had outgrown three buildings and was in the throes of constructing a fourth church complex in the year of my study. After the third facility was completed in 1987, it grew 40 percent in the first year and has added approximately 1,000 new members every year since. Vaughan (1993: 121–27) mentions Riverland Heights as the seventeenth fastest-growing church in the United States between 1989 and 1990.

15. The $78 million church complex cost more than the new football stadium that was built for the University of Louisville in the same year. Finished in 1998, it is the fifth largest church facility in the United States. It has 776,000 square feet of floor space, eight acres of metal roofing, seven elevators and eight escalators. It is designed to seat 9,000 people and has fifty acres of parking. A separate 125,000-square-foot complex houses a youth and activity center with a gymnasium, racquetball courts, and various exercise and multipurpose rooms. Another expansion is underway in 2003.

16. The average age of church members at Riverland Heights is thirty-nine.

17. Similarly, adults who volunteered to work with youth were not automatically slotted into the program, as they are in many congregations who experience a shortage of adults willing to give their time to the youth program. At Riverland Heights, adults who volunteered filled out applications, were interviewed, had their references checked, and attended training for sponsors. They were asked not to consume alcohol or to date any of the youth.

18. Theorists of Christian *paideia*, such as C. Ellis Nelson, Charles R. Foster, William Myers, Michael Warren, and Richard Osmer have explored extensively the processes by which religious commitment is nurtured in teens. Popular literature and applied resources on the bookshelves in the offices of youth ministers exhibited greater wear from more frequent usage. (See above, especially note 10.)

19. While there was a sense that Riverland Heights was reinventing youth ministry, in fact there were many continuities with youth ministry strategies used by older programs such as Young Life, Youth for Christ, and Christian Endeavor. Progressive levels of commitment characterized the Christian Endeavor movement, for example.

20. Dean (1991) and Roehlkepartain and Benson (1993) document the difficulties in obtaining leadership for religious youth programs, such as low pay, limited resources

and interest, and poor quality training. "Whether clergy or lay, full-time youth ministers are often charismatic but overworked paragons of dedication ripe for burnout, giving in excess of sixty hours a week to their vocation," William R. Myers summarizes (cited in Dean and Yost, 1991: 75–76). He estimates that 80 percent of those working with youth work without pay, often in addition to other full-time jobs.

21. Coincidentally, all three of the churches in my sample were engaged in building projects during the year of my study. Transfiguration was remodeling its sanctuary. Riverland Heights broke ground on a new facility in another part of town. Of the three youth programs, First United Methodist's was most disrupted by its building program, because their renovation involved tearing up areas the teens used (Sunday school classrooms, the gym, and the fellowship hall) to add what became a state-of-the-art "youth wing" of the building.

22. It is noteworthy that youth in this church were trained in choral church music and exposed to classical musical literature from a young age, performing it before the congregation when they were preschoolers. Unchurched teens without this experience tend to find contemporary music more accessible. This has been argued as the case with baby boomer adults on the basis of observation in the Willow Creek congregation in the book *Inside the Mind of Unchurched Harry and Mary*. Strobel says the number-one reason previously unchurched baby boomers give as to why they come to church is: "'They played my music'" (Strobel 1993: 180). It is perhaps true that the majority of unchurched seekers, as compared to the church-reared subjects of this study, do prefer contemporary music because it is popularized in mass culture. Trueheart (1996: 45) observes, "It is music, more than any other issue or symbol, that divides congregations on the cusp of growth."

Chapter 2: What Attracts Teens to Churches

1. Csikszentmihalyi and Larson (1984: 236). They used a beeper system that enabled them to track teens throughout the day, wherever they were and whatever they were doing. They were able to identify when and under what circumstance they experienced "flow."

2. Plato, *Laws*, Book 6, 797, translated by Sanders (1970: 276).

3. Roof (1978) finds in his study of Episcopalians that they commit to their congregations for the associational ties and the shared worldview that their church offers.

4. Social scientific understandings of the social bases of religion trace back to Durkheim (1915), who stressed the society's need for communal integration through religious rites and beliefs. While the structures of society and the nature of solidarities in late-twentieth-century America are drastically altered, the inseparable unity of social life and religion is a constant.

5. According to Erikson (1968: 128–35), adolescents are absorbed in a process of clarifying identity confusion by testing their social identities in group identification.

6. Talcott Parsons (1965, cited in Ianni [1989: 11]) noted that the peer group became a part of the environment after World War II as a basic unit of a separate social system more persuasive to youth than family or school. James Coleman (1961) is known for his classic study on the role of peers, emphasizing (like Parsons) the uniqueness and separateness of adolescent society. Recent studies have suggested a more moderate view of peer influence by noting a high degree of overlap between parental and peer values and standards of behavior. Part of this congruence between parents and peers

derives from a recognition that parents play an important role in shaping the adolescent peer environment (Foster-Clark and Blyth [1991: 768]).

7. Search Institute (1996) finds that more than nine in ten congregations of all religions report trouble keeping high school students involved. On the other hand, a National Commission on Children survey conducted in 1990 finds that teens are more involved in activities at their church or temple than they are playing a team sport at school (82 percent as compared to 79 percent). It is difficult to reconcile conflicting assessments of the degree to which teens are engaged in their religious institutions. Recent studies offering estimates of how teens spend their time are: Girl Scouts (1989), Barna (1991), Youth Indicators (1991), Bibby (1992), Gallup (1992), Miller (1996), Chadwick and Heaton (a compilation of many studies, 1996), Search Institute (1996), Farkas (1997), *New York Times* and CBS News (1998).

8. Dean and Yost (1991: 45).

9. In contemporary discussions of youth ministry, for example in De Vries (1994), the "youth group" structure is critiqued as one that segregates and marginalizes youth from the life of the whole congregation. Christian educators, such as Sara Little, John Westerhoff, and Michael Warren, propose an integrated model of youth ministry where youth are encouraged to participate in the life of the whole church rather than to separate as a group (Dean and Yost [1991]).

10. In 1997, total parish revenue at Transfiguration exceeded $1 million. Riverland Heights had an annual budget of $14 million. First United Methodist had receipts of $1.24 million. In that same year, Transfiguration had 3,307 communicant members. Riverland Heights had ten to eleven thousand in worship each week. First United Methodist had 2,300 on its membership rolls.

11. Search Institute study cited in Dean and Yost (1991).

12. Riverland Heights' increase in size caused it to shift from being a "functional" community, where people in the social network know one another in face-to-face interaction, to a "value community," which is a collection of people who exhibit value consistency but do not personally interact in a social network with closure (Coleman [1988]). Without closure—that is, the teen's parents knowing the teen's friends' parents—less "social capital" is available to the teen. One of the social benefits of a bounded solidarity with closure is the enforcement of effective norms. Without closure, teens are more likely to slip out of the church social network and drop out of their religious tradition. It should be noted that the definition of "social capital" (shorthand for the positive consequences of sociability) has been extended in different ways by social theorists such as Bourdieu, Loury, and Coleman (Portes [1998]). Coleman (1988), for example, uses social capital to mean the positive benefit to the parents of having control of the teen that accrues from the sociability of the closed teen/parent network.

13. See Table 3 in chapter 3 for a comparison of the numbers of high school seniors on the mailing lists of the three churches.

14. The cleaning of the youth center was another symbolic battleground. The custodian at the parish did not clean the youth center, and this became a sore point with Angie in particular. By the end of my year of research she had gained a promise from the priest that the youth center would be professionally cleaned like the rest of the church. She understood the promise as an affirmation of the importance of the youth ministry to the church. While Angie felt supported by the priest in her work, she did

not always feel affirmed by the general membership of the congregation. Often she said, "They think I'm a crazy person around here."

15. At Transfiguration, Angie was paid to work full-time with high school and junior high school youth. She used part of her salary to pay two others to help her with the work. Beyond these three, she was assisted by four regular adult volunteers and numerous young adult volunteers, many of them alumni and alumnae of the program. At Riverland Heights, the high school ministry was led by three full-time youth ministers, a full-time student intern, and a full-time coordinator of worship who divided her time between junior and senior highs. They trained approximately forty volunteer "sponsors" each year to assist them. First United Methodist employed a full-time youth minister to work with junior and senior highs and to direct a leisure and recreation ministry. The two full-time choir directors at the church conducted high school choirs as part of their responsibilities. A cadre of adult volunteers, many of them parents, staffed various aspects of the youth program as Sunday school teachers, youth group assistants, and chaperones of the retreats and mission trips.

16. Myers cited in Dean and Yost (1991).

17. Bryk et al. (1995) use the qualitative term "warm" to categorize interactions that suggest a genuine sense of human caring. Search Institute (Benson and Eklin [1990]) use it in a similar way to describe how teens may experience congregations.

18. Thumma (1996).

19. Miller (1997: 20) also notes that pastors tend to be "understated, humble, and self-revealing" in rapidly growing "new paradigm" churches. Riverland Heights fits all twelve of the characteristics Miller identifies except one. Miller says, "Clergy and congregants usually dress informally." At Riverland Heights, clergy do eschew clerical garb, but many congregants dress up for church. As one father in my interview sample commented, "The women dress like it's Derby." I noted the strange mix of formal and informal attire, sometimes even within a single family. It was not unusual to see people dressed in business suits seated next to others wearing jeans.

20. In addition, the importance of building a community of adults to work with teens was made evident to me through a counterexample. The new youth minister hired halfway through the year at First United Methodist joked that he was the "Lone Ranger," because he functioned independently with the help of only one mother whom he called "Tonto." His tenure at the church was short, only two years.

21. Wuthnow (1995: 149) also noted that adults who stepped out of their roles to perform acts of compassion impressed teens in his study of volunteerism.

22. Field Notes, Transfiguration, September 4, 1996.

23. Wuthnow (1998) notes that the general trend is toward too much looseness in community groups, a problem related to larger changes in patterns of social relations he finds among adults.

24. See, for example, the personal story Tate shared on a Transfiguration retreat in Part II of this study.

25. A teacher at one of the Catholic schools coined this term as she described the intensity of the relationships at Transfiguration made evident to her in her students' descriptions of youth group.

26. Jennifer Steinhauer, "Lulu and Her Friends Are, Therefore They Shop," in the *New York Times*, Special Section D, April 29, 1998.

27. It was a "bounded solidarity," with invisible but permeable boundaries. It is harder

for outsiders to penetrate the inside when, as Olson (1993) puts it, the relational networks inside are "saturated."

28. While my research was not longitudinal, I kept in touch with some people after my field research was completed and followed up on some of the teens' stories. Marianna was a sophomore and a loner at First United Methodist during the year of my research. I once observed her sobbing silently during an activity in which she felt excluded. Three years later I heard reports that over time she was better integrated into the youth group, and is now happily engaged in many social activities at college.

29. Jennifer Aniston starred in a television show, *Friends*, that was popular with teens in the year of my research.

30. Coleman (1990) uses the term "multiplex relations" to describe a mechanism of social networks that generates "social capital" for its members. "Social capital" is the aggregate of the resources that are linked to a durable network of institutional relationships. "Multiplex relations" are the transinstitutional connections through which the resources of a relationship in one setting can be appropriated in another. For example, someone who is relied on as a friend at church can also be counted on as someone to save you a seat in the school cafeteria.

31. Hammond (1992).

32. This event is also known as "Meet You at the Pole." Popular across the United States, students meet at the flagpole of their school for prayer before school on designated days. Tragically this gathering has been associated with episodes of violent teen assault.

33. The researchers Reginald Bibby and Donald Posterski (1992) note the importance of people in comparison to programs in his analysis of the religious trends of Canadian teens and young adults. My research supports the strong association between the motivational patterns of teens and their social relationships.

34. Roof (1978: 52).

35. The concepts of segmentation and integration have their roots in Durkheim (1893, in Bellah, ed. 1973). I appropriate these terms as articulated by Nippert-Eng (1995) and as developed by Eiesland (1995).

36. WWJD, an abbreviation for "What Would Jesus Do?" made its debut during the year of this research. In comparison to Catholic and mainline Protestant teens in my sample, evangelical teens used more first-order religious language and wore more religious symbols on their clothing.

37. Interestingly, while the youth leaders at Riverland Heights are adept at articulating the religious goals of their ministry, Craig was stumped by the question I asked each of the youth leaders in the three congregations: "What is your theology of youth ministry?" He replied, "Theology? What do you mean by theology?" At Riverland Heights they talk instead about their "Philosophy of Youth Ministry," reflecting their avoidance of the language and trappings of clericalism. Miller (1997) describes this as characteristic of "new paradigm churches," a category that Riverland Heights fits well.

38. Angie handed me five papers she wrote for graduate-level classes she took in youth ministry at a local Catholic university. These papers describe youth ministry, her theology, her understanding of James Fowler's stage theory, and how her ministry goals grow out of her theology.

39. Dean and Yost (1991) describe four "shapes" that effective youth programs tend to take, representing distinct understandings of youth and faith formation. The "midwifery/adoption model" views "faith as a dormant gift in each young person who

needs to give birth to that faith and foster its development to maturity" (p. 55). The "team model" views "faith as contagious: a teenager 'catches' faith when he or she is around others who 'have' it, and the goal is to give every youth ample opportunity to become 'infected'" (p. 56). In the "kinship model," faith is "something which can only be owned in the context of a worshiping community." It integrates youth so thoroughly into the congregation's daily life that discrete youth activities would be deemed superfluous (pp. 58–59). The most common model, the "corporate/consumer model," views faith as "something youth will choose if it meets their perceived needs" (p. 59). Transfiguration follows the midwifery/adoption model; Riverland Heights follows the team model; First United Methodist follows the corporate/consumer model.

40. This is consistent with what Hoge, Petrillo, and Smith (1982) found in a study of the desired religious outcomes of youth ministers and parents in six denominations.

41. The leaders at Transfiguration and First United Methodist presupposed that teens functioned in an individuative-reflective style, where roles, relations, and self-identity are chosen. The individuative-reflective style is defined by Fowler (1986: 30). At Riverland Heights, leaders designed programs targeted instead to a synthetic-conventional style of faith, where the substance of the teens' self-identity is maintained in the connections and exchanges with others integral to their lives. In the synthetic-conventional style, beliefs and values linking teens to important others take form in a tacit, largely unexamined unity (p. 29).

42. Field Notes, Transfiguration, September 6, 1996.

43. Field Notes, Transfiguration, January 2, 1997.

44. Field Notes, Transfiguration, January 20, 1997.

45. Interview transcription, Youth Minister at Riverland Heights, December 12, 1996.

46. While Riverland Heights uses the term "setting the bar high" to describe how they expect teens to stretch toward developing discipline in Christian practices such as regular worship and Bible study and taking risks to evangelize their peers, it could be argued that the practices of Transfiguration and First United Methodist pose a different kind of "high bar." Transfiguration and First United Methodist expect youth to develop a style of faith that embraces a range of ambiguity and complexity.

47. Dean and Yost (1991: 51) identify the adult/youth relationship as an important "structure" of youth ministry in itself. This structure can take the form of a mentoring relationship (described in the illustration that follows). Young adults also can be "guarantors," showing teens how to handle their circumstances on the basis of their own recent experience as teenagers. Adults also can function as role models for teens, with teens observing and learning from their example even without knowing them personally. Parks (1986), Ianni (1989), Wuthnow (1996), and Richter (1997) are representative of those who have commented extensively on the impact of this structure on teen religious formation.

48. Field Notes, First United Methodist, October 13, 1996.

49. Field Notes, First United Methodist, October 6, 1996.

Chapter 3: The Complex Logic of Why Teens Do (and Do Not) Participate

1. National surveys of teen church attendance patterns that are useful for comparison with my sample are as follows (listed in five age categories): (1) *Thirteen- to Eighteen-Year-Olds.* (a) Barna (1991: 41) reports that for thirteen- to eighteen-year-olds who consider themselves Catholic, Protestant, or Christian, 47 percent attend weekly, 22

percent attend two to three times a month, 11 percent attend once a month, 19 percent do not attend at all, and one percent is not sure. (b) Froehle (1996: 22) reports that of thirteen- to eighteen-year-old Catholic teens who are active in their parish's youth ministry program, 72 percent attend weekly or more often, 12 percent attend once or twice a month, 4 percent attend only on major holidays, and 4 percent never or rarely attend. (2) *High School Seniors*. U.S. Department of Education (1991: 123) reports that 30 percent of all high school seniors attend weekly. Monitoring the Future data (Smith et al. [2002]) show that 33 percent of high school seniors attend weekly; 16 percent attend one to two times per month; 36 percent attend rarely; 15 percent never attend. (3) *Sixteen- to Seventeen-Year-Olds.* (a) Gallup (1992: 36) reports that 39 percent of sixteen- and seventeen-year-olds said they attended church or synagogue in the last seven days, and 61 percent said they did not. (b) A *New York Times*/CBS poll (1998: 25) reports that of sixteen- to seventeen-year-olds, 30 percent attended their place of worship every week, 13 percent attended almost every week, 20 percent attended twice a month, 20 percent attended once or twice a year, 26 percent attended a few times a year, and 11 percent never attended. (4) *Ages Fourteen to Twenty-Eight*. Miller (1996: 150) reports that 43 percent of teens and young adults ages fourteen to twenty-eight attend weekly, 10 percent attend twice a month, 12 percent attend monthly, 18 percent attend yearly, and 14 percent never attend. (5) *Ages Nine to Eighteen*. Girl Scouts (1989: 32) report that of youth ages nine to eighteen, 57 percent attend church or synagogue weekly or more, 22 percent attend once a month or more but not weekly, 15 percent never attend, and 6 percent do not know how often they attend.

2. Since most national surveys aggregate data on older and younger teens, with younger teens exhibiting higher frequencies of church attendance than older teens, the higher frequencies of this sample are not as pronounced as they would be if compared with national survey data sorted by age. Smith et al. (2002: 606), for example, show declining frequencies of church attendance as teens move through their high school years.

3. Ten of the twelve Catholic teens in my interview sample attended Catholic schools where attendance at an all-school mass was required periodically. This mass attendance is not factored in here, just attendance at the parish mass.

4. There is no category for attendance two or three times per month because no one reported that level of attendance. Attendance levels are polarized between the weekly attendees and those who attend on major holidays or never, especially for Catholic and evangelical Protestant high school seniors. Barna (1991) also notes this pattern among teens.

5. In addition, at least one of the schools had daily prayer before school hours, yet it was not well attended by students.

6. Parental influence on teen worship attendance will be explored further in Part IV.

7. A parish survey conducted in 1997 by outside evaluators showed that adults of this parish gave a lower-than-average positive response to questions assessing their general impression of their parish. According to the summary, "About half (fifty-one percent) of the people said they were favorable or very favorable toward the parish, a result that was twenty-four percent below that found in the national sample of parishes [as determined by Leaders-People-National Comparison figures, a nationally normed survey of adult Catholics]." The survey summary noted, "The homilies and the music were the two areas that needed the most attention."

8. Conservative Christian groups generally have higher attendance rates of youth than Catholics or mainline Protestants (Smith et al. [2002: 601–2]).

9. While there were just two preaching ministers, there were forty ministers on staff at Riverland Heights.

10. I did not hear any messages mentioning money the whole year I worshiped there. I wonder if they had stressed giving money the previous year, during the building campaign.

11. The mailing list of high school seniors at Transfiguration began with all confirmed members of the parish. To this the youth director added the names of anyone who attended a youth meeting since freshman year. Since not all Catholic parishes have youth programs, Transfiguration informally served youth from several surrounding parishes. This mailing list sometimes included non-Catholics, even someone I recognized as a very active member at Riverland Heights. The mailing list at Riverland Heights was limited to those who had joined the church or whose parent or parents had joined the church. The twenty-four person mailing list at First United Methodist was the tightest and most accurate, comprised of teens who had been confirmed or who were the teenage children of church members.

12. At Transfiguration this event was the annual Senior Mass held on a Sunday evening. Seniors planned and executed the service. They were recognized by name and given silver crosses in a distinctive design worn by all Transfiguration youth group alumni/ae. At Riverland Heights seniors were recognized by name and given a gift at the last meeting of Vision. First United Methodist hosted a breakfast honoring seniors, and afterward recognized them by name during the morning worship service.

13. This does not fit the pattern noted in national survey data that finds church attendance and youth group participation highly correlated (Smith et al. [2002: 602]). It is also notable that in real numbers Transfiguration had more seniors attend this closing event than the megachurch Riverland Heights, fifty-four seniors as compared to Riverland Heights' forty-four seniors. Again, this does not fit with national survey data that show that conservative religious traditions tend to garner higher participation levels than Catholics or mainline Protestants (Smith et al. [2002: 604]).

14. Search Institute (1996) survey data support the general sense that churches have greater difficulty keeping older teens involved. Eighty percent of congregations of all religions report having "some" or "a lot" of trouble keeping teens in grades seven through nine involved. That figure increases to 93 percent as teens reach grades ten through twelve. National survey data analyzed by Smith et al. (2002: 602) also indicate that, like church attendance, youth group participation declines with the age of the teen.

15. Transfiguration excelled in nurturing the sense of belonging to the youth group and in honing leadership skills in teens. It was weaker in nurturing a Catholic sense of obligation to attend mass and in shoring up the plausibility of Catholic belief. Riverland Heights focused its attention on beliefs, and was strong in developing a proportionally small group of teens who elected to join the high commitment Focus program. Riverland Heights attracted large numbers of unchurched teens through its concerted efforts in evangelism. The sense of belonging to a tight social group was weak at Riverland Heights. First United Methodist was strongest in offering belonging, believing, and competence to those who were interested in music. First United Methodist was not as successful at holding teens who did not join the choir.

Part II: How Churches Hold Teens

Chapter 4: Religious Socialization and Religious Experience

1. Miller (1981).
2. I use the term "religious experience" to denote what subjects broadly consider a direct encounter with "extraordinary" power, meaning, and/or value (Albanese 1992: 6, 11). See also chapter section to follow, "But Have They Experienced God?"
3. Roof (1978), Hammond (1992).
4. See the Introduction for a definition of religious loyalty as operationalized as a dependent variable in this research. For a discussion about the agency of the teen as compared to the power of institutions to shape the teen's appropriation of the religious tradition, see Appendix J.
5. I began my analysis by reviewing the faith biographies that teens had shared with me in interviews. I grouped them according to different characteristics to see if they formed patterns. I checked to see whether there were correlations between religious loyalty and over thirty variables, and I eliminated the variables that did not correlate significantly. For example, I found no association between religious loyalty and faith stages, as described by Fowler (1981, 1986). Likewise, I found no association between religious loyalty and having experiences of an injury or a health problem and/or an experience of the untimely death of a friend or family member. There was association between religious loyalty and membership in a religious group outside the church, but in most cases this membership is a secondary effect of the loyalty already fostered through church and home. While there was no association between religious loyalty in teens and characteristics of their siblings, there was with characteristics of parents, and this is discussed in Part IV.
6. Interestingly, Dudley (1999: 116) finds in a longitudinal study of Seventh Day Adventist high school seniors that the teenagers' statements that they intend to remain in the church when they are "out on their own" is the best predictor of the set who did remain ten years later.
7. Even Catholic teens read into my question about "church" a query about involvement in a local congregation instead of attachment to the universal Catholic church, offering further evidence of a "de facto congregationalism" that dominates American religion (Warner 1994).
8. Teens in my interview sample exhibited high levels of praying and Bible reading compared to national samples of teens measured by Gallup polls of teen religious practices. Fifty-six percent of the teens in my sample pray every day as compared to the 46 percent of sixteen- and seventeen-year-olds who "pray frequently" that Gallup and Bezilla (1992) surveys. Forty-four percent of Protestants and no (0 percent) Catholics in my sample read the Bible every day as compared to 17 percent of Protestants and 5 percent of Catholics reported by Gallup and Bezilla (1992). Because of the distinct emphases of the particular traditions of each church, these are sorted here by church rather than by loyalty type.
9. I expected that most teens in my sample would exhibit at least a basic knowledge of their tradition because I limited my sample of teens to those who were reared in churches that had a record of retaining high numbers of teens. This is not representative of American teens in general. Gallup and Bezilla (1992: 12) say that there is a glaring lack of knowledge of the Ten Commandments and of the basic religious tenets

like the meaning of Easter. Ravitch and Finn (1988) find that American seventeen-year-olds were more likely to offer correct answers to multiple-choice questions about Shakespeare than about the Bible.

10. At least one-third of the Catholic teens in my sample said they accept "Catholic beliefs" about God but disagree with the social teachings of the church. Evangelicals, as compared to Catholics and mainline Protestants, expressed greatest compatibility with the beliefs of their church, as they understood them. Compared to teens in the Catholic and evangelical samples, mainline Protestant teens in my sample were the least consistent with each other. There were teens at First United Methodist who were biblical literalists and socially conservative, holding pro-life and creationist views; there were others who said they knew little about the Bible, and were pro-choice and critical of the lay ecumenical Chrysalis movement because it was too evangelical.

11. Some of these terms have been contested lately, particularly the term "practices." For the purposes of this study, I offer the following distinctions among some of the terms. Symbols are the smallest units of tradition; they are single concepts or images. Rituals are dramaturgical enactments of tradition. Narratives are parts of the tradition conveyed in story. Sacred texts are written tradition endorsed through the years as authoritative. The word "practice" signifies two things. It is religious behavior, such as praying; it is also the largest unit of activities clustered around the pursuit of an intrinsically desirable good (MacIntyre [1984], Dykstra and Bass in Bass [1997]), such as the practice of hospitality. Habits are smaller, more idiosyncratic units of action practiced by individuals that may not be orthodox enough to be considered "practices" (Stephen Turner [1994]).

12. I also determined which teens had experienced consistency in their socialization over the course of their seventeen or eighteen years. I considered what each teen said about the continuity and intensity of the exposure to his or her religious tradition. I matched what teens said with what their parents reported about how consistent they were in church participation and in religious socialization in the home. I also compared these reports with what others in the church told me about particular families. From all of the above, and focusing on the actual knowledge and practices of church attendance and prayer and/or Bible reading that the teens exhibited, I classified each teen's religious socialization as consistent or as intermittent.

13. Beginning with G. Stanley Hall (1904), "religious awakening" or conversion, either sudden or gradual, was seen as a normative experience of American Protestant adolescents. Elkind (1971) studied religious experience in teens more broadly. Hoge and Smith (1982) describe six categories of experience that may be defined as religious: appreciation, meditation, lamentation, initiation, revelation, and salvation. Potvin and Lee (1982) and Potvin and Sloane (1985) explore how religious experience or "internal religiousness" in adolescents is affected by different practices and by parental control.

14. While I proceeded in this research pragmatically, not seeking to settle the question whether God is the actual source of what is experienced by teens, what I found is consistent with that theological assumption. William James, in his classic lectures *The Varieties of Religious Experience*, argues that doctrine and dogma are secondary accretions of religious experience. Religious experience is the foundation of religious life (James [1990]; original lectures delivered in 1901–02).

15. Victor Turner (1969, 1974, 1982) argues that a heightened awareness of the transcen-

dent occurs in the alternating movements between "antistructure" (a time of play when persons are liberated from the normative constraints of social statuses and/or social roles) on the one hand, and the structure of norm-governed institutions with their established classifications on the other hand. Antistructure cannot stand alone to meet the material and organizational needs of human beings. Likewise, structure needs revitalization through periodic, intense experiences of antistructure, taking persons beyond the regularities of everyday life. In addition, parallel alternating rhythms have been noted by other scholars: by phenomenologist Alberoni between "the nascent state" and the institutional "church"; by Robert Ellwood between "emergent religion" and "established" religion; by Mary Douglas between "effervescence" and "ritualism"; and by Max Weber between "charisma" and "routinization" (Warner [1988: 45–46]).

16. Antistructure, as described by Turner, has some of the same characteristics of "flow" described by Csikszentmihalyi and Larson (1984), especially the centering of attention illustrated here (Victor Turner [1982: 56–57]). While "flow" shared characteristics with antistructure, flow differs from antistructure in that is it not conceived by Csikszentmihalyi and Larson (1984) to be part of a dialectical process, as Turner describes antistructure working with structure to mark transitions.

17. Berger (1997: 205) calls the comic "a signal of transcendence."

18. Field Notes, Transfiguration, March 9, 1997.

19. Turner (1969: 95).

20. Turner (1969: 94–98).

21. The percentage of teens in my interview sample who reported a religious experience (49 percent) is higher than the 32 percent of sixteen- and seventeen-year-olds who responded affirmatively in a Gallup poll to the question "Have you ever personally experienced the presence of God?" (Gallup and Bezilla [1992]).

22. Nelson (1989) builds on the ideas of "the structure of consciousness" and the "sifting" process described by Mary Douglas.

23. Nelson (1989: 125).

24. Nelson (1989: 55). This is similar to Geertz's circular relationship between worldview and ethos (1974: 141), or as Tipton (1982: 174–75) expresses it, between "is and ought." See, however, Appendix O for stories that do not fit the pattern of combined religious socialization and religious experience.

25. The view that religious experience is solitary, individual, and unfettered by religious institutions can be traced to William James. Yet unlike James, and in the tradition of Max Weber, my research confirmed that personal encounters with God are not necessarily disconnected from institutions. Following Weber's framework, I observed how institutional religion lives in the tension between substance and structure. On the one hand, when highly structured "routinized" forms and procedures substitute for the primal religious experiences, religious experience is stifled. On the other hand, the substance of religious experience—the direct, spontaneous, and immediate encounter with God—needs structure for it to be communicated to prospective converts and youthful adherents. The substance is assisted by the structure of the church.

26. This was heightened by the liminality of the setting.

Chapter 5: How Three Congregations Hold Teens in Distinctive Ways

1. Sixty-eight percent in my interview sample were loyalists, 12 percent were provisional loyalists, and 21 percent were unlikely loyalists. In contrast, a 1992 Gallup poll

finds that a lower percentage, only 25 percent, express a high degree of confidence in organized religion. Barna (1991) finds overall that more teens wanted a close relationship with God than wanted to be part of a local church (56 percent as compared to 43 percent).

2. Beyond that, the role of parents as their "children's first teachers in the faith" is emphasized in sermons from the pulpit. The priest and religious educator at Transfiguration made a concerted effort to convey to parents the idea that they were their children's most important teachers in faith. Most parents I talked to, however, saw the church and the parochial school as their children's most important teachers in Catholic life. (See Part IV.)

3. Froehle (1996).

4. The percentage of teens attending Catholic high school in one national survey of Catholics was only 25 percent (Froehle [1996]).

5. For example, in a discussion about marriage, the teacher did not offer a sacramental view of it. She broadly endorsed interreligious marriage. The views she presented were similar to those of "Golden Rule Christians" (Ammerman [1997]). "What matters," she said, "is that you see spirituality as important, that you know that there is a God, and that you love your neighbor as yourself."

6. Entry into these schools is by application and is competitive.

7. In McNamara's study of a parochial high school in Arizona, he noted that the school in his study did not offer enough socialization in Catholic ritual, nor did it offer retreats (1992: 162). I agree with his assessment that these omissions had a negative effect on the experience of Catholics teens in his sample. For the Catholics in my sample, these two elements were considered critical to their experience as Catholics.

8. The 1996 Notre Dame Study of students at Catholic colleges and universities reported similar low ratings that students gave to religious education offered by Catholic educational institutions. Less than 50 percent judged the undergraduate schools positively in areas such as presenting material on the Bible and presenting church teaching (Weigert and Miller [1996]).

9. See Part I for a description of the colored ribbon ceremony incorporated into the confirmation retreat led by high school teens for eighth-grade confirmands.

10. Teens who grew up at Riverland Heights remember when the youth complex was the church. The complex of buildings used for junior and senior high ministry was the space used by the church before they built the larger set of buildings a quarter mile down the street. When I interviewed teens in the meeting room of the youth complex, they often remarked that they remembered playing in that room when it was the church nursery.

11. The enormous dimensions and the size, making it the fifth largest church building in the country, are described in Part I.

12. I intentionally use this metaphor of train tracks used by Bourdieu (1977) to define habitus. At Riverland Heights, the notion of growth was part of the habitus.

13. Craig noted his inconsistency that he sent his own children to the Christian school.

14. Field Notes, Riverland Heights, November 13, 1996.

15. See Part I for definition of "big church."

16. Worship at the Riverland Heights youth complex illustrated what Durkheim (1915) called collective effervescence in the seasonal ceremonies of the Central Australians.

17. Field Notes, Riverland Heights, May 11, 1997.

18. "And Now, a Gross-Out from Our Sponsor," *New York Times*, Sunday, July 25, 1999.
19. Field Notes, Riverland Heights, September 22, 1997.
20. Miller (1997: 64–66).
21. Miller (1997) and Trueheart (1996).
22. Wheeler (1996), Olson (1993), Roof (1978).
23. Kelley (1972), Roof (1978).
24. Olson (1993) and Wheeler (1996) have observed this as well.
25. Field Notes, First United Methodist, June 15, 1997.
26. *ER*, *Friends*, and *Seinfeld*, the "Thursday night lineup," were named as the television shows most watched by teens in my sample. The amount of time that teens in my sample spent watching television was lower than what Harris Poll researchers found in a national survey of high school students (Girl Scouts 1989). The percentages who watched four or more hours per day: 0 percent (my sample), 21 percent (Harris); two to three hours per day: 10 percent (my sample), 28 percent (Harris); less than two hours per day: 49 percent (my sample), 41 (Harris); never: 41 (my sample), 8 percent (Harris). The three top movies among teens in my sample were (in order of preference) *The Shawshank Redemption*, *A Time to Kill*, and *Romeo and Juliet*. In general, first-run movies were considered expensive by teens in my sample, and moviegoing in theaters did not occur with great frequency. Five of the teenaged boys in my interview sample played in bands, and for all of them it was a main focus of their lives. One of the five belonged to a band that played Christian music exclusively. Musical tastes ranged across all stylistic categories, with no clear top preference of style.
27. Lynn Schofield Clark (1999) argues that media are not external, but integrated into everyday life. The public is in the home, especially through television. While the content of media may run counter to the values of particular religions, and while the commercial aspect of media is objectionable to many, media are ubiquitous and inextricably tied into private and public discourses about religion and values that occur with and among teens.
28. One of my questions to teens in their interview asked who most represented to them an image or model of mature Christian faith. See Appendix L.
29. Every adult I interviewed who worked with teens could tell a similar personal story about feeling indebted to someone who reached out to them when they were a teen, about someone they admired who had a significant influence on teens, or about some experience that gave them a special sympathy for teens or their parents.
30. Myers (1991b), Parks (1986), Keating (1990).
31. Similarly, in Wuthnow's (1995) study of teen volunteerism he found that teens might perform community service and afterwards fashion their understandings of the reasons why they did it, often through the telling of stories in conversation with others.
32. McNamara (1992).
33. Daloz et al. (1996).
34. Field Notes, First United Methodist, June 15, 1997.
35. I also was attentive to stories that teens might have offered about religious experiences in the course of the interview, and specifically in response to the following questions: "Has your image of God—your relation to God—changed over the years? Are there events that stand out as especially important as you think of changes in what you think about God?" (See Appendix L.)

Chapter 6: Special Challenges of the Senior Year

1. Barna's findings substantiate this pivotal change during the adolescent years. "A massive shuffling of priorities occurs at age 18. . . . Many of the issues that plague them so deeply as younger teens—peer relationships, spiritual development, materialism, physical health—cease to have great importance to them" (1991: 17–18). Barna documents the declines that are notable at age eighteen—the declines in closeness to parents, in descriptions of themselves as religious, in religious activities, and in their desire to know God. At the same time, stress levels increase (1991).
2. Roethke, T. (1956) (in Eisner [1979: 256]). These ambiguous feelings could be compared to Malinowski's description of how the bereaved Melanesians feel in both the longing and the repulsion for the corpse of a dead loved one. Religious rituals assist them to move through their period of mourning (1925: 34).
3. Ianni (1989).
4. Takanishi (1993), Feldman and Elliott (1990).
5. McGuire (1981) and Osmer (1996) note this, and that it is true with the bar mitzvah and bat mitzvah ritual for Jewish teens.
6. The director of religious education at Transfiguration was trying to change confirmation to make it more voluntary and not tied to the eighth-grade year.
7. See Part I for a description of the involvement of high school youth as leaders of the confirmation retreat for eighth-graders.
8. Bill West, the head minister at Riverland Heights, explained in a sermon that believer baptism by immersion is necessary for eternal salvation.
9. Infant baptism by immersion has become the new norm at Transfiguration since the time of my study. The renovation of their sanctuary included the installation of a baptismal pool to replace the font and to make possible baptism of infants and adults by immersion.

Part III: Seven Styles of Being Religious . . . or Not

Chapter 7: Religious Tradition and Teen Self-Identity

1. This finding comes from a 1999 Gallup survey cited in Smith et al. (2002: 609).
2. This is David Tracy's (1981) term for the focal meaning of the Christian tradition, the event of Jesus Christ as witnessed to in the classic Christian texts.
3. See the Introduction for a discussion of Giddens's "posttraditional self."
4. Giddens (1991: 6).
5. Coleman (1990: 585) explains how the decrease in mutual dependency between generations reduces the incentive for parents to invest in child rearing. With the rise in pension funds, retirement insurance, and the shift of the care of the dependent aged to commercial residences, there is less incentive for parents to invest social capital in their offspring, who in earlier times would have cared for them in old age. From the perspective of the teens, the incentive to offer filial loyalty to the parent is reduced as they anticipate the end of their dependence on their parents for nurture. For most teens, however, economic dependence on parents continues, especially with the high expense of secondary education.
6. Giddens (1991: 7).
7. Giddens's use of the term "practices" is similar to Bourdieu's. Practices are individual

and collective patterns of action evolving from taken-for-granted dispositions (habitus) stratified by class that structure relations, language, and other understandings of the world. The practices that result from habitus and its structures produce, in turn, more habitus within the same class (Bourdieu [1977], Giddens [1991: 82]).

8. Giddens (1991: 81).

9. Giddens, like Bourdieu, has a more deterministic view of structures and practices as shaping dispositions, relations, language, and other understandings of the world. Sewell's (1992) critique of Giddens's structuralism helpfully counterbalances Giddens with an understanding of actors' agency to control structures and to understand their complexity and contradictions. (See Appendix J.)

Chapter 8: Self-Identity in Seven Religious Types of Church-related Teens

1. Csikszentmihalyi and Larson document that seniors, compared to freshmen, spend ten hours a week less with their family, and ten hours more with their friends. Throughout the high school years psychic energy shifts to peer relationships from family relationships (1984: 271).

2. Becker (1999) names "family" as one of four models that typify how congregations understand their core tasks, mission, and identity.

3. Smith (1998) notes how evangelicals in comparison to fundamentalists are in tune with styles and trends of the culture.

4. Some of these questions about ethics were as follows. "Do you think actions can be right or wrong?" "If so, what actions are always right?" "Are there certain moral opinions that everyone should agree on?" (See Appendix L.)

5. A national study conducted by the National Center for Health Statistics in 1995 found that 50 percent of girls and 55 percent of boys ages fifteen to nineteen had had sexual intercourse (*New York Times*, May 3, 1997). Search Institute (1996) data show that sexual activity is lower among teens who attend church.

6. Giddens (1991: 103–8).

7. Of the four Classics I got to know best, two went to public schools, one attended a Catholic school, and one attended an elite private school. All four did not consider their school environment "religious," even C.J., an evangelical, who attended a Catholic school.

8. Examples of the student-run Christian clubs besides Fellowship of Christian Athletes were Young Life, Campus Life, and Campus Crusade.

9. "Thirteeners" is a term for a birth cohort similar to Generation X. It was coined by Howe and Strauss to encompass those born from 1961 to 1981 (Howe and Strauss [1992]).

10. "Hold on to Jesus," James Isaac Elliott, Steven Curtis Chapman, © Copyright 1996. Cabinetmaker Music/ASCAP (admin. By ICG)/Peach Hill Songs/BMI. All rights reserved. Used by permission.

11. One of the Catholic girls' high schools developed an especially popular program based on Mary Pipher's best-selling book *Reviving Ophelia*. Selected high school girls lead sixth-grade girls in exercises geared toward building self-esteem and positive gender identity.

12. Bellah et al. (1985).

13. Fifty percent of the Catholics in my interview sample were Marginalizers. (See table 6.)

14. See Part I for a definition of multiplex relations. Briefly, it is when relationships

exceed the boundaries of the institutions. For example, church friends see each other outside church functions and invite each other to parties.

15. The two who went on instead to public high schools also maintained friendships with their friends from their Catholic school years, but these friendships weakened over time as current friends from a different web of connections based in public schools and part-time jobs displaced old friends in importance.
16. Csikszentmihalyi and Larson (1984: 271).
17. Giddens (1991: 110).
18. Wuthnow (1991).
19. Roof (1993) develops this term to describe a different generation, baby boomers, but the characteristics fit the teens of this type as well.
20. See Giddens's definition earlier in the chapter.

Part IV: Nurturing Teen Religious Loyalty in the Family

Chapter 9: How Parents Influence Teen Faith

1. Benson and Eklin (1990) document a trend of high church participation in young adolescence diminishing in late adolescence. Osmer (1996) notes how the drop-off is linked with confirmation as "graduation" from the religious education program of the church.
2. I take the definition of "religious loyalty" as operationalized in the Introduction and use the typology that resulted from teens in my interview sample. To handle the data with greater ease, in this chapter I reduce the five categories to three: the loyalists are the "unshakables" and "tentatives"; the provisional loyalists are the "conditionals"; the unlikely loyalists are the "postponed" and the "alienated."
3. In a national survey of Catholic teens, 86 percent report that they learned about faith from their family (Froehle [1996]). Barna (1991: 39) documents that 54 percent of young adults attribute their acceptance of Christ as Savior to the influence of their parents. Another 24 percent attribute it to the church, 13 percent to clergy, and 4 percent to teachers and counselors.
4. According to a *New York Times* and CBS News poll, the person most teens ages sixteen to seventeen admire most is their mother. Thirty-three percent name their mother; 17 percent name their father; 5 percent and 6 percent name their grandmothers and grandfathers respectively. The next highest category was "best friend," receiving 5 percent (1998: 20).
5. See Part I for a discussion of the role of the mentor, an experienced adult who challenges, supports, and inspires the teen, and of that of the guarantor, an older peer or young adult who acts as a role model for the teen.
6. While teens claim to be more influenced by their parents, they say they turn more often to same-age peers for support and advice about right behavior. According to a Barna survey (1991: 22), sources of support named by teens ages thirteen to eighteen were: friends (72 percent); mother (54 percent); father (38 percent); siblings (33 percent); Bible (13 percent); teachers and counselors (13 percent); ministers and priests (13 percent). Similarly, according to a Harris poll conducted for the Girl Scouts, 58 percent of teens turn to peers for advice; 53 percent turn to parents; 20 percent turn to a brother or sister; 3 percent turn to a youth leader; 2 percent turn to a religious leader (1989: 7).

7. See Part II for a discussion of national survey data reporting teen responses to questions about religious experience.

8. A Barna survey (1991: 23) of teens ages thirteen to eighteen finds that "those having a lot of influence on thoughts and actions" are: mothers (70 percent), fathers (60 percent), clergy (29 percent), siblings (29 percent), and teachers (26 percent). Craig Miller (1996: 33) surveys teens and young adults ages fourteen to twenty-eight to ask where they have learned their core values. The response is family (70 percent), church (13 percent), friends (10 percent), school (4 percent), media (2 percent). DeVaus (1983: 147) makes the distinction between parents and teens as follows: parents influence values, ideals, and beliefs; peers influence self-concept.

9. A Harris poll conducted for the Girl Scouts (1989: 16) reports that the adults who have been a source of disappointment to teens are: parents (56 percent); other family (28 percent); teachers (21 percent); neighbors (11 percent); counselors (5 percent); religious leaders (5 percent); youth group leaders (4 percent).

10. Public Agenda reports on national survey data showing that 49 percent of the general public says fewer families are teaching their children religious faith and that this is a very serious problem, even more serious than how children are suffering because of economic pressure on their parents (Farkas and Johnson [1997: 13]).

11. Public Agenda reports that only one in five of the general public says that it is common to find parents who are good role models for their children (Farkas and Johnson [1997: 13]).

12. The other question I asked parents that sometimes prompted tears was, "What does Christian faith mean to you?"

13. Roof and Gesch note that having an active coreligionist spouse is one of the strongest predictors of adult church participation (1995: 76). Ploch (1998) also supports that finding.

14. Paulson and Sputa (1996) find that both adolescents and parents perceived that levels of parenting dropped between ninth and twelfth grades, except in values toward achievement, which did not change.

Chapter 10: Three Families, Three Outcomes

1. Their family income was $55,000 per year.

2. By "parent/teen social network," I refer to a particular kind of social capital defined by Coleman (1990) that exists for a teen when there is closure in the teen's network of relationships, that is, when the teen's parents know the teen's friends' parents.

3. In my interview sample there was a positive correlation between teen loyalty and having parents who were involved in some kind of religious small group. Wuthnow finds that small groups are noted by participants as important sources for caring and support. Religious small groups cultivate spirituality and empower the individual to take responsibility for faith. In 1991, 40 percent of all Americans were involved in some kind of small group. Fifty-seven percent of those in small groups belonged to a church or synagogue-related small group (Wuthnow [1994]).

4. Steinburg's study of over two hundred families in which the oldest child was on "the cusp of adolescence" finds that over 40 percent of parents suffer a precipitous decline in mental health that was linked strongly to the child's changing sense of self (reported in Sandmaier [1996]).

5. I take the definition of "religious loyalty" as operationalized in the Introduction and

use the typology that resulted from teens in my interview sample. To handle the data with greater ease, in this chapter I reduce the five categories to three: the loyalists are the "unshakables" and "tentatives"; the provisional loyalists are the "conditionals"; the unlikely loyalists are the "postponed" and the "alienated."

6. At Transfiguration the instrumentation of music at corporate worship was usually piano, violin, and flute. After they moved into the renovated sanctuary they used the organ instead of the piano. Phil's mistaking it for "guitar" reflects his sense that the style of music and worship is too informal, regardless of the actual instruments they used.

7. Roof (1993), Hoge, Johnson, and Luidens (1994).

8. Roof and Gesch (1995: 75).

9. Larson and Richards describe how individual members can have very divergent views of the same family unit. "Each family member comes home each night to a different family. Mother, father, and adolescent children experience dissimilar families" (1994: vii).

10. The political rhetoric of the religious right is noted for promoting the view that broken families are responsible for the weakening of traditional family values in the upcoming generation.

11. Hoge, Petrillo, and Smith (1982).

12. Hoge, Petrillo, and Smith note, "Any simple model of parent-to-child value transmission is almost useless" (1982: 578). Like these authors, I make an argument for associations, not for causality.

13. Empirical studies (for example, Carroll and Roof [1998], Barna [1991], Hart [1986]) support the finding that there tends to be lower levels of religious socialization of children in nonintact families.

14. Marler (1995).

15. Wuthnow (1996).

16. Taffel (1996) cites economist Lester Thurow as estimating that parents now spend 40 percent less time with their children than they did thirty years ago.

Chapter 11: How Families Influence Religious Loyalty in Teens

1. Brusco (1995) and Brasher (1998) are two of several authors who have documented the ways evangelical and conservative Christian women exercise power in *paterfamilias* and in male-led churches. In my interviews I noted several cases where the subordinate marital partner dominated the joint interview with her husband.

2. For this group of peer-style parents, "traditional family values" is defined either as a structure (as for hierarchical and traditional-style parents) or as morality (as for democratic-style parents). Peer-style mothers accepted gender-defined roles as an ideal, yet their circumstances dictated that they adopt a more pragmatic approach to roles within their own families.

3. I initially named this style of parenting "chaotic," because almost all the parents in my sample who manifested this style associated it with negative feelings of being out of control. There were two sets of parents, however, who found some positive aspects to this laissez-faire style. As one father expressed it, "We try to be as open as we can."

4. Taffel (1996).

5. Sandmaier (1996: 23).

6. Wuthnow (1998).

7. Browning et al. (1997: 9).

8. Wuthnow (1998).
9. Larson and Richards (1994) name closeness and warmth as today's ideal for families. The parent-child relationship is judged by the presence of congenial affective states. More than just spending time together, spending time together *in leisure* is associated with fewer negative states in teens (1994: 214). Barna finds that teens who say their relationship with God is very important are much more likely to describe their bonds with parents as "very close" (1991: 9).

    In my interviews, I measured the family climate by the teen's answer to the question, "How would you describe your relationship with your parents?" Answers such as "close," "good," and "we get along well" were considered for the purposes of this research as indicating a warm climate. I also rated it "warm" if the teen said that he or she had a good relationship with one parent and not the other. If there was ambiguity, parent responses to a similar question were taken into account.
10. Greeley and Gockel find that "when a home is characterized by an atmosphere of congeniality, then parental values are most effectively communicated. When the orientation of the family is religious, then the impact of outside religious factors is minimized except to reinforce what the home has already established" (1971: 264).
11. Erikson (1968), Youniss and Smoller (1985), Montemayor and Flannery (1991).
12. A teen in my sample estimated that 80 percent of the seniors at her high school had the full use of a car. I was surprised at how lower-income families like the Marlboros found a way to provide a car for their teens.
13. In 1997, teens spent $122 billion, according to Teen-age Research Unlimited, a national market research company based in Illinois—quoted in the *Courier-Journal*, Louisville: February 5, 1999.
14. A 1985 study by Potvin and Sloane confirms that high parental control becomes "dysfunctional" in fostering religious participation in higher-age teens, those ages sixteen to eighteen.
15. Attitudes are attached to these cultural elements, what Bourdieu calls "habitus" or durable dispositions. Habitus is formed in relation to the structures of the family in the early stages of childhood. I investigated family culture and habitus by visiting teens' homes and by paying attention to the comments made by both teens and parents about family symbols, rituals, or practices that had any religious significance. I excluded the practice of church attending in this variable since it was important enough to consider separately. So what evidence is there of habitus replicated from parent to teen? In a few cases I noticed that some teens used the same words as their parents to describe their attitude toward the church. Another example is the way Parker Marlboro, a Customizer (see Part III), puts together his religion. It is something he selects piece by piece from his two traditions, just as his mother says she does. (See the Introduction for a discussion of how the determinism of Giddens's [1991] "structures" is reinterpreted by Sewell [1992] and augmented with an understanding of human agency to exercise control over structures. Similarly, Sewell [1992] corrects the overdeterminism of Bourdieu's notion of habitus to build in the possibility of change. See also Appendix J.)
16. Historian Margaret Bendroth notes that levels of family religious practice in America have never been high (1996: 51). Evangelical families are noted for open dialogues about faith. Catholic piety is expressed mainly in attending mass. The liberal Protestant family is guided more by ungrounded parental authority and practical logic

(Browning et al. [1997]). A Search Institute study (Benson and Eklin [1990]) finds that the family practices of having conversations about faith and reading the Bible together are among the best predictors of adult religious participation. Saying grace as a family has a relatively weak effect on adult church attendance.

17. Overall, nearly 59 percent of teens in this study attend corporate worship regularly, that is, generally every week. More than 12 percent report that they attend on average one, two, or three times a month. Over 29 percent attend only once or twice a year, if at all. Note that the frequencies I observed are higher than what most national surveys of teens report, because (1) my sample is of teens who are on the rolls of a church, and (2) my sample of teens comes from churches regarded as "successful" with youth. On the other hand, the frequencies in this sample are only for seventeen- and eighteen-year-old teens. Since most national surveys aggregate data on older and younger teens (with younger teens exhibiting higher frequencies of practice than older teens), the higher frequencies of this sample are not as outstanding as they would be if compared with national survey data sorted by age.

18. In my study I encountered several teens for whom grandparents were the primary supporters of their participation in the church. Teens sometimes named a grandparent as the person who best exemplified mature Christian faith.

19. Ten percent of teens in the Monitoring the Future national survey listed participating in religious activities as one of the top three activities they enjoy most with family (Bachman, Johnston, and O'Malley [1993], quoted in Chadwick and Heaton [1996]).

20. A 1991 Barna survey reports that 34 percent of teens say they personally feel it is very important to participate actively in a Christian church. Forty-four percent say they believe their parents feel this way. Only 13 percent say they believe their friends hold this view.

Chapter 12: Parenting in Particular Religious Traditions

1. Greven defines "temperament" as a pattern of feelings, thoughts, and sensibilities (1977: 12). The term is similar to Bourdieu's "habitus" without the material implications and linkages of class variables.

2. Greven (1977: 13).

3. Mainline Protestant parents' attitudes about child rearing exhibit the persistence of philosopher John Locke's notions of the need to apply a steady hand in shaping children's supple wills before they have memories so that their compliance to worthy goals will seem natural.

4. See the Introduction, pages 2–4, for Andrea's description of the religiosity of the generations of her family.

5. R. G. Goldman, Robert Coles, and David Elkind are three of the more well known researchers investigating the development of religious belief in early childhood.

6. Ozorak (1989) calls this "the polarization effect." Her study lends empirical support to an earlier polarization thesis of Isenberg.

7. Bendroth (1996).

8. While the phenomenon of switching has been blamed for weakening commitment to religious institutions, switching may represent increased religious commitment or ongoing sanctification, as some shift to higher-demand churches. As Smith (1998: 48) demonstrates, evangelicalism, as compared to fundamentalism and mainline

Protestantism, has the greatest drawing power for those who switch out of other Christian traditions. Ammerman (1997) demonstrates that switching is a form of natural selection that strengthens the probability of survival in the better examples of "the species."

9. Carroll and Roof (1998) found that religious involvement and understanding is not strikingly different between Xers and boomers. Both cohorts are very different from pre-boomers, however. Xers and boomers are more interested in autonomy, freedom, independent thought, and religious exploration, and not committed to institutional religious involvement. Similarly, U.S. Department of Education (1991) finds that youth and parent views on religion and most other topics are closer today than they were in 1975. Surveys from 1975 and 1990 show that the percentage of high school seniors indicating that they agree with their parents about religion is up slightly from 65 percent to 69 percent.

Conclusion

1. Lipset (1963) cited in Marty (1983: 273).
2. In the Introduction I reviewed how the general trend of heightened personal autonomy has been documented and nuanced in particular ways by many scholars, for example, by Luckmann (1967), Bellah (1970), Roof (1978, 1993), Berger (1979), Marty (1983), Bellah et al. (1985, 1991), Roof and McKinney (1987), Hammond (1992), Coalter, Mulder, and Weeks (1992), Wuthnow (1993, 1997), Gilkey (1994), Lippy (1994).
3. Sheila Larson is an ideal type developed by Bellah et al. to represent a certain kind of religiosity found in their study sample of middle-class Americans (1985: 221). She typifies how religious individualism can evolve into a belief in self as God, in "Sheilaism" in her case. Her religious expression is idiosyncratic and not linked to religious traditions of historic religious communities and their contemporary institutions.
4. Giddens (1991: 82).
5. Roof (1978), Carroll and Roof (1998).
6. See Part III.
7. See Part IV.
8. Bellah et al. noted, "Mysticism is probably the commonest form of religion among those we interviewed, and many who sit in the pews of the church and the sects are really religious individualists" (1985: 246).
9. See Part III.
10. See Part III.
11. See Part IV.
12. See Part I and Part III.
13. See Part III.
14. See Part II.
15. See Part III.
16. See Part III.
17. See Part III.
18. The National Commission on Children 1990 Survey of Parents and Children (cited in Chadwick and Heaton [1996: 238]) finds that more teens are involved in activities of religious institutions than with sports, lessons in music, dance, and karate, extra

school activities such as a play or choir, and clubs such as scouts and 4-H. For example, 82 percent of thirteen- to seventeen-year-olds said they attended an activity at their church or temple as compared to 79 percent who said they played a team sport at school.

19. Marler (1995); Carroll and Roof (1998).
20. See Part IV.
21. While America has never been unitary in a Durkheimian sense of having a single shared worldview (Durkheim [1915]), the social fabric of community life in suburban metropolitan areas like Louisville was more unitary three decades ago when teens from a particular church tended to go to the same high school and live in proximity to one another.
22. See the Introduction.
23. See the Introduction.
24. It is the exception rather than the rule for Catholic parishes to have youth groups. The CARA (Froehle [1996]) national survey of youth activity in Catholic parishes does not even list belonging to a parish youth group as one of the options to check.
25. These are Angie's terms describing her strategy for youth ministry. See Part I.
26. See Part I.
27. These are the expressions of the music director. See Part I.
28. See Part I.
29. This is the term used by Csikszentmihalyi and Larson to convey the capture of teens' attention and the intense focus of their attention they call "flow" (1984).
30. This is a metaphor used by one of the teen's fathers in Part IV.
31. See Part IV.
32. See Part IV.

Part V: Appendixes

Appendix A: Validity, Reliability, and Generalization of the Findings
1. Babbie (1992: 132).
2. Lofland and Lofland (1995: 22).
3. Since the time of my study, outbreaks of student violence in Paducah, Columbine, Fort Worth, and other places have altered the lives of high school seniors. The use of the Internet by teens has dramatically increased in the years since I collected my data. The scandals linked to Clinton during his presidency drastically alter the way teens view authority. The calamity of 9/11 increases the vulnerability teens experience.
4. Geertz, in Emerson (1983: 105).
5. Becker and Eiesland (1997: 19).
6. Myers (1991a).
7. Csikszentmihalyi and Larson (1984: 2).

Appendix B: Criteria Used for Selecting Three Congregations and How My Sample Matched Them
1. Ammerman (1987).
2. Roof and McKinney (1987: 81–105).
3. Roof and McKinney (1987: 6).
4. Melton (1989: 479–80).

Notes 275

Appendix C: Theoretical Models of Faith Transmission

1. Berger (1967), Hoge, Johnson, and Luidens (1994).
2. Olson (1993) develops this theory based on Fischer's (1982) analysis of rural and urban social networks.
3. Greeley (1989) argues that it is rational for most people to opt for their own religious heritage because the "consumption of a given religious heritage rises with exposure to the heritage because the marginal utility of time spent on the heritage rises with exposure" (p. 122). Sherkat and Wilson (1995) find a correlation between the persistence of a given religion and the constraints placed on choice.
4. Berger (1967); Hoge, Johnson, and Luidens (1994). Recently, greater attention has been paid to invisible processes that shape identity and moral values. These processes counter traditional formations of religious identity and meaning, and are evolutionary. The following are examples of evolutionary processes, conventional processes, and global processes. Habermas (1974) speaks of an evolutionary process by which ego development becomes increasingly rational as it parallels changes in collective identity that occur with new material and historical conditions (pp. 106ff). New Institutionalist theory, represented by the collection of essays edited by Powell and DiMaggio (1991), describes the symbolic role of conventions in the environment to inculcate what is taken for granted as rules and "scripts" to follow for career paths, social relations, and attitudes about them. Anthony Giddens (1991) argues that the nonconscious strategies on which actors rely most to negotiate everyday life in their local contexts are actually formed by global sources, ones that are incompatible with religious traditions.
5. Erikson (1968), Allport (1961), Rogers (1972), both cited in Dudley and Dudley (1986).

Appendix D: Previous Studies, New Empirical Research, and My Analysis of Religious Loyalty

1. The categories come from Hyde (1990).
2. McNamara (1992) finds that some elements of the religious tradition persist, and some are set aside. The selective process is affected by classroom dialogues with their teachers.
3. Ozorak's (1989) quantitative study finds that past affiliation, family religiousness, and grades are strongest factors correlating with religious commitment.
4. Olson (1993) finds that modernization favors a shift from taken-for-granted cultural religious identity to chosen subcultural religious identity. Social ties and religious institutions are stronger in subgroups with more distinctive identities. Conservative denominations tend to have denser fellowship ties than mainline Protestant religious denominations.
5. Myers (1991a) conducts ethnographic research in teens in a church setting, but he focuses on the style of youth ministry, not the youth's experience of faith transmission per se. Reiff (1995) studies families in the congregational context, but he concentrates on the parents.
6. Coleman (1961), Csikszentmihalyi and Larson (1984), Ianni (1989).
7. Feldman and Elliott (1990).
8. Dean and Yost (1991).
9. D'Antonio et al. (1982).
10. Davidman (1991).
11. Kohn (1969).
12. Myers (1991a).

13. Nelson and Potvin (1980).
14. Potvin and Lee (1982), Roof (1981).
15. Wuthnow (1993: 106).
16. Studies have produced conflicting findings on the interaction of gender and religion. Hunsberger and Brown (1984) and Ozorak (1989) find no significant differences in religious beliefs and participation between male and female respondents. D'Antonio (1996), Williams and Davidson (1996), Dillon (1996), and Hoge and Smith (1982) find variations by gender.
17. Dudley and Dudley (1986), Kieren and Munro (1987), Hunsberger and Brown (1984), Chadwick and Heaton (1996).
18. Benson (1990), Carnegie Corporation (1992), Thornton and Cambrun (1989).
19. Wuthnow (1995), Hodgkinson and Weitzman (1994).

Appendix E: Adolescence

1. For example, by Ianni (1989), Roberts (1993), and Richter (1997).
2. In the eighteenth century, Rousseau used the term "second birth" to refer to the transition to adulthood.
3. In 1901 William James described religious conversion as "a normal adolescent phenomenon, incidental to the passage from the child's small universe to the wider intellectual and spiritual life of maturity" (James [1990: 186]). This is "regeneration" in Calvin's terms. Today evangelicals quote a finding of Barna (1996) that "six out of ten people say they made their decision to accept Christ before age eighteen. The median age is sixteen" (p. 73). This is quoted, for example, by the noted evangelical authors Josh McDowell and Bob Hostetler (1994).
4. Mirel (1991: 1153). For a fuller discussion of the evolution of adolescence in twentieth-century America, see Eisenstadt (1961), Parsons (1961), Keniston (1961), Kett (1977), Koteskey (1991), Mirel (1991), Palladino (1996). Mitterauer (1992) discusses the same subject in a worldwide context.
5. It is widely agreed that adolescence begins with the onset of puberty, yet this is occurring earlier now, on average at age twelve for girls in 1990, as compared to age sixteen 150 years ago. It occurs approximately two years later for boys (Atkinson 1997: 6). The end point of adolescence is not marked biologically. Some bracket it by the departure of the adolescent from the family home, which may occur at the end of high school. Others mark the end by marriage, the formation of a new family unit. Not all adolescents are leaving home, however, even if they marry.
6. Coleman (1961).
7. Parsons (1961), Erikson (1968), Strommen (1971). Keeley (1976) found Strommen's study of teens to exaggerate the generation gap.
8. U.S. Department of Education (1991) shows that youth's and parents' views on religion and most other topics are closer in 1990 than they were in 1975. Brown (1990) demonstrates that the generation gap ideas were a historical aberration of the 1960s. Ianni (1989) reports that over 90 percent of the teens in his sample in the late 1970s and 1980s reported that their relationship with parents was good. See also Keeley (1976), Takanishi (1993), Foster-Clark and Blyth (1991), Offer and Church (1991), Chadwick and Heaton (1996). There is evidence that could be construed to support the contrary. For example, Farkas and Johnson (1997) report that adults have an overwhelmingly negative view of teenagers and younger children, with only 37 per-

cent saying today's youth will eventually make the country a better place. On balance, the empirical evidence does not weigh in favor of the generation gap hypothesis.
9. Coleman (1961: 9).
10. For example Davies (1991).
11. Brown (1990), Feldman and Elliott (1990), Kakutani (1997), and Clark (1998) find a blurring between adolescence and adults in cultural tastes and styles.
12. Palladino (1996) quotes sources saying that by 2006 the worth of the teenage consumer market should be $89 billion, almost ten times what it reportedly was worth in 1957, when Elvis Presley was at his zenith (p. xii). She reports that one-third of teens own their own cars (up from 7 percent in 1968), 25 percent have their own phones, and 50 percent own personal computers (p. 257).
13. Kakutani (1997: 22).
14. Kegan (1982, 1994), Jurgen Habermas (1974).
15. Developmental theorists do not claim that these stages are immune from historical factors, which may alter them. Erikson (1968), for one, cautions that his stages may need to be revised in time. He also allows that his stages describe male development more than female. Initiated by psychologist Carol Gilligan (1982), a body of literature critiques Kohlberg's moral development theory as gender-biased.
16. Fowler (1981). Dykstra and Parks (1986) offer critiques of this understanding. Parks adds a stage to Fowler's scheme between stages three and four. Dykstra offers arguments against one of Fowler's assumptions, that faith is universal.
17. Fowler (1981: 318).
18. Meyrowitz (1985).
19. Meyrowitz (1985) synthesizes Erving Goffman's understanding of "backstage" and foreground social interaction with Marshall McLuhan's accounts of the impact of electronic media on social change.
20. The concept of the life cycle refers to the demarcations in a person's status related to changing institutional contexts and roles, such as leaving home, completing education, entering the workforce, getting married, and having children. I regard this as a helpful way to discuss some culturally constructed tasks that characterize a particular group more than a universal description of any period of maturation. Mitterauer (1992), Montemayor and Flannery (1991), Osmer (1996).
21. Of the forty-one youth I interviewed, forty were attending college in the fall, and only three were planning to live at home while attending college. The remaining youth I interviewed was joining the U.S. Marines.

Appendix F: Faith Tradition as Religious Culture
1. Geertz (1973: 89).
2. Geertz (1973: 90).
3. Ibid.
4. Wuthnow (1987).
5. Tillich (1963).
6. Niebuhr (1951).

Appendix G: Cohort Effects
1. Mannheim (1952).
2. Roof (1993: 3).

3. Cf. Greeley, McCready, and McCourt (1976) and D'Antonio et al. (1996).
4. Csikszentmihalyi and Larson (1984) show that high school freshmen tend to socialize in groups of same-sex friends, while seniors spend the majority of their time with friends in mixed-sex dyads or small groups.
5. The counterculture of the 1960s and early 1970s in America is an example of a phenomenon that shaped the baby boomer generation, one that is both historical and cultural in nature. The historical effect of the Vietnam War cannot be isolated from cultural effects like increased drug usage and more liberal sexual attitudes. Both of these effects are related to a concurrent reassessment of the sources of moral authority (Tipton [1982]). Walrath (1987), building on Mannheim, stresses that it is both the historical and the cultural phenomena to which adolescents are exposed that mold relatively permanent effects.
6. Cited by Chaves (1991).
7. Glen (1987).
8. Roof (1993).
9. Willits and Crider (1988, 1989).
10. Hoge, Johnson, and Luidens (1994).
11. Of the parents whose age I knew, 92 percent were baby boomers; the remaining ones were slightly older. This baby boomer generation are characterized religiously (in comparison to their parents) as more interested in autonomy, freedom, independent thought, and religious exploration. They are less committed to institutional religious involvement (Carroll and Roof [1998]).
12. Cf. Tipton (1982), Roof (1993), Hoge, Johnson, and Luidens (1994), Reiff (1995), Carroll and Roof (1998). Catholic researchers studying baby boomers tend to look at them as a historically defined cohort, "Post Vatican II." Cf. Greeley, McCready, and McCourt (1976), McNamara (1992), D'Antonio et al. (1996).
13. This is the name used most often by the popular and scholarly press for the cohort born between 1962 and 1982, numbering eight million in the U.S. Other names are "GenX" and "the 13th Generation." They are approximately 70 percent white, 13 percent African American, 12 percent Latino, 4 percent Asian, and 1 percent native American or other ethnicity. The majority are from a middle-class background. They are better educated and more racially and ethnically diverse than any previous generation (Beaudoin 1998). Barna (1992) studies an overlapping cohort that is slightly smaller, one he calls "baby busters," born 1965–83. They tend to be less involved in organized religion than the baby boomers. Bibby and Posterski (1992) describe the "Charter Generation," born 1973–77, immediately before those in my sample. They show declining involvement in religion but rising interest in spirituality. Carroll and Roof (1998) narrow the cohort of "Xers" to those born between 1964 and 1979. They find religious involvement and understanding are not "strikingly" different between Xers and boomers, but very different from "pre-boomers."
14. McNamara gathers qualitative and quantitative data in a middle-class suburban Catholic high school to look for the elements of the Catholic tradition that persist in teens' lives.
15. McNamara (1992).
16. Myers gathers qualitative data on teens in two middle-class mainline Protestant congregations in the Chicago area, one black and one white.
17. Myers (1991a).

18. Barna (1996) offers national poll data reporting on teens' religious views. His data include responses from the cohort in my sample. Bibby's (1992) poll of Canadian teens includes questions about religion. Farkas and Johnson (1997) polls children, youth, and parents of a wide range of opinions, but has scant data on religious beliefs, practices, and attitudes. The latest Gallup report on teens (Gallup and Bezilla [1992]) offers valuable statistics on religious opinions from members of my sample's cohort, though they are surveyed in their early teenage years and their responses are mixed with those of teens five years older. The Girl Scouts Survey (1989) conducted by Harris researchers polls high school seniors and younger youth in my sample's cohort, but surveyed at an earlier age. The Girl Scouts Survey asks general questions about morality more than religion. The latest Search Institute (1996) data on children and youth were collected on youth grades seven through twelve in 1990 and address the issues of my research. The study of Johnston, Bachman, and O'Malley (1983) offers longitudinal data on a national sample of high school seniors collected from 1975 to 1983. The National Study of Youth and Religion directed by Christian Smith of the University of North Carolina at Chapel Hill began to publish in 2001 analyses of three existing national data sets on teens, religion, and spirituality.

Appendix J: Agency and Religious Socialization

1. Like Bourdieu, Stephen Turner (1994) speaks of "reproducing practices" instead of "transmission."
2. Bass (1994).
3. Swidler (1986).
4. Bourdieu (1977).
5. Powell and DiMaggio (1991).
6. John Meyer in Powell and DiMaggio (1991).
7. Selznick (1992).

Appendix O: Cases Where Socialization and Religious Experience Were Not Exhibited Together

1. The issue of boredom reported by teens points to the lack of religious experience. This is behind the aphorism "The greatest sin is boring a kid," found, for example, in Strobel's *Inside the Mind of Unchurched Harry and Mary* (1993), which was referenced several times by ministers at Riverland Heights. Boredom indicates that the "sin" is the routinization of the charisma, as Weber described it (in Gerth and Mills [1946]).
2. One of the characteristics of new-paradigm churches is that they minimize the institutional feeling of the church so that religious experiences are perceived to be unfettered by the institution. As Miller describes them, they discard attributes of establishment religion, appropriate contemporary cultural forms, create a new genre of worship music, and restructure the organizational character of the institution to be more democratizing (1997).

Appendix P: Comparing Loyalty among Churches and to National Sample

1. There is no national survey data more recent than the 1987 Gallup-Castelli study that compares religious loyalty in Catholic, evangelical Protestant, and mainline Protestant teens. However, Barna develops a category called "born again" that sorts

by evangelical orientation in its questions about being "born again" and having a personal relationship with God. He finds that teenagers aligned with a Protestant church are twice as likely to be born again as those aligned with the Catholic church. Barna considers 30 percent of those aligned with the Catholic faith to be born again (1991: 36).

Appendix Q: Data Related to Parenting Variables

1. I asked parents and teens separately: "Is attendance at church or mass an individual choice or is church attendance a family activity?"
2. Roof and Gesch (1995).
3. The drift toward greater voluntarism in matters of faith is reflected in a 1978 Gallup poll that shows that 81 percent agree that "one should arrive at his or her own religious beliefs independent of a church or synagogue," and 78 percent agree that "one can be a good Christian or Jew without attending a church or synagogue."
4. Roof and Gesch (1995: 63–67).
5. Roof and Gesch (1995: 72).

References

Albanese, Catherine L. 1992. *America: Religions and Religion*. Belmont, Calif.: Wadsworth Publishing.
———. 1996. "Religion and Popular American Culture: An Introductory Essay." *Journal of the American Academy of Religion* 59 (Winter): 733–43.
Ammerman, Nancy Tatom. 1987. *Bible Believers: Fundamentalists in the Modern World*. New Brunswick; N.J.: Rutgers University Press.
———. 1990. *Baptist Battles: Social Change and Religious Conflict in the Southern Baptist Convention*. New Brunswick, N.J.: Rutgers University Press.
———. 1997. *Congregation and Community*. New Brunswick, N.J.: Rutgers University Press.
Atkinson, Harley. 1997. *Ministry with Youth in Crisis*. Birmingham, Ala.: Religious Education Press.
Babbie, Earl. 1992. *The Practice of Social Research*. Belmont, Calif.: Wadsworth Publishing.
Barna, George. 1991. *Today's Teens*. Glendale, Calif.: Barna Research Group.
———. 1992. *The Invisible Generation: Baby Busters*. Glendale, Calif.: Barna Research Group.
———. 1995. *Generation Next: What You Need to Know about Today's Youth*. Ventura, Calif.: Regal Books.
———. 1996. *Index of Leading Spiritual Indicators*. Dallas: Word Publishing.
Bass, Dorothy C. 1994. "Congregations and the Bearing of Traditions." In *American Congregations*. Edited by James P. Wind and James W. Lewis. Chicago: University of Chicago Press.
———, ed. 1997. *Practicing Our Faith*. San Francisco: Jossey-Bass.
Bass, Dorothy C., and Craig Dykstra. 1999. "Life Abundant: A Theological Understanding of Christian Practices." Unpublished paper (November 12).
Beaudoin, Thomas More. 1998. *Virtual Faith: The Irreverent Spiritual Quest of Generation X*. San Francisco: Jossey-Bass.
Becker, Penny Edgell. 1999. *Congregations in Conflict: Cultural Models of Local Religious Life*. Cambridge: Cambridge University Press.
Becker, Penny E., and Nancy L. Eiesland. 1997. *Contemporary American Religion: An Ethnographic Reader*. Walnut Grove, Calif.: AltaMira.

Bellah, Robert N. 1970. *Beyond Belief.* New York: Harper and Row.

———, ed. 1973. *On Morality and Society.* Chicago: University of Chicago Press.

———. 1997. "Care of Souls in Today's America." San Antonio, Tex.: Presbyterian Church Redevelopment Training Network.

———. 1998. "Is There a Common Culture?" In *Journal of the American Academy of Religion* 66, no. 3: 613–25.

Bellah, Robert N., Richard Madsen, William M. Sullivan, Ann Swidler, and Steven M. Tipton. 1985. *Habits of the Heart.* New York: Harper and Row.

———. 1991. *The Good Society.* New York: Vintage Books.

Bendroth, Margaret L. 1996. "Families and Faith Formation, 1930–1990." Unpublished paper.

Bendroth, Margaret Lamberts. 2003. *Growing Up Protestant: Parents, Children, and Mainline Churches.* New Brunswick, N.J.: Rutgers University Press.

Benson, Peter L. 1990, 1993. *The Troubled Journey: A Portrait of 6th–12th Grade Youth.* Minneapolis: Search Institute.

Benson, Peter L., and Carolyn H. Eklin. 1990. "Effective Christian Education: A National Study of Protestant Congregations—A Summary Report on Faith, Loyalty and Congregational Life." Minneapolis: Search Institute.

Benson, Peter L., Dorothy L. Williams, and Arthur L. Johnson. 1987. *The Quicksilver Years: The Hopes and Fears of Young Adolescents.* San Francisco: Harper and Row.

Berger, Peter L. 1967. *The Sacred Canopy: Elements of a Sociological Theory of Religion.* New York: Doubleday.

———. 1979. *The Heretical Imperative: Contemporary Possibilities of Religious Affirmation.* Garden City, N.Y.: Anchor Press.

———. 1983. "From the Crisis of Religion to the Crisis of Secularity." In *Religion and America: Spirituality in a Secular Age.* Edited by Mary Douglas and Steven M. Tipton, 14–24. Boston: Beacon Press.

———. 1992. *A Far Glory: The Quest for Faith in an Age of Credulity.* Garden City, N.Y.: Doubleday.

———. 1997. *Redeeming Laughter: The Comic Dimension of Human Experience.* New York: Walter De Gruyter.

———. 1998. "Protestantism and the Quest for Certainty." *Christian Century*, August 26–September 2, 78–96.

Berger, Peter L., and Thomas Luckmann. 1966. *The Social Construction of Reality.* Garden City, N.Y.: Doubleday.

Bezilla, Robert, ed. 1988. *America's Youth 1977–1988.* Princeton, N.J.: Gallup Organization.

———. 1993. *America's Youth in the 1990s.* Princeton, N.J.: George H. Gallup International Institute.

Bibby, Reginald W., and Donald C. Posterski. 1992. *Teen Trends: A Nation in Motion.* Toronto: Stoddart Publishing.

Bourdieu, Pierre. 1977. *Outline of a Theory of Practice.* Cambridge, N.Y.: Cambridge University Press.

Brasher, Brenda E. 1996. "Thoughts on the Status of the Cyborg: On Technological Socialization and Its Link to the Religious Function of Popular Culture." *Journal of the American Academy of Religion* 64, no. 4: 809–30.

———. 1998. *Godly Women: Fundamentalism and Female Power.* New Brunswick, N.J.: Rutgers University Press.

Brown, B. Bradford. 1990. "Peer Groups and Peer Culture." In *At the Threshold: The Developing Adolescent.* Edited by S. Shirley Feldman and Glen R. Elliott. Cambridge, Mass.: Harvard University Press.

Browning, Don S. 1991. *A Fundamental Practical Theology: Descriptive and Strategic Proposals.* Minneapolis: Augsburg Fortress.

———. 1994. "Congregational Studies as Practical Theology." In *American Congregations.* Edited by James P. Wind and James W. Lewis. Chicago: University of Chicago Press.

———. 1995. "Religion and Family Ethics." In *Work, Family, and Religion in Contemporary Society.* Edited by Nancy Tatom Ammerman and Wade Clark Roof. New York: Routledge.

Browning, Don S., Bonnie J. Miller-McLemore, Pamela D. Couture, K. Brynolf Lyon, and Robert M. Franklin. 1997. *From Culture Wars to Common Ground: Religion and the American Family Debate.* Louisville; Ky.: Westminster John Knox Press.

Brusco, Elizabeth E. 1995. *The Reformation of Machismo: Evangelical Conversion and Gender in Colombia.* Austin, Tex.: University of Texas Press.

Bryk, Anthony S., Valerie E. Lee, and Peter B. Holland. 1995. *Catholic Schools and the Common Good.* Cambridge, Mass.: Harvard University Press.

Burawoy, Michael. 1991. "Reconstructing Social Theories." In *Ethnography Unbound.* Edited by Michael Burawoy. Berkeley: University of California Press.

Carnegie Corporation of New York. 1995. "Great Transitions: Preparing Adolescents for a New Century." New York: Carnegie Corporation of New York.

Carnegie Corporation of New York, and Carnegie Council on Adolescent Development of Washington, D.C. 1992. "A Matter of Time: Risk and Opportunity in the Nonschool Hours." New York: Carnegie Corporation of New York.

Carroll, Jackson W., and Wade Clark Roof. 1998. "Family Disruption and Churchgoing Habits." *Christian Century,* January 7–14: 9.

Chadwick, Bruce A., and Tim B. Heaton, eds. 1996. *Statistical Handbook on Adolescents in America.* Phoenix, Ariz.: Oryx Press.

Chaves, Mark. 1991. "Family Structure and Protestant Church Attendance: The Sociological Basis of Cohort and Age Effects." *Journal for the Scientific Study of Religion* 30 (December): 501–14.

Chidester, David. 1996. "The Church of Baseball, the Fetish of Coca-Cola, the Potlatch of Rock 'n' Roll: Theoretical Models for the Study of Religion in American Popular Culture." *Journal of the American Academy of Religion* 64, no. 4: 743–61.

Clark, Lynn Schofield. 1998. "Identity, Discourse, and Media Audiences: A Critical Ethnography of the Role of Visual Media in Religious Identity-Construction among U.S. Adolescents." Ph.D. diss., University of Colorado.

———. 1999. "If You Stay Away from Nintendo, You'll Read the Qur'an More: Media, the Family, and Muslim Identity." Boulder: University of Colorado Press.

———. 2003. *From Angels to Aliens: Teenagers, the Media, and the Supernatural.* New York: Oxford University Press.

Coalter, Milton J., John M. Mulder, and Louis B. Weeks. 1992. *The Re-Forming Tradition: Presbyterians and Mainstream Protestantism, The Presbyterian Presence.* Louisville; Ky.: Westminster/John Knox Press.

Coleman, James S. 1961. *The Adolescent Society: The Social Life of the Teenager and Its Impact on Education.* New York: Free Press.

———. 1974. *Youth: Transition to Adulthood*. Chicago: University of Chicago Press.

———. 1988. "Social Capital in the Creation of Human Capital." *American Journal of Sociology* 94 (Supplement): S95–S120.

———. 1989. *Public and Private High Schools: The Impact of Communities*. New York: Basic Books.

———. 1990. *Foundations of Social Theory*. Cambridge, Mass.: Harvard University Press.

Csikszentmihalyi, Mihaly, and Reed Larson. 1984. *Being Adolescent: Conflict and Growth in the Teenage Years*. New York: Basic Books.

Daloz, Laurent A. Parks, Cheryl H. Keen, James P. Keen, and Sharon Daloz Parks. 1996. *Common Fire: Lives of Commitment in a Complex World*. Boston: Beacon Press.

D'Antonio, William V., James D. Davidson, Dean R. Hoge, and Ruth A. Wallace. 1996. *Laity: American and Catholic: Transforming the Church*. Kansas City, Mo.: Sheed and Ward.

D'Antonio, William V., William M. Newman, and Stuart A. Wright. 1982. "Religion and Family Life: How Social Scientists View the Relationship." *Journal for the Scientific Study of Religion* 21, no. 3: 218–25.

D'Antonio, William V., and Joan Aldous, eds. 1983. *Families and Religions, Conflict and Change in Modern Society*. Beverly Hills, Calif.: Sage Publications.

Davidman, Lynn. 1991. *Tradition in a Rootless World: Women Turn to Orthodox Judaism*. Berkeley: University of California Press.

Davies, James A. 1991. "Adolescent Subculture." In *Handbook of Youth Ministry*. Edited by Donald Ratcliff and James A. Davies. Birmingham, Ala.: Religious Education Press.

Davis, Patricia H. 1996. *Counseling Adolescent Girls*. Minneapolis: Fortress.

Dean, Kenda Creasy, and Ron Foster. 1998. *The Godbearing Life: The Art of Soul Tending for Youth Ministry*. Nashville: Upper Room Books.

Dean, Kenda Creasy, and Paul R. Yost. 1991. "A Synthesis of the Research on, and a Descriptive Overview of, Protestant, Catholic, and Jewish Religious Youth Programs in the United States." Washington, D.C.: Carnegie Council on Adolescent Development.

DeVaus, David A. 1983. "The Relative Importance of Parents and Peers for Adolescent Religious Orientation." *Adolescence* 18: 147–58.

DeVries, Mark. 1994. *Family-Based Youth Ministry*. Downers Grove, Ill.: InterVarsity Press.

Dillon, Michele. 1996. "The Persistence of Religious Identity among College Catholics." *Journal for the Scientific Study of Religion* 35, no. 2: 165–70.

Dolan, Jay P. 1992. *The American Catholic Experience*. Notre Dame, Ind.: University of Notre Dame Press.

Dudley, Roger L. 1999. "Youth Religious Commitment over Time: A Longitudinal Study of Retention." *Review of Religious Research* 41: 109–20.

Dudley, Roger L., and Margaret G. Dudley. 1986. "Transmission of Religious Values from Parents to Adolescents." *Review of Religious Research* 28, no. 1: 3–15.

Dudley, Roger L., and C. Robert Laurent. 1989. "Alienation from Religion in Church-related Adolescents." *Sociological Analysis* 49, no. 4: 408–20.

Dudley, Roger L., and H. Phillip Muthersbaugh. 1996. "Social Attachment to Religious Institutions among Young Adults." *Review of Religious Research* 38, no. 1: 38–50.

Durkheim, Emil. 1915. *The Elementary Forms of the Religious Life*. New York: Macmillan.

———. 1973. *On Morality and Society*. Edited by Robert N. Bellah. Chicago: University of Chicago Press.

Dykstra, Craig. 1981. *Vision and Character: A Christian Educator's Alternative to Kohlberg.* New York: Ramsey.

———. 1985. "No Longer Strangers: The Church and Its Educational Ministry." *Princeton Seminary Bulletin* 6: 188–200.

———. 1986. "Faith Development and Religious Education." In *Faith Development and Fowler.* Edited by Craig Dykstra and Sharon Parks. Birmingham, Ala.: Religious Education Press.

———. 1986. "What Is Faith? An Experiment in the Hypothetical Mode." In *Faith Development and Fowler.* Edited by Craig Dykstra and Sharon Parks. Birmingham, Ala.: Religious Education Press.

———. 1987. "The Formative Power of the Congregation." *Religious Education* 82: 530–46.

———. 1989. "A Fresh Awakening?" *Theology Today* 46 (July): 127.

———. 1991. "Reconceiving Practice." In *Shifting Boundaries: Contextual Approaches to the Structure of Theological Education.* Louisville, Ky.: Westminster/John Knox Press.

Dykstra, Craig, and Sharon Parks, eds. 1986. *Faith Development and Fowler.* Birmingham, Ala.: Religious Education Press.

Dykstra, Robert C. 1997. *Counseling Troubled Youth.* Louisville, Ky.: Westminster John Knox Press.

Eiesland, Nancy L. 1995. "A Particular Place: Exurbanization and Religious Response in a Southern Town." Ph.D. thesis, Emory University.

———. "Contending with a Giant." 1997. In *Contemporary American Religion: An Ethnographic Reader*, 191–219. Edited by Penny Edgell Becker and Nancy L. Eiesland. Walnut Creek, Calif.: AltaMira.

Eisenstadt, S. N. 1961. "Archetypal Patterns of Youth." In *Youth: Change and Challenge.* Edited by Erik H. Erikson. New York: Basic Books.

Eisner, Elliot W. 1979. *The Enlightened Imagination: On the Design and Evaluation of School Programs.* 2d ed. New York: Macmillan.

Elkind, David. 1971. "The Development of Religious Understanding in Children and Adolescents." Pages 655–85 in *Research on Religious Development.* Edited by Merton P. Strommen. New York: Hawthorn Books.

———. 1984. *All Grown Up and No Place to Go.* Reading, Mass.: Addison-Wesley Publishing.

Emerson, Robert, ed. 1983. *Contemporary Fieldwork.* Boston: Little, Brown.

Erikson, Erik H. 1961. "Youth: Fidelity and Diversity." In *Youth: Change and Challenge.* Edited by Erik H. Erikson. New York: Basic Books.

———. 1968. *Identity, Youth and Crisis.* New York: W. W. Norton.

———. 1977. *Toys and Reasons: Stages in the Ritualization of Experience.* New York: W. W. Norton.

Farkas, Steve, and Jean Johnson. 1997. "Kids These Days: What Americans Really Think about the Next Generation." New York: Public Agenda.

Feldman, S. Shirley, and Glen R. Elliott. 1990. "Progress and Promise of Research on Adolescence." In *At the Threshold: The Developing Adolescent.* Edited by S. Shirley Feldman and Glen R. Elliott. Cambridge, Mass.: Harvard University Press.

Fischer, Claude S. 1982. *To Dwell among Friends: Personal Networks in Town and City.* Chicago: University of Chicago Press.

Foster, Charles R. 1990. "Education in the Quest for the Church." In *Theological Approaches to Christian Education.* Edited by Jack L. Seymour and Donald E. Miller. Nashville: Abingdon Press.

———. 1994. *Educating Congregations: The Future of Christian Education*. Nashville: Abingdon Press.

Foster-Clark, Frederick S., and Dale A. Blyth. 1991. "Peer Relations and Influences." In *Encyclopedia of Adolescence*, 767–71. Edited by Richard M. Lerner, Anne C. Petersen, and Jeanne Brooks-Gunn. New York: Garland Publishing.

Fowler, James W. 1981 *Stages of Faith: The Psychology of Human Development and the Quest for Meaning*. San Francisco: Harper and Row.

———. 1986. "Faith and the Structuring of Meaning." In *Faith Development and Fowler*, 15–42. Edited by Craig Dykstra and Sharon Parks. Birmingham, Ala.: Religious Education Press.

———. 1996a. "Adolescence in the Trinitarian Praxis of God." In *The 1996 Princeton Lecture Series on Youth and the Church*, 13–21. Princeton, N.J.: Princeton Theological Seminary.

———. 1996b. "Grace, Repentance, and Commitment: Youth Initiation in Care and Formation." In *The 1996 Princeton Lecture Series on Youth and the Church*, 23–34. Princeton, N.J.: Princeton Theological Seminary.

———. 1996c. "Perspectives on Adolescents, Personhood, and Faith." In *The 1996 Princeton Lectures on Youth, Church, and Culture*. Princeton, N.J.: Princeton Theological Seminary.

Froehle, Bryan T. 1996. "New Directions in Youth Ministry: A National Study of Catholic Youth Ministry Program Participants." Washington, D.C.: Center for Applied Research in the Apostolate.

Gallup, George, and Jim Castelli. 1987. *The American Catholic People*. New York: Doubleday.

———. 1989. *The People's Religion: American Faith in the 90s*. New York: Macmillan.

Gallup, George, and Sarah Jones. 1989. *100 Questions and Answers: Religion in America*. Princeton, N.J.: Princeton Religion Research Center.

Gallup, George H. Jr., and Robert Bezilla. 1992. *The Religious Life of Young Americans*. Princeton, N.J.: George Gallup International Institute.

Gallup, George H. Jr., and Wendy Plump. 1996. *Scared: Growing Up in America: And What the Experts Say Parents Can Do about It*. Harrisburg, Pa.: Morehouse Publishing.

Garland, Diana, R. 1999. *Family Ministry: A Comprehensive Guide*. Downers Grove, Ill.: InterVarsity Press.

Geertz, Clifford. 1973. *The Interpretation of Cultures*. New York: Basic Books.

Gerth, H. H., and C. Wright Mills, eds. 1946. *From Max Weber*. New York: Oxford University Press.

Giddens, Anthony. 1991. *Modernity and Self-Identity: Self and Society in the Late Modern Age*. Stanford, Calif.: Stanford University Press.

Gilkey, Langdon. 1994. "The Christian Congregation as a Religious Community." In *American Congregations*. Edited by James P. Wind and James W. Lewis. Chicago: University of Chicago Press.

Gilligan, Carol. 1982. *In a Different Voice: Psychological Theory and Women's Development*. Cambridge, Mass.: Harvard University Press.

Gillis, John R. 1996. *A World of Their Own Making: Myth, Ritual, and the Quest for Family Values*. New York: Basic Books.

Girl Scouts of the United States of America. 1989. "Girl Scouts Survey on the Beliefs and Moral Values of America's Children." New York: Girl Scouts of the U.S.A.

Glen, Norvall D. 1987. "The Trend in 'No Religion' Respondents to U.S. National Surveys, Late 1950s to Early 1980s." *Public Opinion Quarterly* 51: 293–314.

Greeley, Andrew. 1972. *The Denominational Society: A Sociological Approach to Religion in America.* Glenview, Ill.: Scott, Foresman and Co.

———. 1989. *Religious Change in America.* Cambridge, Mass.: Harvard University Press.

———. 1997. "Coleman Revisited: Religious Structures as a Source of Social Capital." *American Behavioral Scientist* 40, no. 5 (March/April): 587–94.

Greeley, Andrew M., and Galen L. Gockel. 1971. "The Religious Effects of Parochial Education." In *Research on Religious Development*, 264–352. Edited by Merton P. Strommen. New York: Hawthorn Books.

Greeley, Andrew M., William C. McCready, and Kathleen McCourt. 1976. *Catholic Schools in a Declining Church.* Kansas City, Mo.: Sheed and Ward.

Greven, Philip. 1977. *The Protestant Temperament: Patterns of Child-Rearing, Religious Experience, and the Self in Early America.* New York: Alfred A. Knopf.

Habermas, Jurgen. 1974. "Moral Development and Ego Identity." In *Communication and the Evolution of Society.* Boston: Beacon Press.

Hadaway, C. Kirk. 1990. "Denominational Defection: Recent Research on Religious Disaffiliation in America." In *The Mainstream Protestant "Decline": The Presbyterian Pattern.* Edited by M.J. Coalter, J.M. Mulder, and L.B. Weeks. Louisville, Ky.: Westminster/John Knox Press.

Hadaway, C. Kirk, and Penny Long Marler. 1996. "The Problem with Father as Proxy: Denominational Switching and Religious Change, 1965–88." *Journal for the Scientific Study of Religion* 35, no. 2: 156–64.

Hadaway, C. Kirk, and David A. Roozen. 1995. *Rerouting the Protestant Mainstream.* Nashville: Abingdon Press.

Hall, G. Stanley. 1904. *Adolescence: Its Psychology and Its Relations to Physiology, Anthropology, Sociology, Sex, Crime, Religion, and Education.* 2 vols. New York: Appleton.

Hammond, Philip E. 1988. "Religion and the Persistence of Identity." *Journal for the Scientific Study of Religion* 27, no. 1: 1–11.

———. 1992. *Religion and Personal Autonomy: The Third Disestablishment in America.* Columbia: University of South Carolina Press.

———. 1998. *With Liberty for All: Freedom of Religion in the United States.* Louisville, Ky.: Westminster John Knox Press.

Hart, Stephen. "Religion and Changes in Family Patterns." 1986. *Review of Religious Research* 28, no. 1: 51–70.

Herberg, Will. 1956. *Protestant, Catholic, Jew, An Essay in American Religious Sociology.* Garden City, N.Y.: Doubleday.

Hersch, Patricia. 1998. *A Tribe Apart: A Journey into the Heart of American Adolescence.* New York: Ballantine Publishing Group.

Hertel, Bradley R., and Michael J. Donahue. 1996. "Parental Influences on God Images among Children: Testing Durkheim's Metaphoric Parallelism." *Journal for the Scientific Study of Religion* 34, no. 2: 186–99.

Hodgkinson, Virginia, and Murray Weitzman. 1994. "Giving and Volunteering in the United States: Findings from a National Survey." 1994 ed. Washington, D.C.: Independent. Sector.

Hoge, Dean R. Esther Heffernan, Eugene F. Hemrick, Hart M. Nelsen, James P. O'Connor, Paul J. Philbert, and Andrew D. Thompson. 1982. "Desired Outcomes of Religious Education and Youth Ministry in Six Denominations." In *Religious Education Ministry with Youth*, 132–48. Edited by D. Campbell Wyckoff and Don Richter. Birmingham, Ala.: Religious Education Press.

Hoge, Dean R., Benton Johnson, and Donald A. Luidens. 1994. *Vanishing Boundaries: The Religion of Mainline Protestant Baby Boomers*. Louisville, Ky.: Westminster John Knox Press.

Hoge, Dean R., and Gregory H. Petrillo. 1978. "Determinants of Church Participation and Attitudes among High School Youth." *Journal for the Scientific Study of Religion* 17: 359–79.

Hoge, Dean R., Gregory H. Petrillo, and Ella I. Smith. 1982. "Transmission of Religious and Social Values from Parents to Teenage Children." *Journal of Marriage and the Family* 44: 569–80.

Hoge, Dean R., and David A. Roozen, eds. 1979. *Understanding Church Growth and Decline 1950–78*. New York: Pilgrim Press.

Hoge, Dean R., and Ella I. Smith. 1982. "Normative and Non-normative Religious Experience among High School Youth." *Sociological Analysis* 43, no. 1: 69–82.

Howe, Neil, and William Strauss. 1992. "The New Generation Gap." *Atlantic Monthly*, December: 67–89.

Hunsberger, Bruce, and L. B. Brown. 1984. "Religious Socialization, Apostasy, and the Impact of Family Background." *Journal for the Scientific Study of Religion* 23, no. 3: 239–51.

Hyde, Kenneth E. 1990. *Religion in Childhood and Adolescence: A Comprehensive Review of the Research*. Birmingham, Ala.: Religious Education Press.

———. 1991. "Adolescents and Religion." In *Handbook of Youth Ministry*. Edited by Donald Ratcliff and James A. Davies. Birmingham, Ala.: Religious Education Press.

Ianni, Francis A.J. 1989. *The Search for Structure*. New York: Free Press.

Institute in Basic Life Principles, Advanced Training Institute International. 1993. *How to Conquer the Addiction of Rock Music*. Rock Brook, Ill.: Institute in Basic Life Principles.

James, William. *The Varieties of Religious Experience*. 1990. The Gifford Lectures, Delivered in 1901–1902 in Edinburgh. New York: Vintage Books.

Johnston, Lloyd D., Jerald G. Bachman, and Patrick M. O'Malley. 1983. *Monitoring the Future*. Ann Arbor, Mich.: University of Michigan Press.

Kakutani, Michiko. 1997. "Adolescence Rules!" *New York Times*, (May 11): 22.

Keating, Daniel P. 1990. "Adolescent Thinking." In *At the Threshold: The Developing Adolescent*. Edited by S. Shirley Feldman and Glen R. Elliott. Cambridge, Mass.: Harvard University Press.

Keeley, Benjamin J. 1976. "Generations in Tension: Intergenerational Differences and Continuities in Religion and Religion-related Behavior." *Review of Religious Research* 17 (Spring): 221–31.

Kegan, Robert. 1982. *The Evolving Self*. Cambridge, Mass.: Harvard University Press.

———. 1994. *In over Our Heads: The Mental Demands of Modern Life*. Cambridge, Mass.: Harvard University Press.

Kelley, Dean M. 1972. *Why Conservative Churches Are Growing*. New York: Harper and Row.

Keniston, Kenneth. 1961. "Social Change and Youth in America." In *Youth: Change and Challenge*. Edited by Erik H. Erikson. New York: Basic Books.

Kentuckiana Interfaith Community. 1993. "Directory of Churches, Faith Communities, Congregations and Community Ministries." Louisville, Ky.

Kett, Joseph F. 1977. *Rites of Passage: Adolescence in America 1790 to Present.* New York: Basic Books.

Kieren, Dianne K., and Brenda Munro. 1987. "Following the Leaders: Parents' Influence on Adolescent Religious Activity." *Journal for the Scientific Study of Religion* 26, no. 2: 249–55.

Kohn, Melvin. 1969. *Class and Conformity: A Study in Values.* 1977 ed. Chicago: University of Chicago Press.

Koteskey, Ronald L. 1991. "Adolescence as a Cultural Invention." In *Handbook of Youth Ministry.* Edited by Donald Ratcliff and James A. Davies. Birmingham, Ala.: Religious Education Press.

Larson, Reed, and Maryse H. Richards. 1994. *Divergent Realities: The Emotional Lives of Mothers, Fathers, and Adolescents.* New York: HarperCollins.

Lippy, Charles H. 1994. *Being Religious, American Style: A History of Popular Religiosity in the United States.* Westport, Conn.: Greenwood Press.

Lofland, John, and Lyn H. Lofland. 1995. *Analyzing Social Settings.* Belmont, Calif.: Wadsworth Publishing.

Luckmann, Thomas. 1967. *Invisible Religion.* New York: Macmillan.

MacIntyre, Alasdair. 1984. *After Virtue.* 2d ed. Notre Dame, Ind.: University of Notre Dame Press.

Malinowski, Bronislaw. 1925. "Magic, Science, and Religion." In *Science, Religion, and Reality.* Edited by Joseph Needham. London: SPCK.

Mannheim, K. 1952. "The Problem of Generations." Chap. 7 in *Essays on the Sociology of Knowledge.* Edited by P. Kecskemeti. London: Routledge.

Marler, Penny Long. 1995. "Lost in the Fifties: The Changing Family and the Nostalgic Church." In *Work, Family and Religion in Contemporary Society.* Edited by Nancy Tatom Ammerman and Wade Clark Roof. New York: Routledge.

Marty, Martin E. 1971. "Religious Development in Historical, Social, and Cultural Context." In *Research on Religious Development.* Edited by Merton P. Strommen. New York: Hawthorn Books.

———. 1983. "Religion in America since Mid-century." In *Religion and America: Spirituality in a Secular Age.* Edited by Mary Douglas and Steven M. Tipton. Boston: Beacon Press.

———. 1993. "Where Energies Go." In *Religion in the Nineties.* Edited by Wade Clark Roof. Newbury Park, Calif.: Sage Publications.

Maxwell, Carol J., and Ted G. Jelen. 1995. "Commandos for Christ: Narratives of Male Pro-Life Activists." *Review of Religious Research* 37, no. 2: 117–31.

McDowell, Josh, and Bob Hostetler. 1994. *Right from Wrong: What You Need to Know to Help Youth Make Right Choices.* Dallas: Word Publishing.

McGuire, Meredith B. 1981. *Religion: The Social Context.* Belmont, Calif.: Wadsworth Publishing.

McNamara, Patrick H. 1992. *Conscience First, Tradition Second.* Albany, N.Y.: SUNY Press.

Melton, J. Gordon. 1989. *The Encyclopedia of American Religions.* Detroit: Gale Research, Inc.

Meyrowitz, Joshua. 1985. *No Sense of Place: The Impact of Electronic Media on Social Behavior.* New York: Oxford University Press.

Miller, Craig Kennet. 1996. *Post Moderns: The Beliefs, Hopes and Fears of Young Americans, 1965–1981.* Nashville: Discipleship Resources.

Miller, D. E. 1981. "Lifestyle and Religious Commitment." *Religious Education* 76: 49–63.

Miller, Donald E. 1997. *Reinventing American Protestantism*. Berkeley: University of California Press.

Mirel, Jeffrey E. 1991. "Twentieth-Century America, Adolescence in." In *Encyclopedia of Adolescence*, 1153–63. Edited by Richard M. Lerner, Anne C. Petersen, and Jeanne Brooks-Gunn. 1153–63. New York: Garland Publishing.

Mitterauer, Michael. 1992. *A History of Youth*. Translated by Graeme Dunphy. Cambridge, Mass.: Basil Blackwell.

Montemayor, Raymond, and Daniel Flannery. 1991. "Parent-Adolescent Relations in Middle and Late Adolescence." In *Encyclopedia of Adolescence*, 729–34. Edited by Richard M. Lerner, Anne C. Petersen, and Jeanne Brooks-Gunn. New York: Garland Publishing.

Myers, William R. 1991a. *Black and White Styles of Youth Ministry: Two Congregations in America*. New York: Pilgrim Press.

———. 1991b. "Youth between Culture and Church." *Theology Today* 47, no. 4: 400–40.

Nelson, C. Ellis. 1967. *Where Faith Begins*. Richmond: John Knox Press.

———. *How Faith Matures*. 1989. Louisville, Ky.: Westminster/John Knox Press.

———. 1992. *Helping Teenagers Grow Morally*. Louisville, Ky.: Westminster/John Knox Press.

Nelson, H.M., and R.H. Potvin. 1980. "Toward Disestablishment: New Patterns of Social Class, Denomination and Religiosity among Youth?" *Review of Religious Research* 22: 137–54.

New York Times and CBS News. 1998. "National Teenagers Survey, April 2–7, 1998."

Niebuhr, H. Richard. 1929. *The Social Sources of Denominationalism*. New York: Henry Holt.

———. 1951. *Christ and Culture*. New York: Harper and Row.

Nippert-Eng, Christina E. 1995. *Home and Work: Negotiating Boundaries through Everyday Life*. Chicago: University of Chicago Press.

Offer, Daniel, and R.B. Church. 1991. "Generation Gap." In *Encyclopedia of Adolescence*, 397–99. Edited by Richard M. Lerner, Anne C. Petersen, and Jeanne Brooks-Gunn. New York: Garland Publishing.

Olson, Daniel V.A. 1993. "Fellowship Ties and the Transmission of Religious Identity." In *Beyond Establishment*. Edited by Jackson W. Carroll and Wade Clark Roof. Louisville, Ky.: Westminster/John Knox Press.

Osmer, Richard Robert. 1996. *Confirmation: Presbyterian Practices in Ecumenical Perspective*. Louisville, Ky.: Geneva Press.

Ozorak, Elizabeth Weiss. 1989. "Social and Cognitive Influences on the Development of Religious Beliefs and Commitment in Adolescence." *Journal for the Scientific Study of Religion* 28: 448–63.

———. 2003. "Love of God and Neighbor: Religion and Volunteer Service among College Students." *Review of Religious Research* 44, no. 3: 285–99.

Palladino, Grace. 1996. *Teenagers: An American History*. Basic Books.

Parks, Sharon. 1986. *The Critical Years: The Young Adult Search for a Faith to Live By*. San Francisco: Harper and Row.

Parsons, Talcott. 1952. *The Social System*. Glencoe, Ill.: The Free Press.

———. 1961. "Youth in the Context of American Society." In *Youth: Change and Challenge*. Edited by Erik H. Erikson. New York: Basic Books.

Paulson, Sharon E., and Cheryl L. Sputa. 1996. "Patterns of Parenting during Adolescence: Perceptions of Adolescents and Parents." *Adolescence* 31 (Summer): 369–82.

Pipher, Mary. 1994. *Reviving Ophelia*. New York: Ballantine.

Plato. *The Laws*. 1970. Translated by Trevor J. Sanders. London: Penguin Books.

Ploch, Donald R., and Donald W. Hastings. 1998. "Effects of Parental Church Attendance, Current Family Status, and Religious Salience on Church Attendance." *Review of Religious Research* 39, no. 4 (June): 309–20.

Portes, Alejandro. 1998. "Social Capital: Its Origins and Applications in Modern Sociology." *Annual Review of Sociology* 24: 1–24.

Potvin, Raymond H., Dean R. Hoge, and Hart M. Nelsen. 1976. *Religion and American Youth with Emphasis on Catholic Adolescents and Young Adults*. Washington, D.C.: Publications Office, United States Catholic Conference.

Potvin, Raymond H., and C.F. Lee. 1982. "Adolescent Religion: A Developmental Approach." *Sociological Analysis* 43, no. 2: 131–44.

Potvin, R. H., and D. M. Sloane. 1985. "Parental Control, Age, and Religious Practice." *Review of Religious Research* 27: 3–14.

Powell, Walter W., and Paul J. DiMaggio, eds. 1991. *The New Institutionalism in Organizational Analysis*. Chicago: University of Chicago Press.

Ravitch, Diane, and Chester Finn Jr. 1988. *What Do Our 17-Year Olds Know?* New York: Harper and Row.

Reiff, Joseph T. 1992. "A Practical Theology of Congregational Studies, Ecclesiology and Formation/Commitment in the Congregation." Ph.D. thesis, Emory University.

———. 1995. "Nurturing and Equipping Children in the Public Church." In *Work, Family, and Religion in Contemporary Society*, 199–218. Edited by Nancy Tatom Ammerman and Wade Clark Roof. New York: Routledge.

———. "Commitment in a Congregation of 'Cultural Left' Baby Boomers." *Journal of Pastoral Theology*, no. 6 (Summer): 93–119.

———. 1996–97. "The Resurrection of a Congregation: The Story of St. Paul United Methodist Church." *The Quarterly Review* (Winter): 325–41.

Richter, Don. 1982a. "A Bibliographical Survey of Youth and Youth Ministry." In *Religious Education Ministry with Youth*, 1–53. Edited by D. Campbell Wyckoff and Don Richter. Birmingham, Ala.: Religious Education Press.

———. 1982b. "The Creative Process in Adolescent Development." In *Religious Education Ministry with Youth*, 208–41. Edited by D. Campbell Wyckoff and Don Richter. Birmingham, Ala.: Religious Education Press.

———. 1997. "Roots and Wings: Practicing Theology with Youth." Unpublished paper.

Roberts, Donald F. 1993. "Adolescents and the Mass Media: From 'Leave It to Beaver' to 'Beverly Hills 90210.'" In *Adolescence in the 1990s*. Edited by Ruby Takanishi. New York: Teachers College Press.

Roehlkepartain, Eugene C. 1993. *The Teaching Church*. Nashville: Abingdon Press.

Roehlkepartain, Eugene, and Peter L. Benson. 1993. *Youth in Protestant Churches*. Minneapolis: Search Institute.

Roof, Wade Clark. 1978. *Community and Commitment: Religious Plausibility in a Liberal Protestant Church*. New York: Elsevier.

———. 1981. "Alienation and Apostasy." In *In Gods We Trust: New Patterns of Religious Pluralism in America*, 87–99. Edited by Thomas Robbins and Dick Anthony. New Brunswick, N.J.: Rutgers University Press.

———. 1993. *A Generation of Seekers: The Spiritual Journeys of the Baby Boom Generation*. San Francisco: HarperCollins.

Roof, Wade Clark, and Lyn Gesch. 1995. "Boomers and the Culture of Choice." In *Work, Family, and Religion in Contemporary Society*. Edited by Nancy Tatom Ammerman and Wade Clark Roof. New York: Routledge.

Roof, W. Clark, and W. McKinney. 1987. *American Mainline Religion*. New Brunswick, N.J.: Rutgers University Press.

Sandmaier, Marian. 1996. "More than Love." *Networker* (May/June): 21–33.

Search Institute. 1996. "Study Finds Churches Not Holding On to Teen-agers." Louisville, Ky.: *Louisville Courier-Journal*.

Selznick, Philip. 1992. *The Moral Commonwealth: Social Theory, and the Promise of Community*. Berkeley: University of California Press.

Sewell, William J. Jr. 1992. "A Theory of Structure: Duality, Agency, and Transformation." *American Journal of Sociology* 98, no. 1 (July): 1–29.

Sherkat, Darren E., and John Wilson. 1995. "Preferences, Constraints, and Choices in Religious Markets: An Examination of Religious Switching and Apostasy." *Social Forces* 73: 993–1026.

Smith, Christian. 1998. *American Evangelicalism: Embattled and Thriving*. Chicago: University of Chicago Press.

———. 2003. "Religious Effects among American Adolescents." *Journal for the Scientific Study of Religion* 42, no. 1 (March): 17–30.

Smith, Christian, Melinda Lundquist Denton, Robert Faris, and Mark Regnerus. 2002. "Mapping American Adolescent Religious Participation." *Journal for the Scientific Study of Religion* 41, no. 4 (December): 597–612.

———. 2003. "Mapping American Adolescent Subjective Religiosity and Attitudes of Alienation toward Religion: A Research Report." *Sociology of Religion* 64, no. 1 (Spring): 111–33.

Smith, Christian, and Robert Faris. 2002a. "Religion and American Adolescent Delinquency, Risk Behaviors and Constructive Social Activities." *National Study of Youth and Religion*. No. 1. Chapel Hill, N.C.: University of North Carolina Press.

———. 2002b. "Religion and the Life Attitudes and Self Images of American Adolescents." *National Study of Youth and Religion*. No. 2. Chapel Hill, N.C. University of North Carolina Press.

Stolzenberg, Ross M., Mary Blair-Loy, and Linda Waite. 1995. "Religious Participation in Early Adulthood: Age and Family Life Cycle Effects on Church Membership." *American Sociological Review* 60 (February): 84–103.

Strobel, Lee. 1993. *Inside the Mind of Unchurched Harry and Mary*. Grand Rapids: Zondervan Publishing House.

Strommen, Merton P., ed. 1971. *Research on Religious Development: A Comprehensive Handbook*. New York: Hawthorn Books.

———. 1974. *Five Cries of Youth*. San Francisco: Harper and Row.

Strommen, Merton P., and Richard A. Hardel. 2000. *Passing on the Faith: A Radical New Model for Youth and Family Ministry*. Winona, Minn.: St. Mary's Press.

Swidler, Ann. 1986. "Culture in Action: Symbols and Strategies." *American Sociological Review* 51 (April): 273–86.

Taffel, Ron. 1996. "The Second Family." *Networker* (May/June): 36–45.

Takanishi, Ruby. 1993. "Changing Views of Adolescence in Contemporary Society." In *Adolescence in the 1990s*. Edited by Ruby Takanishi. New York: Teachers College Press.

Thornton, Arland, and Donald Cambrun. 1989. "Religious Participation and Adolescent Sexual Behavior and Attitudes." *Journal of Marriage and the Family* 51 (August): 641–53.

Thumma, Scott G. 1996. "The Kingdom, the Power, and the Glory: The Megachurch in Modern American Society." Ph.D. Thesis, Emory University.

Tillich, Paul. 1963. *Systematic Theology*. Vol. 3. Chicago: University of Chicago Press.

Tipton, Steven M. 1982. *Getting Saved from the Sixties: Moral Meaning in Conversion and Cultural Change*. Berkeley: University of California Press.

———. 1987. "Conversion and Cultural Change." In *Individualism and Commitment in American Life: Readings on the Themes of Habits of the Heart*. Edited by Robert N. Bellah, Richard Madsen, William M. Sullivan, Ann Swidler, and Steven M. Tipton. New York: Harper and Row.

Tracy, David. 1981. *The Analogical Imagination: Christian Theology and the Culture of Pluralism*. New York: Crossroad Publishing.

Trueheart, Charles. 1996. "Welcome to the Next Church." *Atlantic Monthly* (August): 37–58.

Turkle, Sherry. 1995. *Life on the Screen: Identity in the Age of the Internet*. New York: Simon and Schuster.

Turner, Stephen. *The Social Theory of Practices: Tradition, Tacit Knowledge, and Presuppositions*. Chicago: University of Chicago Press, 1994.

Turner, Victor W. 1969. *The Ritual Process*. Chicago: Aldine Publishing.

———. 1974. *Dramas, Fields, and Metaphors: Symbolic Action in Human Society*. Ithaca, N.Y.: Cornell University Press.

———. 1982. *From Ritual to Theater*. New York: PAJ Publications.

Urban, and Associates. 1994. "Report for the Louisville Metro Area." Louisville, Ky.: Louisville Market Services.

U.S. Bureau of the Census. 1990. "Census of Population and Housing, 1990." U.S. Printing Office.

U.S. Department of Education. 1991. "Youth Indicators, 1991: Trends in the Well-being of American Youth." Washington, D.C. U.S. Printing Office.

Vaughan, John N. 1993. *Megachurches and America's Cities: How Churches Grow*. Grand Rapids: Baker Books.

Walrath, D. A. 1987. *Frameworks: Patterns for Living and Believing Today*. New York: Pilgrim Press.

Warner, R. Stephen. 1988. *New Wine in Old Wineskins: Evangelicals and Liberals in a Small Town Church*. Berkeley: University of California Press.

———. 1993. "Work in Progress toward a New Paradigm for the Sociological Study of Religion in the United States." *American Journal of Sociology* 98, no. 5: 1044–93.

———. 1994. "The Place of the Congregation in the Contemporary American Religious Configuration." In *American Congregations*. Edited by James Wind and James Lewis. Chicago: University of Chicago Press.

Warren, Michael. 1992. "Imitating Jesus in a Time of Imitation." In *Schooling Christians*. Edited by Stanley Hauerwas and John H. Westerhoff. Grand Rapids: Wm. B. Eerdmans Publishing Co.

Weigert, Kathleen Mass, and Sharon L. Miller. 1996. "The Cara Report: Research on American Catholics and the U.S. Catholic Church." University of Notre Dame.

Wheeler, Barbara G. 1996. "You Who Were Far Off: Religious Divisions and the Role of Religious Research." *Review of Religious Research* 37, no. 4: 289–301.

Whyte, William Foote. 1984. *Learning from the Field*. Beverly Hills, Calif.: Sage Publications.

Wigger, J. Bradley. 2003. *The Power of God at Home: Nurturing Our Children in Love and Grace*. San Francisco: Jossey-Bass.

Wilder, Esther I. 1996. "Socioeconomic Attainment and Expressions of Jewish Identification, 1970 and 1990." *Journal for the Scientific Study of Religion* 35, no. 2: 109–27.

Williams, Andrea, and James D. Davidson. 1996. "Catholic Conceptions of Faith: A Generational Analysis." *Sociology of Religion* 57, no. 3: 273–89.

Willits, Fern K., and Donald M. Crider. 1989. "Church Attendance and Traditional Religious Beliefs in Adolescence and Young Adulthood: A Panel Study." *Review of Religious Research* 31, no. 1 (September): 68–81.

Willits, Fern K., and Donald M. Crider. 1988. "Religion and Well-being: Men and Women in the Middle Years." *Review of Religious Research* 29, no. 3 (March): 281–94.

Wuthnow, Robert. 1976. "Recent Pattern of Secularization: A Problem of Generations?" *American Sociological Review* 41: 850–67.

———. 1987. *Meaning and Moral Order: Explorations in Cultural Analysis*. Berkeley: University of California Press.

———. 1988a. *Loose Connections: Joining Together in America's Fragmented Communities*. Cambridge, Mass.: Harvard University Press.

———. 1988b. *Restructuring of American Religion*. Princeton, N.J.: Princeton University Press.

———. 1989. *The Struggle for America's Soul*. Grand Rapids: Wm. B. Eerdmans Publishing.

———. 1991. *Acts of Compassion: Caring for Others and Helping Ourselves*. Princeton, N.J.: Princeton University Press.

———. 1993. *Christianity in the 21st Century: Reflections on the Challenges Ahead*. New York: Oxford University Press.

———. 1994. *"I Come Away Stronger": How Small Groups Are Shaping American Religion*. Grand Rapids: Wm. B. Eerdmans Publishing Co.

———. 1995. *Learning to Care: Elementary Kindness in an Age of Indifference*. New York: Oxford University Press.

———. 1996. "Religious Upbringing: Does It Matter and, If So, What Matters?" In *The 1996 Princeton Lecture Series on Youth and the Church*, 67–101. Princeton, N.J.: Princeton Theological Seminary.

———. 1997. "Contemporary American Spirituality." Paper presented at Louisville Presbyterian Theological Seminary. Louisville, Ky.

———. 1998. *After Heaven: Spirituality in America since the 1950s*. Berkeley: University of California Press.

Youniss, J., and J. Smoller. 1985. *Adolescent Relations with Mother, Father, and Friends*. Chicago: University of Chicago Press.

Zinnbauer, Brian J., and Kenneth I. Pargament. 1997. "Religion and Spirituality: Unfuzzying the Fuzzy." *Journal for the Scientific Study of Religion* 36, no. 4: 549–64.